James Philip

F.S. JACKSON

A Cricketing Biography

Copyright © James P. Coldham writing as James Philip
1989 & 2017.   All rights reserved.

Cover concept by James Philip
Graphic Design by Beastleigh Web Design

Other Cricket books by James Philip

F.S. Jackson

James Philip is also the Editor of the
James D. Coldham Series

Contents

Prologue 9
1 | F.S. Jackson 13
2 | The Early Years (1870-1884) 21
3 | Harrow Days (1884-1889) 30
4 | Trinity and Cambridge (1889-1891) 52
5 | Captain of Cambridge (1892) 73
6 | Lord Hawke's Team in India and Ceylon (1892-1893) 95
7 | From Parker's Piece to Lord's (1893) 114
8 | The County of the Broad Acres (1894-1895) 134
9 | The Return of the Australians (1896) 149
10 | Yorkshire Pride (1897-1898) 165
11 | The End of an Era (1899-1901) 187
12 | The Return of the Soldier (1902) 206
13 | The Gentleman Cricketer (1903-1904) 225
14 | An Appointment with Destiny (1905) 237
15 | Life after Cricket (1906-1926) 255
16 | Life after Cricket (1927-1946) 270
Epilogue 278
Statistical Section 282
Bibliography 313
Author's Endnote 318

Other Books by James Philip 320

"A Flannelled Fighter"

Prologue

Sergeant Leonard Hutton was in Pinderfields Hospital on the outskirts of Wakefield in 1942. He had broken his left forearm in a fall on the last day of a Commando course and was having to come to terms with the likelihood that he would never again play first-class cricket. He was in the hands of Mr Reginald Broomhead, a pioneering orthopaedic surgeon who was slowly expanding the frontiers of bone-graft surgery in the treatment of serious fractures.

Hutton had undergone two operations, and after the second - involving the removal of a 3-inch piece of bone from his right leg which was then implanted in his arm - he was bed-bound, alone with his thoughts and his pain. There was always pain, sometimes more, sometimes less, but there was always pain; pain, doubt, and hour upon hour of trying not to think about what might have been.

He was feeling very low one day when the ward sister approached his bed.

'A gentleman would like to see you', she told him.

Hutton had not been expecting a visitor and he was somewhat taken aback when he discovered that his visitor was none other than the President of the Yorkshire County Cricket Club, Sir Stanley Jackson.

The well-wisher spent about an hour at Hutton's bedside. The talk was mostly of cricket, for both men were Yorkshire born and bred, and both men had, in their own ages, taken the field for England and put an Australian attack to the sword. Sir Stanley reminisced about the players of his era. He was a man who had played under the captaincy of W.G. Grace, bowled at the great Trumper in full flow, had been Archie MacLaren's captain at Harrow, and Ranjitsinhji's at Cambridge, had served as Lord Hawke's faithful lieutenant for a dozen years, and once - on a famous day in 1902 - in league with George Hirst, bowled out Joe Darling's Australians at Headingley for 23 runs.

From afar, the Yorkshire President could seem a little aloof, a rather daunting figure (as befitted a former Chairman of the Unionist Party and Governor of Bengal, who, it was said had no time for fools). Yet as he shared some cricketing memories his kindness and concern left a lasting impression on the young Hutton.

Hutton was then twenty-six, and to men of his generation Sir Stanley Jackson was hardly less a giant of the game than W.G. Grace or Victor Trumper. In 1905 he had captained England with brilliant success against a formidable Australian side, and for good measure topped both the English batting and bowling averages in the Test Matches.

Sir Stanley confided that his one regret was never having toured Australia. He had often been on the verge of going, but something had always cropped up. The conversation soon turned to bowlers, as often happens when batsmen get together.

Sir Stanley recounted tales of the great Australians he had faced: Spofforth, Jones, Cotter, Turner, Trumble and Gregory. F.R. Spofforth was aptly named 'the Demon' for his mastery of variation of pace, but Ernest Jones (who once sent a ball whistling through W.G.'s beard and said, with a shrug, 'Sorry, Doc, she slipped') gained his vote as the fastest bowler he had ever encountered. In that same match at Sheffield Park in 1896 - when Ernest Jones had ruffled the Great Cricketer's whiskers - he also contrived to crack two of Sir Stanley's ribs.

Hutton had many visitors in hospital, but this visit came when he was at a low ebb and for a short while it took him out of himself, out of the lonely inner world of pain and doubt. As Sir Stanley spoke of his own playing days he breathed life into the legends of that golden age before the First World War. There was nothing in his manner to suggest he had the slightest doubt that when cricket started up anew after the war, a certain L. Hutton would be opening the batting for Yorkshire.

Sir Stanley lived in London and travelling was no easy matter in 1942. Hutton knew the journey up to Yorkshire - by some quirk of fate a round trip of 364 miles - could only have been a difficult and wearying affair for a man who was in his seventy-second year. He was touched that the great Jackers had gone to so much trouble on his account.

The old man's heart must have gone out to the young man trapped in that hospital bed with his left arm encased in plaster from fingertip to shoulder. He had lived his life to the full and the thought of a career such as Hutton's withering before his eyes must have seemed infinitely sad.

Lord Hawke, Sir Stanley's predecessor as Yorkshire President, had declared in an ill-considered moment; 'Pray God, no professional shall ever captain England!' Hawke had no stauncher friend and ally than Stanley Jackson, but Stanley Jackson was never a man who blindly submitted to the shackles of tradition. Had Sir Stanley known on that day in 1942 that the pale young man in the hospital bed was destined to become the first professional of the modern era to captain England, he would have been the first to offer his heartfelt congratulations.

Although Sir Stanley Jackson did not live to see that day, he and Sir Leonard Hutton stand shoulder to shoulder in cricket's hall of fame: two sons of Yorkshire, captains of England both, and winning captains, too.

1 | F.S. Jackson

Sir Stanley Jackson captained Harrow School, Cambridge University and England in a golden epoch of English cricket. It is no bad thing to place the man and his age in perspective before the telling of his story. Our subject played his cricket in an age lost to us forever, an age wreathed in legend.

Cricket has been blessed with many golden ages. The claims of one era can be set against those of another almost at will. Such debates are - and always have been - part and parcel of the joy of cricket, at once the guardian of one's good humour on a damp and dismal Test Match Saturday at Lord's, and the bane of the long-suffering cricket widow's life. To the cricket lover every age seems like a golden age, and each new season a fresh gem to set in King Willow's crown. Yet if ever there was a golden age among golden ages it must have been the quarter of a century leading up to the Great War, for this was the age of the amateur batsman par excellence.

In those years before the cataclysm, cricket flowered as

not only the foremost national game - the halcyon days of association football were in the future - but as the very expression of the age. The batsmanship of W.G. Grace, K.S. Ranjitsinhji, A.C. MacLaren, C.B. Fry, L.C.H. Palairet, R.E. Foster, G.L. Jessop and a host of others reached heights of dash and dominance in those days that have rarely been surpassed. Late Victorian and Edwardian Britain was a proud and confident land, a nation unafraid of its divisions and inequalities. It was an age of opulence and poverty, of inexplicable complacency and wishful optimism as yet untouched by the horrors that were to come in 1914. Cricket, then as now, tended to mirror the mores of the wider world beyond the boundary rope.

If, like the age in which it was played, cricket was an exuberant, exciting affair, it was also true to say that sometimes there was a brittleness beneath the surface. The world of 1914 could not continue as it was, and neither could cricket. Nothing could ever be the same after that war, and so it was with cricket. The game was different when it started up again in 1919, not simply because the players had been away to war, nor because some of them had never returned: something had been lost. The truest reflection of the spirit of the age before the fall had been in the ethos of the amateur, and 1914 had mortally undermined his dominance of the game. There were still great amateur batsmen and bowlers in England after the war, but the balance had swung towards the professional. Times had changed for the amateur and the reality of those post-war years was not always kind. What had been lost would never be refound.

Those who lament the passing of the amateur spirit risk

the accusation that they are living in the past. This is most unfair. The crack amateur batsmen of the golden age before the Great War were amateurs only in the sense that they were not actually paid for playing the game they loved; in most respects they were thoroughly professional performers who strove every bit as hard as any real professional for the cause of their side. To the top amateurs, cricket was anything but a hobby; for most of them it was the consuming passion of their lives.

Off the field the amateur was expected to set an example; on the field he competed day in and day out with professionals to whom winning and losing was sometimes, quite literally, a bread-and-butter issue. It ought not to be forgotten that by the turn of the century the overwhelming majority of the players appearing in first-class cricket were professionals, and the amateur who did not, or could not, pull his weight was rarely retained for long. As any cricketer will readily affirm, there are few hiding places on the field of play. Remember, if this was the age of the amateur batsman, it was also an age in which bowlers of the quality of T. Richardson, W. Lockwood, G.A. Lohmann, S.F. Barnes, A. Mold, T. Wass, J. Briggs, G.H. Hirst, W. Rhodes, S. Haigh, R. Peel and C. Blythe, among others, were competing for places in the England XI. It was an era in which C.J. Kortright, an amateur who was reputed to be the fastest bowler of his time, never won an England cap, when mediocrity with bat or ball was, without exception, liable to be mercilessly punished.

This, then, was the age in which Stanley Jackson's cricketing star was in the ascendant. He first played for England in 1893 and from then until the end of his career he was an automatic choice for any Test Match side either for his batting or his bowling. He was the finest all-round amateur cricketer of the golden age.

As a batsman he combined native Yorkshire grit with an orthodox technique and a penchant for forcing strokes in front of square on both sides of the wicket; he was a particularly gifted exponent of the cut, and his driving, notably off his legs, invariably savaged the slightest lapse in line or length. In an age when every county had at least one genuine fast bowler on its books, he was regarded by many as being as good a player of fast bowling as any batsman in the land. His response to anything pitched short was robustly uncomplicated; occasionally he might duck or sway out of the path of the ball, but more often than not he cut or hooked the ball to the boundary.

As a bowler, he operated off a run that was never over-long, and bowled at a brisk fast-medium pace with a high, easy action that tended to make the ball come off the wicket appreciably faster than a batsman anticipated. While he was never an out-and-out fast bowler, in his earlier days his fast ball could be a somewhat disconcerting delivery. Even near the end of his career he could still produce a very awkward 'faster' ball. He was a bowler who liked to attack the stumps, or pitch on a nagging length in the batsman's area of maximum uncertainty, just outside his off-stump - and from his first days he earned a reputation for being one of the meanest bowlers of his type in the game. The deadliest weapon in his armoury was the ball he cut back into the right-handed batsman from a good length. He was a thoughtful bowler who relied on line and length and subtle changes of pace to undo batsmen; the sort of bowler who was always liable to bowl the occasional wickedly unplayable delivery that every batsman dreads.

Strangely, it was on bad wickets, or wickets damaged by rain, that he often produced his best batting. It seemed sometimes that only adversity - be it a glue-pot of a rain-ruined wicket, or the threat of an imminent England collapse - summoned forth his best form with the bat. Although sporadically he scored as freely as any man in normal county cricket, he undoubtedly reserved his most indomitable performances for the Test Match arena, or for those times when his side was struggling and in need of his particular gifts. In time he became renowned as 'the man' for a crisis. He was the batsman most likely to play a long innings just at the moment when an Australian attack was rampant, the man to send in to hold the line on a wet wicket. As a bowler he became the man his captain would bring on to break a dangerous partnership between two well-set batsmen, the bowler whose unerring length and direction could be confidently relied upon to frustrate, torment and finally defeat both the best of opening batsmen and the most dogged of tail-enders.

Stanley Jackson's feats on the cricket field were considerable, but he and his amateur brethren brought more to the game than a torrent of runs and prodigious wicket-taking. He was a man of many interests who, after laying down his bat, went on to achieve great things in later life. Cricket was his recreation, not the be all and end all. He and other amateurs brought not merely their talents to cricket, but also a broader perspective on matters in general. In professional sport it is too easy for the protagonists to forget that the real world surrounds their game, and not vice versa.

Like many amateurs, Stanley Jackson's commitments outside the game often limited the amount of cricket he was able to play, and, after he came down from Cambridge, effectively ruled out touring overseas. This meant that it was only possible for him to join one tour abroad, that of Lord Hawke's team to India and Ceylon in the winter of 1892-93. In 1903 he was reluctantly obliged to decline the England captaincy because he was unable to tour Australia that winter.

His first-class career spanned the years 1890 to 1907, although he played only one match in 1900, missed the whole of the 1901 season when away in South Africa fighting the Boers, and played in just four matches in the 1906 and 1907 seasons. Had he played continuously and been available to tour abroad he would probably have played in well over five hundred matches; instead he appeared in 309 first-class fixtures, in which he scored 15,901 runs at an average of 33.83, claimed 774 wickets at 20.37 apiece, and held 195 catches in the field.

His fame, and his place amongst cricket's immortals, rests on his batting in Test Matches. Between 1893 and 1905 he played 20 times for England against Australia, scoring 1,415 runs at an average of 48.79. In Test Matches played on English soil in those years he scored almost as many runs as the next two most successful Englishmen combined, T.W. Hayward and A.C. MacLaren. To this day, no English batsman has bettered his total of five three-figure innings against Australia in England, a record that has been equalled but once, by another remarkable Yorkshireman, a certain G. Boycott, in 1981.

He was a gentleman cricketer but he was no idle son of the new industrial aristocracy of the West Riding.

During his playing days he became a director of his father's business, Messrs W.L. Jackson and Co., one of the largest tanning and currying concerns in the country. He also acquired a directorship of the Yorkshire Post, was increasingly involved in local Unionist politics in Leeds, rose to the rank of Captain in the 3rd (Militia) Battalion of the Royal Lancaster Regiment, and from 1899 served Yorkshire cricket in the capacity of Vice-President, often representing the club's interests at Lord's. In later years he was to become a director of the Great Northern Railway, enter Parliament as the Member for the Howdenshire Division of Yorkshire, thereafter holding the posts of Financial Secretary to the War Office (1922-23), Chairman of the Unionist Party (1923-26) and Governor of Bengal (1927-32).

Cricket was never far from his heart; he was elected President of the Marylebone Cricket Club for 1921, and when his sojourn in India was over he was co-opted to be Chairman of the England selectors in the aftermath of the 'Bodyline' crisis. He never really retired from public life; he succeeded to the Presidency of the Yorkshire Club in 1938 upon the death of Lord Hawke and in 1942, after serving for many years as a governor, he was invited to become Chairman of the Governors of his old school, Harrow.

The Honourable F.S. Jackson - as he was when he swept all before him in 1905 - was unashamedly a man of his times, a great Edwardian, a man who always looked to the future, to whom duty and service to family, friends and, ultimately, country, was something wholly intrinsic.

His approach to the game he loved was, dare one say, marvellously old-fashioned: 'Adopt a dynamic attitude towards the game whether batting, bowling or fielding.'

He might have been articulating his view of the bigger game, the game of life.

'Aim,' he declared, 'for victory from the first ball, and maintain enterprise until the last over is finished.'

No story about the golden age of the amateur batsman would be complete without F.S. Jackson, and no biography of F.S. Jackson complete without a portrait of the age in which he played.

Here then is his story.

2 | The Early Years (1870-1884)

Francis Stanley Jackson was born on Monday 21st November 1870 at Chapel Allerton, near Leeds. He was the seventh child and second son of Grace and William Lawies Jackson, later the first Baron Allerton of Chapel Allerton.

It was a date of particular significance in the history of Anglo-Australian cricket, for on that same day in November 1870, half a world away, at Glen Osmond, Adelaide, a son was born to Scottish emigrants who had settled in South Australia in 1853: his name was Joseph Darling.

If ever two cricketers' destinies were inextricably linked then it was those of Stanley Jackson and Joe Darling. It was said of them that they were cricketing twins; for though they were different kinds of cricketers, and perhaps different kinds of men, they had everything that is best in cricket in common, although they were never friends.

They did not meet until they were in their mid-twenties and by then were already well-established Test cricketers. Set apart by temperament and tradition, they were natural opponents. It was one of the cruel ironies of the golden age that when, in 1905, Jackson belatedly succeeded to the England captaincy, it was Darling's rightful place among the ranks of the great captains of Australia that was at stake. There never has been, nor will there ever be, room for sentimentality in the cauldron of the Test Match arena. Cricket at the highest level has never been simply a demonstration of sporting excellence: it has always been about winning and losing. Then, as now, the acid test of a captain, irrespective of whether he was an English man or an Australian, was whether or not he was a *winning* captain.

Such harsh realities lay in the distant future as the young Stanley Jackson grew up on the family estate at Chapel Allerton. He was the baby of the family, doted over by his five sisters. No doubt he was bullied from time to time by his elder brother George, but there was no major impediment to his happiness and general well-being during his first years. His infancy passed serenely in the bosom of his family, an old and respected Yorkshire family over which his redoubtable father towered.

The family fortune was derived from the tanning and currying works of Messrs W.L. Jackson and Co. which were situated at nearby Buslingthorpe in Leeds. The Jacksons of Chapel Allerton were country folk who enjoyed their country pursuits. They had won their position in the county of the broad acres at the beginning of the Industrial Revolution, and had long since adopted the attitudes and manners of the gentry of the West Riding. Country life: riding, hunting and outdoor sports of all kinds were the normal recreations of the sons of the household, and Stanley began to excel in the rough and tumble from an early age.

The Jackson clan was a confident, forward-looking family. At its head stood William Lawies Jackson, a leader of men who's every act bespoke a sureness of touch and a clarity of purpose that was quite awesome. He was the eldest son of William Jackson, and was born on 16 February 1840 at Otley. He was educated privately at Adel and then later at the Moravian School at Fulbeck, but his education was cut short when, at the tender age of seventeen, his father died and bequeathed him the family business.

William Jackson had founded the Buslingthorpe works in the boom years after the end of the Napoleonic Wars. More recently, the firm had fallen on hard times. The business had not kept up with progress, and for some  years it had only survived by the good graces of its creditors. When William Lawies Jackson [pictured *left*] inherited the company it was, to all intents, bankrupt.

Faced with a situation that would have driven a battle-hardened captain of industry to despair, the boy of seventeen responded to the great crisis of his life in a fashion which was to become his hallmark. Rising early, he would work all day and late into the night; the world was against him and his only asset was the fearless vitality of his youth. His single-mindedness wholly discounted the possibility of failure. In a relatively short time - to the astonishment of his creditors - the family business, now Messrs W.L. Jackson and Co., was back on its feet and its new proprietor was looking to develop and expand it. The firm's return to solvency and its long-term prosperity was not achieved overnight, and many of its creditors had to wait several years to be repaid in full. But, from the first day William Lawies Jackson took on his father's mantle, he never took a step backward. He quickly won a reputation for probity and commercial acumen in the hard-headed business community of the West Riding, and after a few short years the Buslingthorpe works sprawled across some eight or nine acres and employed well over two hundred hands as it grew into one of the largest tanning and currying concerns in the country.

A young man in his position might easily have been forgiven for marrying into money, but William Lawies Jackson did not bow to conventional wisdom in these matters. When he married at the age of twenty, it was to Grace Tempest, another native of Otley whom he had known from childhood. Her family was as staunchly Conservative as his and, not unnaturally, they were involved in work for the Unionist cause from the outset of their marriage. Even when still in his twenties, Jackson sought new outlets for his seemingly boundless energies. He was a restless spirit all his life, at his happiest when he could throw himself heart and soul into an enterprise.

'The busiest man is the man who has the most leisure to undertake further work,' he would say - and promptly bury himself in his next project.

He launched himself into his political career in 1869 when, at the age of twenty-nine, he was elected to Leeds Council as the representative for Headingley. He was to serve eleven years on the Council, in which time he transformed the minority Tory Group to its position of control in later years and completely modernised the finances of the Council.

His political aspirations went far beyond Headingley, and in 1876 he stood for Parliament, narrowly failing to be elected. Undismayed, he stood again in 1880 and was returned as a Member for Leeds.

As a back-bencher in the House of Commons his financial expertise was soon recognised, and it was this, and the friendship and patronage of Lord Randolph Churchill which in 1885 resulted in his appointment as Financial Secretary to the Treasury in Lord Salisbury's Government. He held the post until 1891, when he succeeded Balfour as Chief Secretary for Ireland, having already been sworn a Privy Councillor in 1888. His time in high office effectively ended in 1892 with the defeat of his party, but his career in public service continued. [In common with his youngest son, W.L. Jackson, became a subject for Spy in Vanity Fair, pictured *right*]. He was a tireless worker behind the scenes, sitting on committees dealing with such diverse matters as the Indian railways, financial arrangements between the Indian and home governments, bankruptcy law, and War Office contracts.

For the average man one career is usually more than enough. William Lawies Jackson was not the average man. He never lost control of the family business, nor contact with his social, commercial and political roots in the West Riding. He was Chairman of the Great Northern Railway from 1895 to 1908 and a major force in the reforming Building Societies Act, 1894, which was promulgated in the aftermath of the failure of the Liberator Building Society in 1892. He was appointed Chairman of the inquiry into the Jameson Raid in 1896, and Chairman of the Royal Commission on the coal resources of the United Kingdom, 1901-1905. Elevated to the peerage in 1902, he interested himself less in party politics, and devoted more time to Leeds and his beloved West Riding. He became the first Conservative Mayor of Leeds, a Fellow of the Royal Society, and, among other distinctions, Provincial Grand Master of the Freemasons of West Yorkshire, a body of men responsible for a great many honourable and charitable deeds in his lifetime, most notably the establishment of the West Yorkshire Masonic and Educational and Benevolent Fund in 1897. In 1908 he was granted the freedom of the city of Leeds - his name being only the fifth on the roll - an honour he cherished as much as any he received in his career in public service.

Stanley Jackson was his father's son.

While it would be true to say that a son of William Lawies Jackson could not help but feel that he had a great deal to live up to, two factors combined to rescue young Stanley from the darkness of his father's long shadow. Firstly, he was the younger son, a state not without its advantages in most families. His brother George was the heir, and so the greater burden of expectation fell upon him. In a sense, Stanley was a free man; he could succeed or fail, make his mark or sink without a trace. He was not just the younger son, but the baby of the family, and parents tend to view the youngest of their brood with a patience and indulgence that infuriates the other siblings. And secondly, although his father's shadow was indeed long, its darkness was more apparent than real.

William Lawies Jackson was in many ways a very modern man. He always sought compromise; he looked for pragmatic answers, would search for the least line of resistance in debate, and appreciated that there were very few things in the world worth the risking of life, reputation and fortune - a lesson he taught his sons.

He had fought tooth and nail for everything that was rightfully his, but in throwing off the millstone of his own flawed inheritance he had also conquered his own 'inner demons'. He made sure his sons were given the opportunities he had never had, he sent them to public school, thence to Cambridge, introduced them into the commercial circles of the West Riding, and educated them in the ways of the Buslingthorpe works. His sons respected and admired him; he was always 'the guv'nor'. Some great men are ogres to their families; William Lawies Jackson was not.

Stanley Jackson was not the man to rue being his father's son. He accepted the responsibilities of his station in society just as he accepted the advantages attendant upon it. Throughout his life he set himself the highest of standards, and if he had a secret, it was that sometimes he lived up to the standards he set himself. In the vernacular of the present day, one might say he was a well-adjusted child. He was by no means a 'victim' of the good fortune of his birth - at least not until he was banished from the family home, waving his farewells to his sisters, Alice, Ella, Annie, Evelyn and Grace, and despatched into exile at the Reverend D.M. Draper's

Preparatory School at Locker's Park near Hemel Hempstead in Hertfordshire.

The Reverend Draper was by all accounts a man who saw in cricket the truest manifestation of the inner meaning of 'muscular Christianity', and it was under his wing that Stanley Jackson showed the world the first glimpses of a precocious cricketing talent.

In the 1870s and 1880s cricket was by no means the dominant national game that it was to become in the 1890s, and its importance was not yet universally acknowledged by the great public schools. Locker's Park was a cricketing school, and one cannot help but suspect that William Lawies Jackson would not have sent his son to a cricketing school by accident.

The underlying purpose of schools like Locker's Park was to introduce its pupils to the majority of the privations they could expect to experience at Winchester, Eton or Harrow. The days were long, dormitory life was harsh, and the discipline was severe. Schools like Locker's Park existed solely to ready a boy for the ordeals of the remainder of his education; a boy's first real inkling of what lay ahead of him in the public school *gulag*. There was only one saving grace, and that was granted to the select few who excelled at sport. Young Stanley was a natural games player who relished the heat of battle. For little men like him, there were times when school life seemed almost bearable.

The Reverend Draper liked to play cricket with his little men. On one occasion he offered a bottle of ginger beer to any boy who could bowl him out, and took guard at the wicket. Whereupon, young Stanley proceeded to bowl him out no less than eighteen times!

Afterwards, it was a somewhat chastened cleric who declared: 'That lad will one day captain England!' Perhaps Stanley Jackson's old Headmaster would have felt better had he known then that he had just been bowled by the hand that in years to come would dismiss W.G. Grace seven, and Victor Trumper six times.

3 | Harrow Days (1884-1889)

Stanley Jackson entered Harrow School on Wednesday 17th September 1884. At Harrow there was one reality: the system was always right and the system always won. A boy swam with the tide or he drowned, there was no safe haven. Avenues for personal development were few and far between, and in most things except sport the slur of individualism was the bedfellow of heresy. There was no room for outsiders, a boy was a team man or he was nothing. Harrow was no place for faint hearts. The 'school on the hill' was a world within a world, an enclave fiercely devoted to its own very particular view of civilisation. It was a closed society in which behaviour that was in any sense different was (with one notable exception) treated as a threat to the whole community and ruthlessly stamped out.

The one exception to the dictum of rigid conformity which otherwise oppressed every boy, was, of course, games. In the Victorian public school prowess at games had an almost mystical significance; the system's *raison d'etre* was to turn boys not just into young men, nor even gentlemen, but rather to make of its boys men to whom the burden of Empire could safely be entrusted. To a Victorian the hurly-burly of games was a metaphor for life's battles. The building blocks of the *Pax Britannica* had been forged on the playing fields of the great public schools, and nobody was allowed to forget it.

Harrow was a daunting, bewildering place for a new boy, but Stanley Jackson came to the school on the hill with advantages that few boys before or since have enjoyed on their first day at Harrow. It was not a case of family influence, wealth, or favouritism; he simply came to the school with a god-given talent for all manner of games, and a youthful assurance that bordered on arrogance in one so young.

Equipped with these attributes, he had a head start on the majority of his contemporaries and never looked back. If he suffered the same rigours of school life as his peers, his sporting prowess won him the compensations his fellows were denied. By the time he left Harrow he was the best all-round schoolboy cricketer of his generation, and the school rewarded its own in its own ways.

Yet it would be wrong to pretend that the young Stanley Jackson was anything less than thoroughly intimidated on his first day. Entering Harrow was a step into the unknown at a stage in his life when he was at his most impressionable. Let it not be thought that he sailed through his Harrow days without a care in the world; he was a new boy, and everything is strange and frightening to a new boy on his first day.

There is a myth that the great public schools are unchanging, wholly monolithic institutions, bastions of reaction dedicated solely to the promotion of the status quo. There may well be a deal of truth in the proposition, but then, as now, Harrow survived and prospered by meeting the demand for its product.

The type of education available at Harrow, as a result, altered considerably over the years, and in this sense the school that Jackson joined in September 1884 was not the same school it had been even ten years before. The school was no longer the exclusive preserve of the sons of the aristocracy. The Industrial Revolution had altered the British in more ways than they knew, and in no way more profoundly than in the matter of the educational needs of their children. For a young man being groomed to take on his family's business the value of a purely classical education was in question. While nobody denied that such an education was 'the making of a gentleman,' it was becoming equally clear that the effective administration of the world's first industrial society required rather more than a passing knowledge of Greek and Latin. Harrow was among the first of the premier public schools to bend with the times, moving cautiously towards offering a curriculum that was recognisably modem.

Most of the boys at Harrow in Jackson's day were classics men, but he was a modernist whose education, although it still included the divinity and the Latin of the classicist, excluded Greek and consequently gave more weight to modem languages (French and German), mathematics and the natural sciences.

In Jackson's time there were some six hundred boys at Harrow, two-thirds of whom were classicists. The modernists were divided into two groups: general scholars like Jackson, and boys studying for military entrance examinations.

Over five hundred boys were boarders in one or other of

the school's seventeen houses. New boys were usually sent to a 'small' boarding house, of which there were six, and transferred to a 'big' house of which there were eleven, as and when space became available. The big houses had about forty boys in them - excepting the Head Master's which had sixty - and the small houses held nine or ten. The balance of the school population comprised boys who lived or were lodged locally, some fifty in number.

A boy's house was the dominant social structure in his school life. George Townsend Warner in *Harrow School* (1898) describes a boy's perception of house and school thus:

> To old Harrovians in particular, and to the world in general, the school is a school; but to a boy in it, it is primarily a collection of houses, of which his own is, *ipso facto*, "the best house in Harrow", and the rest are mainly unknown ground.
>
> To the ordinary boy the history of a term, putting aside the inevitable "swot", is domestic history; foreign politics are represented by the relations of his house with other houses, by house matches in cricket and football, second and third Elevens, and rivalry in sports. Only once in each year does the idea of school thoroughly dominate the idea of house, and that is in the presence of a common foe at Lord's.

However, if a boy's idea of 'house' ruled his day to day existence Warner goes on to warn against drawing the wrong conclusion:

If any stranger imagines this strong house feeling overpowers school loyalty, that the school is not united as a school, he would be grievously mistaken. Let him attempt to hint, I will not say the superiority, but even the equality, of any other school, and he will be at once enlightened. The school feeling is there: you may hear it asserting itself in the holidays, if Harrow is not treated with the respect it deserves in an Harrovian's opinion; you may find it in the warm applause that rewards the school cricket Eleven in its battles against visiting teams; you may behold it with a bunch of cornflowers in its buttonhole at Lord's; but as a rule, the feeling is dormant.

In Harrow it is taken for granted; there is nothing to provoke it to show itself, and, consequently, interest is centred on the smaller field - on the affairs of the house.

When Jackson entered the school in September 1884, he was placed in form IV(3) under the general charge of F.E. Marshall, a mathematics teacher, and boarded in one of the small boarding houses called 'High Street' with H.O.D. Davidson, who taught classics and 'modern side'. From the outset he was assigned to Davidson's pupil room for teaching in additional subjects and coaching in others.

He was to remain in Davidson's pupil room until he left Harrow, although he transferred from Marshall's general charge to that of Dr J.E.C. Welldon, the Head Master, early in 1886, at which time he moved from the High Street to the Head Master's House, where he spent the rest of his school career. In his five years at Harrow, Jackson had two House Masters; Marshall for the first eighteen months, then Welldon: throughout his tutor was Davidson.

One might expect any pupil to benefit from such continuity of masters, but alas, this was not the case with Stanley Jackson. As a scholar he never came last, but he never went to any great lengths to come top either. Apart from his first term at Harrow, when he was placed in a form far below his ability, he never shone as a scholar as positions in examinations clearly illustrate.

FORM	TERM	CLASSICS	MODERN LANGUAGES	MATHEMATICS	NATURAL SCIENCES
IV(3)	1884(3)	1	1	1	—
IV(1)	1885(1)	9	8	5	—
Lower Shell	1885(2)	26	12	8	—
Middle Shell	1885(3)	23	22	9	—
Upper Shell	1886(1)	27	13	9	21
Upper Shell	1886(2)	24	19	17	28
Lower Remove	1886(3)	25	23	19	22
Lower Remove	1887(1)	21	4	7	27
Lower Remove	1887(2)	16	24	13	22
Upper Remove	1887(3)	25	11	15	14
V(3)	1888(1)	23	3	22	31
V(3)	1888(2)	(No information available)			
V(2)	1888(3)	(Absent during examinations)			
V(2)	1889(1)	30	30	9	—
V(2)	1889(2)	32	32	9	—

One is tempted to draw a discreet veil over Jackson's academic record at Harrow. Like many boys his energies were expended on the field of play rather than in the classroom, and at Harrow, where sporting excellence was often regarded with reverence, his studies were allowed to suffer by default. He was clearly capable of doing better, as his obvious aptitude for mathematics shows, but he was neither motivated, nor coerced into giving of his best in the academic sphere. Sport was his consuming preoccupation at Harrow. Apart from cricket, he made a name for himself at Harrow football, which is not to be confused with either the Association or Rugby codes, being a robust combination of the two that is quite incomprehensible to an outsider. He represented the school at both fives and rackets, and was a member of the school Philathletic Club from 1888, being a committee member from the Christmas term of that year.

The aim of the Philathletic Club was to promote 'all manly sports and exercises'. It appears that our subject was a trifle forgetful in the matter of paying his membership dues, for after settling his admission charge - the princely sum of thirty-six shillings - he failed to pay his subscription for the next two terms. One might conjecture that his elevation to the club's committee reminded him of the error of his ways, for at the beginning of 1889 he suddenly paid his arrears. The club itself was a considerable force at Harrow, not only in the organisation of games, but in raising funds to support sporting activities.

At first sight it might seem odd that Jackson was permitted to underachieve - in strictly scholastic terms - throughout his time at Harrow. Even if it is assumed that excellence in one field makes up for failings in another, it does rather go against the grain.

The answer probably lies in the philosophy of Dr Welldon, who became Head Master of Harrow School in 1885. Legend has it that Welldon admitted Winston Churchill to the school on the grounds that the future Prime Minister had demonstrated his capacity to write his name, in ink, on the top of the Harrow entrance examination paper. Young Winston's father was Chancellor of the Exchequer at the time, which probably inclined Welldon to give him the benefit of the doubt, but even so, it does suggest he was his own man.

Welldon was still in his thirties when he became Head Master. He was a man of great vigour and presence, a man of vision. He was the second remarkable man whose example touched the young Stanley Jackson in his formative years.

Welldon was not content merely to continue the work of his immediate predecessor, Dr H. Montagu Butler, in modernising the old curriculum; he also took it upon himself to expand the school. It was under his guidance that Harrow School became recognisably the school it is today, both in terms of its buildings, and the education it offers. He realised that Harrow had to provide a broader, more modem education if it was to look to the future with the same confidence and pride as it had done in its past. Sport played a vital role in the process of change. Sport was the catalyst; it identified the very ethos of the old Harrow, embodying the spirit he knew was also essential to the Harrow he was striving to build.

Welldon's stewardship of Harrow School ended in 1898. There were those who thought he was ahead of his times. Other schools, notably Winchester, clung to classicism and the old ways into the 1920s. Welldon's approach modified more than the curriculum and architecture of the school; it began to alter attitudes, adding a liberal touch of humanity to school life and banishing the worst excesses.

However, it should not be forgotten that the purpose of Harrow under Welldon was to prepare its boys to 'take up the white man's burden'. Under Welldon the Harrow regime was - by the standards of the present - unforgiving, needlessly harsh. The system tended to break and remake a boy, beat the spirit out of him and then give him back his pride in penny packets; it was the law of the jungle, the survival of the fittest.

Stanley Jackson thrived at Harrow.

In one of his first house matches he returned a bowling analysis of 4 for 16. From the start he was a dashing batsman with but one flaw, a fondness for hitting across the line of the ball before he was set. At Harrow this was hardly a weakness at all; indeed nothing was more admired than a boy who watched the ball, opened his shoulders, and hit out.

It was at Harrow that Jackson acquired his nickname: 'Jacker', or less commonly, 'Jackers'. As befitted a community that was essentially insular, the school had its own slang, its own arbitrary usage of the mother tongue. J. Fischer Williams in *Harrow* (1901) summed up Harrow English thus:

> As to the language, the inhabitants of Harrow speak, generally, the English tongue. But in this way they are, or were, once peculiar, that they cut short certain words of their last syllable or syllables and substitute the letters "er". Thus Duck Puddle becomes "Ducker", football "footer", and Speech-Room "speecher", blue-coat "bluer".

Hence, Jackson becomes Jacker.

The singular use of language, and the way one wore the Harrow uniform (Eton jacket and black waistcoat for fourth-formers and below, civilised tail-coats for their seniors, and Harrow straw hat - broad at the brim, flat on the crown with a dark blue ribbon about it - or in the summer a short blue flannel coat, or cricket cap with its unmistakable blue and white stripes) and the way one played the game; these marked out a Harrow man. In this age to be an Englishman was a very special thing, and to be a Harrow man as well, was to be an Englishman twice blessed.

It was all very different for the young Joe Darling as he grew up in South Australia; although unlike Jackson he was not banished from his family for the sake of his education. From 1879 to 1886 he attended Prince Alfred College, Adelaide, where he also soon showed his worth as a schoolboy cricketer. From the beginning he was a pugnacious left- handed batsman who was never happier than when thrashing the bowling to the boundary.

The day before his fifteenth birthday Darling scored 252 for his school against the Collegiate School of St Peter, at the Adelaide Oval. He batted for six hours, offering in that time only two chances. When he left the field his hands were blistered and bleeding from gripping his bat - rubber handle grips were an invention of the future - but he had made his mark. A famous innings, surpassing George Giffen's 209 **not** out as a record for the ground, it earned him a place in the South Australia and Victoria XV to play the Australian XI at Adelaide in March, 1886. In that match Darling batted for over an hour for 16 runs, in a manner that moved the then Australian Captain, H. Scott, to say that one day he would play for his country.

At this time Stanley Jackson was on the fringe of the Harrow XI, a budding fast-medium bowler and an overly fearless batsman, as yet untested by players nearer to his own calibre.

But there was a cloud on Joe Darling's cricketing horizon, a cloud of a sort that Stanley Jackson would never have to face. The Honourable John Darling, merchant-farmer and Member of the South Australian Legislative Council, did not entirely approve of his son's obsessions, with cricket in the summer and football in the winter. He felt his son's sport was interfering with his studies, and eventually he acted to remedy the situation, albeit not before Joe had averaged 299 for the Avenue Cricket Club in the season after he left school, and played Rules football for both Adelaide and Norwood.

The axe fell when John Darling packed his son off to the Roseworthy Agricultural School for a year. Afterwards, Joe had a spell working as a bank clerk, before his father again intervened and had him appointed manager of one of the family's wheat farms. Out in the country, far away from Adelaide and civilisation, he was in cricketing exile. His batting prospered on 'the mat', but easy runs are too often a young batsman's ruination. Had it not been for his father's interference Joe Darling might have broken into first-class cricket many years before he finally did, in 1893.

It was the dream of every Harrow boy to one day earn a place in the XI at Lord's. Jackson was in his seventeenth year when he became a regular member of the side. An aggressive, fluent middle order batsman and a naturally fastish bowler, he was good enough to be picked for either his batting or his bowling.

Jackson was joined in the Harrow XI of 1887 by a batsman not yet sixteen, but every ounce as precocious a cricketing talent as he. His name was Archibald Campbell

MacLaren. Although they belonged to the same select first XI clique, and consequently spent much time in each other's company Jackson and MacLaren were never very close during their time at Harrow. Perhaps, it was because Jackson was one crucial year older, or simply because the backgrounds of the two boys were so different. MacLaren's father had risked ruination to send his sons to Harrow, and Archie knew it.

In many ways Archie MacLaren was the embodiment of Harrow batting; a majestic batsman whose bat flowed into the ball whether the stroke was in attack or defence. Moreover, there was something of the lovable rascal in MacLaren even in his Harrow days, whereas Jackson was sometimes a trifle aloof, a rather 'adult' youth whose quiet confidence on the field belied the qualms he sometimes felt in the pavilion.

Winston Churchill was Jackson's (and later also MacLaren's) fag at Harrow, doubtless in consideration of his father's friendship with Lord Randolph Churchill. Jackson and Winston Churchill remained, if not friends, then men with a certain respect for each other, even in political opposition. In later life MacLaren revelled in having had Churchill as his fag, particularly in telling his listeners what a 'snotty little so-and-so' he had been.

That a school side could field two batsmen such as MacLaren and Jackson was a portent of a golden age to come. MacLaren topped the Harrow batting averages in 1887. But Stanley Jackson was marked out as a cricketer of rare promise.

Wisden noted 'we think the best bowler on the side was F.S. Jackson, right hand fast'. James Lillywhite noted he was 'a good bat, with a fine free style, hitting well all round;

a very good fast bowler on his day, coming in from the off, and a capital field anywhere'.

The test of a Harrow cricketer is how he performs against the common foe at Lord's.

In 1887 Harrow went down by 5 wickets to an Eton team that was acknowledged as by far the stronger side before a ball was bowled. Jackson and MacLaren were two of the eight Harrow newcomers to the Lord's fixture. Jackson had a miserable time of it with the bat, batting at number four in the order and accumulating as many runs in the match; 3 in the first innings, and 1 in the second. By one of those ironies cricket throws up, MacLaren, opening with J. St Fair, was top scorer in both innings, with knocks of 53 and 67. The match was won and lost on the first day when Harrow, batting first, lost their last 7 wickets for 18 runs, mainly to the fast left-arm bowling of H.R. Bromley-Davenport, another future England player. Jackson took four wickets in the match but after Harrow's collapse it was to no avail. He bowled 192 balls, but *Wisden* still commented, 'Jackson, the fast bowler, was not sufficiently tried'.

The Eton - Harrow match of 1888 turned out to be the watershed of Jackson's schoolboy career, although before the match the omens were mixed. Harrow's season had until then been something of a disappointment. It had been a dull, wet summer and Harrow cricket was in the doldrums. MacLaren, the star of the previous year's Lord's match, was in the middle of a dismal run which saw him average a mere 9.42 runs. Eton, too, had their problems - exacerbated by a less than inspiring performance in a trial game against Winchester.

Lord's had seen several days of heavy rain before the

Friday when the match was due to commence: Harrow won the toss and elected to bat on a damp wicket. It was an act of bravado - pure Harrow. The decision was very nearly fatal to Harrow's cause; at one stage 5 wickets were down for 17 runs, then 6 down with a meagre 32 on the board. MacLaren was out without troubling the scorers, the first four batsmen scrambled 9 runs between them. Jackson entered the fray at the fall of the third Harrow wicket, and, in the context of what followed the 21 runs he scored (out of 35 while in the middle) were worth their weight if not in gold, then certainly silver. By the time he was seventh out he had stemmed the tide that had swept aside the cream of Harrow batsmanship. Harrow stumbled to 80 all out; many more than had seemed likely earlier that morning.

Prior to the match, William Lawies Jackson had offered his son a shilling for every run he scored, and a sovereign for each wicket he claimed. It was going to be an expensive two days for the great man. Perhaps his father felt his younger son was in need of encouragement after a recent illness from which he was still recuperating, or perhaps he wanted to reward his son for making the XI two years running. In any event Jackson cashed in.

Eton struggled to a total of 106, six of the first eight Etonians falling to Jackson's pace and movement off the pitch. Jackson was inclined to drop the ball a shade too short of a length in his youth, but his line and disconcerting pace on a wicket which gave him ample assistance were altogether too much for Eton. When Harrow batted again that evening 2 wickets fell for 4 runs before R.B. Hoare was joined in a stand of 70 by H.D. Watson. H.W. Studd eventually removed Watson, bowling him for 26, at which point Harrow were 48 runs ahead, and the game finely balanced. Jackson came to the wicket, and by the close of play Harrow had moved on to 167 for 3, Hoare undefeated on 80, Jackson on exactly 50. Their stand of 93 had come in good time with the tempo of scoring accelerating near the end of the day, the last 67 coming in 45 minutes.

Jackson had started solidly and batted with increasing freedom as the evening drew in. On the Saturday morning he added another 9 to his overnight score, assisting Hoare to carry the stand to 114 before Studd broke his wicket. Harrow, largely on the backs of Hoare - whose 195-minute innings of 108 would in any other match have earned him undying fame - and Jackson, amassed 234 runs in their second innings.

Set 209 to win with time to spare the Eton innings began in bad light under ominous skies. In view of what transpired only the intervention of the elements could have saved Eton. The bowling of Jackson and Hoare, the very men who had so recently tormented Eton's bowlers, cut down Eton's batsmen for a humiliating 52 runs. Jackson took 5 wickets, bowling the first four Etonians, and Hoare 4. At one stage Eton's innings stood at a wretched 17 for 8. Harrow's victory was absolute, the margin of 156 runs a revelation after the XI's disastrous batting on the first morning of the match.

Jackson received a cheque from his father in full and prompt settlement of his offer of a shilling per run and a sovereign for every wicket; some fifteen pounds. It was a princely sum in 1888!

The young hero was modesty itself as he basked in the glory of his deeds. Harrow was at his feet. Before his triumph a master had made the comment in his school report that 'Jackson thinks too much of his cricket; in the days after the match the same master wrote to his father: Jackson still thinks too much of his cricket, but I am very glad he does'.

At Harrow Welldon gave E.E. Bowen three days special leave to immortalise Jackson's match-winning performance in verse. The result was a famous Harrow song: 'A Gentleman's A-Bowling'.

O Cabby, trot him faster;
O hurry, engine, on
Come glory or disaster
Before the day be done!
Ten thousand folks are strolling,
And streaming into view,
A gentleman's a-bowling (More accurately, two).

With changes and with chances
The innings come and go,
Alternating advances
Of ecstasy and woe;
For now 'tis all condoling,
And now - for who can tell?
A gentleman's a-bowling –
It yet may be all well.

Light Blue are nimbly fielding,
And scarce a hit can pass;
But those the willows wielding
Have played on Harrow grass

And there's the ball a-rolling,
And all the people see
A gentleman's a-bowling,
And we're a-hitting he.

Ten score to make, or yield her!
Shall Eton save the match?
Bowl, bowler! Go it, fielder!
Catch, wicket-keeper, catch
Our vain attempt's controlling,
They drive the leather - no!
A gentleman's a-bowling,
And down the wickets go.

And now that all is ended,
Were I the Queen to-day,
I'd make a marquis splendid
Of every one of they!
And still for their consoling.
I'll cheer and cheer again
The gentleman a-bowling,
And all the other ten.

Jackson was captain of Harrow School in 1889.

In 1888 the XI had won only two of its ten fixtures and as *Wisden* noted, the victory against Eton 'made up for a great many failures'. In 1889 under Jackson's captaincy the XI had its best season for some years, defeating E.E. Bowen's XI, Harrow Town, Harlequins, Old Harrovians, not to mention the old foe, Eton College. With the exception of losses at the hands of M.C.C. and I Zingari, Harrow cricket dominated its opponents that year. Jackson bore the burden of responsibility with a light heart; he scored more runs and took more wickets that summer than any of his fellows. His batting flourished as never before, highlighted by scores of 125 against the Household Brigade, 88 against Rugby, and a captain's innings of 68 against Eton at Lord's. His season's tally with the bat was 408 runs at an average of 45.33, and with the ball 29 wickets at 14.56 runs apiece.

Wisden, in summing up Jackson's season, struck a cautionary note, which in the context of the season of 1889, seems a little odd:

> F.S. Jackson, the captain, is undoubtedly a cricketer of whom a great deal may be expected, and, unless he should, like others before him, lose his form, we may take it for granted that he will get his Blue at Cambridge. He is a fine free bat, with great punishing powers, and a very good fast bowler. As regarding the actual value of his bowling, however, we must wait until he has been tried against first rate elevens, many public school bowlers of late years having quite failed after their school days to sustain their early reputations.

Hindsight of course, is a luxury that often tends to make a nonsense of caution. If the Lord's match of the previous year saw Jackson's potential come to fruition on the big stage of English cricket, the following season, of 1889, saw his star ascendant in public-school cricket. The Lord's match of 1888 had won him a national fame that is hard to comprehend in the modern age. By the end of his school days he was Harrow's favourite son, hardly a scholar, more a roving ambassador, a young man who struck awe into many of his schoolfellows and opponents on the field of play.

As a captain he was calm, collected, always in command; if his temper was usually even, his displeasure could be very abrupt indeed when the occasion warranted. He was his own man, he knew his own mind and had the conviction - some say, the arrogance - to impose his will both on his team, and its opponents. In short, he had an old head on young shoulders.

Of course, the real test of a Harrow captain, was how he fared in the annual contest with Eton. When the test came on an overcast, close Friday morning in July at Lord's Jackson began as he meant to continue. He won the toss and without a moment's hesitation elected to bat. The Harrow openers were soon back in the pavilion, C.G. Pope for a single and MacLaren who played on when he had made 17. The damage had been partly repaired by a useful stand between R.B. Hoare and C.P. Wells which had carried the score along to 81, when, at twenty-five to one, the former was out bowled, and Jackson entered the fray. The Harrow captain was cheered all the way to the middle by the first-day crowd of over five thousand.

Jackson started slowly. The conditions were far from ideal for batting; the light was variable, with storm clouds threatening a downpour at any moment. At 13 he offered a straightforward catch to J.E. Talbot at cover-point off H.R. Bromley-Davenport's fast left-arm bowling. The chance went down, as did another a little later, this time spilled by W.G. Crum at square-leg as Jackson began to bat with a greater freedom. Even the best batsmen need fortune's bounty, and Jackson, batting with growing authority was 66 not out at the luncheon interval, taken at two o'clock with the Harrow total at 204 for the loss of 4 wickets. Jackson was out just after the resumption, caught one-handed by C.W. Studd at mid-off. His 68, made in an hour and a half was to be the highest individual score of the match, and with his departure the innings gradually subsided until at a little before four o'clock the XI were all out for 272, whereupon, a cloudburst saturated Lord's and further play was impossible.

On the Saturday morning the captains agreed to an extension of play to half past seven that evening, if a finish was in prospect. As it transpired, but for this provision the contest would have ended in a draw. It says much for the spirit of the age that Eton should so readily agree to the proposal, since the question was not whether they could triumph, but rather whether or not they could save the match. The tally of victories in the previous 63 encounters between the schools stood at 27 each and throughout the long day Eton fought a valiant rearguard action to preserve parity in the series. Eton withstood the Harrow attack until twenty-five past three, when they were dismissed for 169 and obliged to follow on. Now their plight was desperate, deepening as time went by; Jackson - who sent down some 280 deliveries that day - bowled the opener W.G. Crum after twenty minutes' dogged resistance for 5 runs, and removed the luckless J.E. Talbot without scoring. G.B. Gosling batted for 155 minutes for 35, H.R. Bromley-Davenport hit out for a brave 42, but as Jackson juggled his tiring bowlers, Eton wickets fell, and Harrow's grip on the match tightened. R.B. Hoare, C.G. Pope, W.B. Anderson, and C.P. Wells shared the wickets with Jackson as Eton tottered to a final tally of 152 at twenty-eight minutes past six, leaving Harrow 50 to win in as many minutes.

C.W. Studd bowled MacLaren for the second time in the match for 16, but C.P. Wells and R.B. Hoare knocked off the runs with ten minutes to spare.

It was the crowning moment of Jackson's schooldays. He had captained the XI to an overwhelming victory, made the highest score on either side, and claimed 5 wickets for 81 runs in the match. If Bowen had not already penned 'A Gentleman's A-Bowling' Welldon would have put him to work there and then. If anybody doubts the awe in which Jackson was now held by many of his schoolboy contemporaries, Sir Pelham Warner's description of his first meeting with Jacker, in *My Cricketing Life* (1921), should dispel such doubts.

Warner turned out for Rugby against a Harrow past and present XI, over the first weekend of August 1889, three weeks after the Eton - Harrow match, directly following the Rugby - Marlborough game at Lord's. The match was held at Althorp Park, the estate of Lord Spencer, a governor of both Rugby and Harrow. In the evenings the teams dined together in the presence of the Earl, and the two Head Masters, Welldon and Percival.

Warner recalls how he was lucky enough to sit beside Jackson: 'He was a tremendous swell at Harrow, the friend and confidant of his Head Master, it was rumoured, but he was most extraordinarily nice to me, and I tingled with pride whenever he spoke to me.' Warner remarked that his own Head Master thought Welldon 'made too much of Jackson'. The young 'Plum' Warner was quite content to bask in the illustrious company of the famous

Jacker; he for one had no doubt whatsoever that Jackson was anything but 'an enormous influence over the Harrow of his day'.

The match itself was drawn, although not without incident. Harrow amassed 302 in their first innings, J. St Fair with 114, and Jackson with 88, batting with an end-of-term abandon. Rugby replied with 249, and then, as the two-day fixture drifted towards the inevitable draw, MacLaren struck 49 of Harrow's carefree 144 on the second afternoon. Jackson came in to bat at number nine in the order, even in those days careless about his average; padless, he was out for 2, cheerfully swiping across the line. The game was the thing and it did not do to take it too seriously, not when the contest was over and all that was left was to play out time.

So ended F.S. Jackson's Harrow days.

4 | Trinity and Cambridge (1889-1891)

Stanley Jackson became a freshman of Trinity College in October, 1889. Cambridge offered freedoms unknown at Harrow, and academic horizons undreamed of at the school on the hill. Yet the University offered him but one great challenge when he passed through the portals of Trinity College for the first time; the quest for a blue at cricket. He still played fives and football, but cricket now dominated his thoughts.

When he arrived at Cambridge some wags dubbed him 'Lord Harrow' on account of his schoolboy feats. It was well meant, but much was expected of him. University life bowed to the same gods of sporting endeavour worshipped in the great public schools. Prowess on the field of play excused poor scholarship; some would say, it encouraged it.

Cambridge cricket was in full bloom in 1890 under the captaincy of the remarkable S.M.J. 'Sammy' Woods. Able to call on H.J. Mordaunt, R.C. Gosling, G. McGregor, C.P.

Foley and J. Ford from the previous year, Woods also had a wealth of schoolboy talent at his disposal amongst his freshmen: Harrow had sent him its captain, accompanied by R.B. Hoare and C.P. Wells; there was R.A. Ward, H.R. Bromley-Davenport, W.G. Crum, and H.W. Studd from Eton; A.J.L. Hill from Marlborough; E.C. Streatfield of Charterhouse; and D.L.A. Jephson, who had already attracted the lively interest of Surrey, from Manor House.

As at Harrow, while Jackson enjoyed all the scholastic opportunities of his fellows, his energies were only spasmodically devoted to matters academic in his time at Trinity. At Harrow he had worked hard enough to matriculate, at Cambridge he aimed for, and achieved an 'ordinary' degree. He won his B.A., for his mind was quick, and, when necessary, he was not afraid of hard work and could undoubtedly have walked away from Trinity College with an 'honours' degree; but it seems he was never convinced of the necessity of setting his academic sights so high, and, besides, his public awaited him on the great stages of English cricket.

His tutor throughout his Cambridge days was Richard Appleton, a man of no mean distinction - a lecturer in mathematics and theology, Secretary and Treasurer of the Cambridge Clergy Training School, and Examining Chaplain to three successive Bishops of Durham - a man of profound religious convictions who influenced many generations of undergraduates at Trinity. Appleton's role was predominantly pastoral, being not so much to teach the men under his care, but to advise and guide, and generally oversee their progress.

The Trinity College freshman's match was held on the last Friday and Saturday of April 1890, although in the event rain forced the abandonment of the game on the Saturday. Jackson opened the batting and the bowling for R.A. Wilson's side against G.T. Foljambe's side; he scored 29, and took 4 good wickets. R.B. Hoare, W.G. Crum and W. Studd from the previous year's Eton - Harrow match at Lord's were among his opponents, and the latter pair fell victim to his bowling. A week later Jackson turned out for the 'Perambulators' against the 'Etceteras', in a game featuring several of the leading Cambridge cricketers, scored 22 and 42, and took 6 for 89 in the match, including the wickets of Gregor McGregor, the Cambridge wicketkeeper, in the first innings, and Sammy Woods, the Cambridge captain, clean bowled in the second.

This fixture was the prelude to the Cambridge University freshman's match, in which Jackson was selected for G. McGregor's XV versus S.M.J. Wood's XIV. He hit 44, the top score in his side's first innings, and 9, although, in opening the bowling he returned a disappointing 1 for 58 in the match. But Sammy Woods and Gregor McGregor had seen enough, recognising that the former Harrow captain was an all-rounder who was worth his place in the University side either as a batsman or a bowler.

Jackson was duly selected and he made his debut in a first-class match at Fenner's Ground, Cambridge on Monday 12 May, 1890, against C.I. Thornton's XI, a scratch side raised by the redoubtable hitter of former days, and promoter of the festivities which crowned each season at Scarborough.

The match was over in two extraordinary days. Sammy Woods and C. Streatfield caught C.I. Thornton's XI on a damp wicket on the first morning and dismissed them for 68. Cambridge struggled to 130 all out, Jackson's share - batting at number five - being 17 hard-earned runs against the pace of Arthur Mold and the hardly pedestrian wiles of Johnny Briggs. It was Briggs who had him caught in the end, the first of the nine occasions on which he was to dismiss Jackson over the coming years. Jackson did not get to bowl in the match, since Sammy Woods bowled out C.I. Thornton's XI single-handed in the second innings, taking all ten wickets, seven of them bowled, for match figures of 15 for 88. *Cricket* takes up the story:

> Cambridge wanted at the end 72 to win, but the bowling of Briggs, Mold and Wright was too good to admit of any liberties, and when the sixth wicket fell, the total was only 48. Mr. Jackson, the Harrow captain of 1889, though, batted with great judgement, as he had in the first innings, and as Mr. Hale and he got the runs still wanting, the University was able to win the match with four wickets in hand.

A week after his baptism of fire in first-class cricket Jackson was in the side that faced A.J. Webbe's team in a 12-a-side match at Fenner's. A.J. Webbe's XII was, like C.I. Thornton's XI, a powerful team, but on this occasion Cambridge was without the services of Sammy Woods. A.J. Webbe's XII, which included several England players, won in the end by a margin of 11 wickets. Jackson, batting sixth in the order, scored 21 and 6, and took his first wickets for Cambridge, running through the opposition's lower order, capturing the wickets of P.J. de

Paravicini, G.F. Vernon, T.S. Pearson, and A.D. Pougher to end with figures of 4 for 75.

At the end of that week Cambridge lost by 9 wickets to M.C.C., Jackson batting well for 20 and 41 in a low-scoring contest and capturing 5 wickets for 94 in the match.

It was at the end of May, in the course of his fourth first-class match that Jackson established himself in the Cambridge team. The match was at Fenner's, and the opponents were, ironically, Yorkshire. The Yorkshire Committee had been watching Jackson since his heroic deeds of 1888, and if any doubts lingered in the county of the broad acres about the ability of the Old Harrovian, they were soon to be dispelled.

The Yorkshire side that visited Fenner's was the same side – except for the absence of Edward Wainwright - that had defeated the Australians by 7 wickets earlier in the week at Bramall Lane, Sheffield. Cambridge were again without Sammy Woods. Yorkshire batted first and reached 80 for the loss of only one wicket, that of Louis Hall bowled by Jackson for 9. At that point a big score was likely, and without Woods, the University's main strike bowler, there seemed little that Cambridge could do about it. It was then that Jackson the bowler came of age. He removed Frederick Lee and Lord Hawke within minutes of each other, both bowled, and shortly afterwards had Robert Frank caught. The back of the Yorkshire innings was broken, George Ulyett battled on to 51 before A.J.L. Hill broke his wicket, Bobby Peel survived for a stubborn 37, but in the end the 'Tykes' were dismissed for 193. Jackson's share of the spoils was 5 wickets for 61 runs.

When Cambridge batted Jackson went in at the fall of the fifth wicket and was out without troubling the scorers.

He had never been out for a duck in an important match, and it preyed on his mind as he sat in the pavilion at Fenner's, pondering the sudden darkness of the world. Out in the middle the University's tail was wagging with a vengeance and the Cambridge score was already well in advance of the Yorkshire total.

'What's the matter with you, Jacker?' demanded a familiar voice. Jackson looked up to find Sammy Woods towering over him. Before he could reply his captain grinned, and declared, laughing: 'If it's that blue you are feeling anxious about, you can have it now if you like, but you know it isn't usual for it to be given until after the next match.'

The Cambridge innings eventually closed with 329 on the board, a lead of 136 on first innings, mostly due to a robust last wicket stand of 101 between A.J.L. Hill and E.C. Streatfield. In those days one of the strengths of Cambridge cricket was that even the bowlers batted like batsmen. Streatfield, coming into the attack as first change was Jackson's henchman in what followed. Jackson had George Ulyett caught in the outfield, and bowled Louis Hall for the second time in the match, this time for 0; Streatfield sent back Lord Hawke and Bobby Peel, and Yorkshire were struggling. Lee battled valiantly until Jackson induced him to edge a catch to the wicketkeeper, and after that, he quickly disposed of the tail. His second innings analysis of 7 for 53 gave him match figures of 12 for 114. In his career he would bowl in another 285 first-class matches, but improve on this return but three times, never bettering 12 wickets in any match.

From that moment Jackson became an automatic

selection for the University. In his four years at Cambridge he never missed a match. When the match against Yorkshire began he had been a new man in the team, unsure of his tenure, looking to consolidate his position, prove himself worthy of the prized blue for which every freshman yearns. Afterwards, a place in the XI was his by right.

Cambridge won by 9 wickets, and Jackson was out in the middle at the death, undefeated, and with 7 runs to his credit. That the University could triumph over the growing might of Yorkshire without its captain and spearhead bowler was testimony indeed to the quality of cricket at Cambridge.

Sammy Woods dominated Cambridge cricket.

His influence on the 'Cantab' XIs in which he played, and later captained, went far beyond merely his own contribution to the team. He was a man who imbued those around him with his own irresistible zest for life. He played the game with a fearlessness that inspired lesser mortals to deeds that often astonished them when they looked back on a match. The great captain is the captain who imposes his will on a game: some captains achieve this by dissecting the strengths and weaknesses of their opponents, others by sleight of hand, some simply by dint of commanding a powerful side; once in a blue moon a captain imposes his influence not just upon his opponents, but on a generation of cricketers by sheer force of personality: such a man was Sammy Woods.

Samuel Moses James Woods was captain of Cambridge University, Somerset and the Gentlemen; he played Test Match cricket for both his native Australia, and for his adopted country, England, for whom he also won thirteen caps on the rugby field as an indestructible flank forward. Born at Glenfield, New South Wales, he was schooled at Royston College, Sydney, where he once performed the incredible feat of taking seven wickets with seven consecutive deliveries. He and his younger brother H.D.L. Woods had been sent to England to be educated at Brighton College. In a match against Lancing College he took 14 for 27, all his victims bowled.

At Cambridge he was a legend. As a batsman he was a ferocious striker of the ball: as a bowler - for a few short years before his pace waned in 1893 - he was a fast bowler with few equals. He had the strength of a bear, the ability to bowl fast for long spells with unerring accuracy, and could deliver at will either a terrifying yorker or a villainously disguised slower ball. He was that most dangerous of fast bowlers; not just a tearaway pace merchant - although he was that too - but an inveterate thinker, also. Plum Warner thought he was the most intelligent fast bowler he had ever faced.

When he went down from Cambridge Sammy Woods played for Somerset for over twenty years, captained the county for most of them, served it as Secretary for three decades and came to speak with a pronounced Taunton accent. Sammy Woods was one of the great characters of the game.

On the night before the Oxford - Cambridge match at Lord's, he was ragging with Gregor McGregor, then, as later, one of his closest friends, and in high spirits threw the Cambridge wicket-keeper through a ground floor plate-glass window. McGregor miraculously survived without a scratch, although Sammy confessed afterwards that it had been one of the worst moments of his life.

One of Sammy's favourite recreations was walking in the country; another was a fondness for cool ale. Looking back on his life he declared: 'There is one thing I have steadily tried to do: to drink more beer for the years I have lived than any other man who has ever come down from Cambridge.' He combined these two pleasures by burying caches of beer bottles along the routes of his long treks.

It was off Sammy's bowling that W.G. Grace made the run that took him to the hundredth hundred of his illustrious career.

'It was the proudest moment of my life', Sammy always maintained.

While at Cambridge he invited six of the opposing C.I. Thornton's XI to join him for breakfast, whereupon he set before them hot lobsters and tankards of beer. When his ungrateful guests demanded bacon and eggs, and tea to wash it down, he proceeded to consume all the lobster and all the beer - a preliminary to taking all 10 wickets in his opponents' second innings: 'to show that a little nourishment is not harmful'.

The moral of the story is that if Sammy Woods thought a chap could play a bit, a chap usually believed him.

As the Oxford - Cambridge Match at Lord's approached, Jackson's batting was inconsistent. He was too inclined to play across the line early in his innings, and, to a degree, he was found out by the professional bowling fraternity. He scored 21 and 5 against the Australians in a drawn match at Fenner's, went for 5 and 0 against Surrey at the Oval, where he was undone by George Lohmann in the second innings, at Brighton against Sussex he scored 7, and then 60 in 65 minutes in a partnership of 132 with Francis Ford, as the University raced to the then record first-class score of 703 for 9 - Cambridge won by the small matter of 425 runs. Immediately before the Oxford - Cambridge match, he registered the third duck of his short first-class career, but in the second innings of a low-scoring encounter he made 38 of the University's 101 all out against M.C.C. at Lord's. His brisk fast-medium bowling was the backbone of his game, although with the return of Sammy Woods to the side after the Yorkshire match, his bowling was less in demand. He took 4 for 69 against the Australians, 1 for 57 against Surrey, 3 for 54 in the Sussex game, and 1 for 37 against M.C.C.

It was at Lord's in the match against M.C.C. that he held the first of his 195 catches in first-class cricket, to dismiss James Wootton, the Kent professional, off the medium pace bowling of Harold Hale, the Australian-born blue who had played for Gloucestershire before coming up to Cambridge.

The 56th Oxford - Cambridge match at Lord's was played on a rain-ruined wicket. It poured before the game began, soaking the surrounds and damaging the wicket. The first day was completely lost to the weather, and the second day was curtailed by some four hours because of the elements. Cambridge, everybody's favourites to win, was the stronger all-round side without obvious weaknesses; Oxford had several capable cricketers, but their form had been generally unconvincing.

When the match finally started on Tuesday 1st July, Oxford, upon winning the toss, took first use of a wicket that was underprepared to begin with, and by then damp. The Oxford captain, The Honourable J.N. Thesiger, no doubt believed that the pitch could only deteriorate as the match progressed, and reasonably, in the circumstances, assumed the side that had first use of it would have the advantage.

He was sadly mistaken.

Sammy Woods and Streatfield, bowling unchanged, skittled out Oxford in 67 minutes for 42 runs in the space of 143 deliveries. Woods ended with 4 for 25, Streatfield with 5 for 14. Of the Oxford batsmen, five were dismissed without scoring, and just one, Ernest Smith, with 22, reached double figures. (Smith, an Old Cliftonian, was like Jackson a native of Yorkshire, and much in the mind of Lord Hawke as he looked to the future of Yorkshire cricket.)

Cambridge went out and batted for some 50 minutes before the heavens opened and put a stop to proceedings, by which time they had lurched to 40 for 3, R.N. Douglas, F.G.J. Ford and G. McGregor back in the pavilion, with Jackson and C.P. Foley attempting to withstand the twin-pronged pace attack of G.F.H. Berkeley and Ernest Smith.

On the next morning - the last morning of the match - the wicket had lost much of its spite, although it was not without its surprises as Jackson and Foley carried the Cambridge score to 60. Berkeley bowled Jackson at 23 to end a careful, watchful innings of about an hour in which he had curbed his natural attacking instincts in the interests of the side. The Cambridge innings soon concluded, the vagaries of the pitch exposing the defensive shortcomings of the later batsmen. The University were out for the grand total of 97, an achievement which gave them a decisive first innings lead of 55.

In reply, Oxford wiped off the arrears at a cost of 3 wickets, mainly due to a staunch partnership by M.R.

Jardine (father of Douglas Jardine) and G.L. Wilson, who scored 24 and 20 respectively. But Oxford could do no more than delay the inevitable on the treacherous wicket; Woods and Streatfield were at them all the time like wolves upon the fold. L.C.H. Palairet batted with grace - his hallmark for the next twenty years - for his 17, but once he was gone Woods scythed through the Oxford tail and the innings closed at 108, leaving Cambridge 54 to win. Jackson had bowled nine overs without taking a wicket; it was not destined to be one of his happier days. Cambridge scored the runs they needed with relative ease, although not before losing Douglas for 17, and Jackson and McGregor for 1 apiece. The 'Cantabs' were indebted on this occasion to Francis Ford, whose solid innings of 32 not out, was largely responsible for seeing them home with seven wickets in hand.

It had been a frustrating match for Jackson. On a bowler's wicket he had struggled as a batsman and had had scant opportunity to show his worth as a bowler. But he was not a man to dwell on such things; he had in any case been invited to join the Yorkshire XI to face Lancashire at Huddersfield later in the month, and in the meantime he gained some useful batting practice playing for I Zingari against the Garrison at Colchester, scoring a handsome 112 out of the touring club's total of 190.

Jackson's first appearance for his native county was destined to be a rather harrowing experience. Yorkshire was put to the sword on an underprepared pitch by Lancashire's Arthur Mold. Mold was a bowler with a suspect action who was destined to be hounded out of the game, but that was many years hence, and on his day he was a terrifyingly fast bowler. Jackson scored 2 and 0, one of Mold's nine victims in the first innings. Yorkshire scored 90 and 57 and lost by an innings and 28 runs. For Jackson there was the minor compensation of taking his first wickets for the county of his birth, those of the Lancashire opener R.G. Barlow and the middle order batsman, G. Yates.

However, within a week, Stanley Jackson put the disappointments of his Championship debut behind him in Yorkshire's match against M.C.C. at Lord's. Batting sixth in the order he was joined by Robert Moorhouse with the score at 28 and half the side back in the pavilion. It was a dire situation, but it called forth the best in the two Yorkshiremen. Their stand lasted 85 explosive minutes in which time 134 runs were added and the course of the match irrevocably altered. Jackson was first out for a robust 68, having scored faultlessly until a wildness came into his hitting near the end of his knock, while Moorhouse went on to complete one of his three centuries in a first-class career of over two hundred matches. The Yorkshire innings closed at 217, whereupon Jackson was soon among the wickets, bowling both M.C.C. openers, C.W. Wright and A. Hearne. Yorkshire won by an innings with their new young fast bowler claiming 5 for 28 in the match.

He played in only one other fixture for Yorkshire that year, a rain-affected match at Bradford against Middlesex, in which 26 wickets fell for just 300 runs and the home side very nearly forced a win. Jackson had a quiet match, bowled by J.T. Rawlin for 8 in the Yorkshire innings, and was no more than an interested observer as Bobby Peel and Edward Wainwright tormented the visitors. Near the end of the season he turned out for I Zingari against the

Gentlemen of England, at Scarborough, where he had the misfortune to run into Sammy Woods in his most destructive form, registering 3 and 0 with the bat in his two short stays in the middle. He was in good company, for Woods' figures were 7 for 47 and 5 for 50, and no one withstood him for long. When Sammy Woods was in full flow, courage and technique counted for very little without an outrageous helping of luck. From Scarborough, he went on to Leeds, where he had been invited to appear for a North of England XI against the Australians, in a match staged to open formally the new Headingley Ground. He was bowled by J.J. Ferris in the first innings for the sixth duck of his brief first-class career, and when he had made 13 in the second, he was run out.

In his debut season in the first-class game Jackson had given a good account of himself, particularly with the ball. In fourteen matches he had struck 385 runs at an average of 16.04, and taken 37 wickets at 17.37 apiece. James Lillywhite was less than charitable in commenting that he had 'hardly sustained his school reputation, though a useful man in any eleven'. This, however, was balanced by *Wisden's* verdict on the University season that of the four freshmen who secured places against Oxford: 'Mr Jackson was probably the best cricketer, his batting and bowling figures being extremely creditable.'

Jackson was content to spend the winter of 1890-91 in relative obscurity. He studied hard, and indulged his passion for shooting. April found him practising hard for the coming cricket season.

Although Sammy Woods was still available to play in the XI, Gregor McGregor was captain of Cambridge in 1891. Before the season began Jackson was elected

Honorary Secretary of the University Club.

The first match of the season against C.I. Thornton's XI at Fenner's was set aside for the benefit of W. Watts, who for thirty years had been the caretaker of the Fenner's Ground. C.I. Thornton's team was a formidable combination, in batting order: J.J. Ferris, J.E. Barrett, W.L. Murdoch, W.G. Grace, R. Peel, A.J. Webbe, J. Briggs, G.F. Vernon, H. Philipson, C.I. Thornton, and A. Mold. The XI was billed in some quarters as C.I. Thornton's England XI, although the first three in the order, Ferris, Barrett and Murdoch were Australians. For Cambridge, on the other hand, Sammy Woods was absent.

The University won the toss and elected to bat. Faced with an attack comprising Ferris, Mold, Peel, Briggs and W.G., Cambridge, due mainly to the efforts of two redoubtable former Dulwich College boys, R.N. Douglas (131) and C.M. Wells (58) reached the dizzy heights of 262 all out in four and a half hours. Despite 54 from W.G., C.I. Thornton's XI struggled in their first innings which closed at 203, a deficit of 59 runs. Mold and Ferris did their level best to redress matters when Cambridge batted again, and at the close of play on the second day the University had been reduced to 107 for 8, Jackson out for a staunch 22. Cambridge was dismissed on the third morning of the match for 135, leaving C.I. Thornton's side 194 for the match. The University's plight was all the worse for the loss of E.C. Streatfield - Jackson's partner with the new ball - struck on the hand by one of Mold's thunderbolts.

Jackson hurled himself into the fray, six of the first eight batsmen fell to him, the other two departing run out. These were no easy pickings, rather the wickets of several of the most renowned international cricketers of the day, but in the end it was to no avail. *Cricket* described the high drama of that Saturday afternoon in May thus:

> Mr Thornton's team made such a good start that 100 went up with only two batsmen out. Afterwards a succession of disasters occurred. Dr Grace was run out, and when the sixth wicket fell, the total was only 143. Mr Webbe and Briggs, however, made a plucky stand, and their excellent cricket practically decided the result. As it was, the University was only beaten after a good fight by one wicket, and had Peel, who was fielding as substitute for Mr Streatfield, not missed a chance just at the close the positions might have been reversed.

Bobby Peel's hands were usually safe. Though he was too fond of his ale, and could often be the bane of friend and foe alike, he deserves, at this remove, the benefit of the doubt even if it was his spilled catch that robbed Cambridge of a famous victory.

Despite the return of Sammy Woods, Cambridge were defeated in their next two games, by the narrow margin of 32 runs by A.J. Webbe's XI, and by 4 wickets by M.C.C. In the latter match Jackson made the highest score in the University's first innings, hitting 41 in a total of 126. Once again, with Sammy Woods back in the side his bowling was briefly in the shade, mainly because it was so little used. When Sammy Woods wanted to bowl, Gregor McGregor - quite understandably - let him get on with it, and Jackson as the junior fast bowler, had to wait his turn.

Three successive defeats hardly constituted an auspicious start to Cambridge's season, even if the manner of those defeats reflected no little glory on the state of the University's cricket. Indeed, with their fair share of luck, Cambridge might have run out the winners in all three matches. Nevertheless, a defeat is a defeat, and three defeats on the trot suggested that perhaps the University was no longer the side it had been the previous season. Not unnaturally doubts were being aired about the Cambridge XI of 1891 when Yorkshire came down to Fenner's at the end of May.

The Tykes were without Lord Hawke and Ernest Smith, but were otherwise at full strength, the first six in their order reading: G. Ulyett, L. Hall, A. Sellars, R. Peel, E. Wainwright and J.T. Brown. The wicket was soft after recent rain, and batting was a less than straightforward business on it during the two days it took to conclude the match. Yorkshire had first use of the wicket, floundering to totals of 118 and 89, with only George Ulyett playing with any freedom, for scores of 51 and 45. Cambridge fared little better in their first innings, struggling to 120, but in their second the University eventually made the 88 runs required for victory with 4 wickets in hand. As in the corresponding fixture of 1890, Yorkshire's downfall was mainly caused by the bowling of Jackson, who took 10 for 65 in the match, 5 for 28 in the first innings and 5 for 37 in the second. He was ably assisted in the destruction by Sammy Woods, who returned match figures of 8 for 98. Yet with the bat Jackson again failed, trapped leg before by Bobby Peel for another 'egg' in his one innings. He was not the first, and certainly not the last, aspiring batsman to be thoroughly bamboozled by the guile of Bobby Peel, but in time he *would* work out Peel. In the final reckoning, Peel dismissed Jackson on six occasions, while Jackson dismissed Peel five times.

After vanquishing Yorkshire, the University went on to the Oval and triumphed by 19 runs over Surrey. Jackson's 62 in the University's first innings was the highest score in the match. *Cricket* reported:

> The score was only 67 when Messrs. Jackson and McGregor became partners on the fall of the fourth wicket. Mr. Jackson hit all round in most determined style until after making twelve off Lockwood's first over he was caught... He was only in an hour and twenty minutes, and his 62 out of 97 made during his stay was a capital display.

There were no easy runs to be made off the Surrey attack; G.A. Lohmann, J.W. Sharpe and W. Lockwood were as daunting a combination as any in England. However, Sammy Woods wrecked both Surrey innings, taking 14 wickets in the match to assure the county side's first defeat of the season.

From Kennington, Cambridge went on to beat Sussex by 48 runs in an extraordinary, high-scoring game at Brighton. 1,402 runs were scored in the match, Cambridge registering 359 and 366, Sussex 314 and 363. Jackson contributed a modest 46 runs to the feast of batsmanship, 4 and 42 respectively in the University totals, but with the ball he proved the most successful bowler on either side, taking 8 for 220 in the course of 74 five-ball overs.

After the match at Brighton, there remained only the

traditional fixture against M.C.C. at Lord's before the annual clash with Oxford. The University rested Sammy Woods and C.M. Wells and on the first day restricted the home side to a total of 283. Overnight rain then ruined the wicket and Cambridge were bowled out for a dismal 36 by J.T. Hearne and William Attewell. Following on the University reached the respectability - on that wicket - of 113, the match being lost by an innings and 134 runs. Jackson scored 0 and 10, taking 2 for 76 on the first day when the wicket was at its most benign. It was the worst possible prelude to the Oxford - Cambridge match.

In fact Jackson's season was already in eclipse. His fifty against Surrey and his bowling triumph against Yorkshire were the highlights of the season. His batting was rarely needed by Cambridge, or, for that matter, by his native Yorkshire; likewise, at Cambridge, his bowling was overshadowed by Sammy Woods, competing for the new ball with E.C. Streatfield, while in Yorkshire he was second or third change after Bobby Peel and Edward Wainwright, and sometimes even Ernest Smith was preferred ahead of him in the county's attack.

His apprenticeship was strewn with all the normal pitfalls that spoil so many promising cricketers, and the Oxford - Cambridge game rather typified the latter half of his season. He scored 10 and 2, and bowled economically without much luck in taking 1 for 24 and 1 for 46, while Sammy Woods was helping himself to wickets and glory at the other end. Sammy's tally in the match was 11 for 132, and, as if this were not enough, he came to the wicket in the Cambridge second innings padless, smashing the match-winning boundary to give the University victory by two wickets in a desperate finish.

After the match Jackson, along with Woods, McGregor and R.N. Douglas from the triumphant Cambridge XI, were invited to play for the Gentlemen against the Players at the Oval. In an age when the fixture was every bit as important a contest as any Test Match, his early selection for the Gentlemen has a particular significance. Other than to play for one's country, there was no higher honour in the game than to represent either the Gentlemen or the Players. To appear in the fixture was to be at one remove from the England XI.

In the event Jackson failed to do himself justice with the bat; caught at the wicket by his fellow Yorkshireman, David Hunter, off the bowling of Johnny Briggs for 5; although when he bowled, the one wicket he took in his 45 deliveries was the prized wicket of Arthur Shrewsbury, then at the height of his powers, comprehensively bowled by a ball that cut back into the Nottinghamshire opener off the wicket for 17.

He played six matches for Yorkshire during July and August, making several useful contributions with the bat without ever threatening to set the world on fire, and bowling economically and competently when required. His season ended with an appearance for the North against the South at Scarborough. In a very low-scoring match, he scored a robust 27 in the first innings, and fell leg before for a duck in the second.

His batting remained an enigma. After two seasons and 30 matches in the first-class game he had made just three half-centuries in his 55 innings. His bowling was a different matter: in the 26 matches in which he had actually bowled, he had taken 82 wickets at an average cost of 18.98, and, moreover, taken his wickets at the highly respectable strike rate of one wicket every 44 balls. But if it was his bowling that had impressed most and had earned him his invitation to play for the Gentlemen in the Oval match, in July, the potential of his batting had also been noticed. At this stage of his career he was one of those infuriating batsmen who always seem much better than their average suggests. He looked the part and appeared full of runs, but somehow they stubbornly refused to materialise. During that summer of 1891 there were tantalising glimpses, signs that his batting was about to blossom - most notably his innings against Lohmann, Sharpe and Lockwood in June, but at the end of the season his batting was a conundrum awaiting a solution.

Of course, he rightfully played in the middle of the Cambridge batting order, his place unquestioned. His bowling had already won a string of matches, sometimes alone, as often as not the perfect foil to Sammy Woods or Streatfield. In the matter of the Cambridge captaincy, he had long been regarded as the natural successor to Woods and McGregor, and it came as no surprise when that autumn he was duly elected Captain of the Cambridge University Cricket Club.

When a lady had complimented him on his second innings knock of 59 in the 1888 Eton - Harrow Match at Lord's, Jackson had said, 'Yes, it is jolly, isn't it? Not so much for one's self, you know, but it will give the guv'nor such a lift!' No doubt he took the accolade of the Cambridge captaincy in his stride in the self-same spirit.

5 | Captain of Cambridge (1892)

When Jackson assumed the Cambridge captaincy there were those who wondered whether the glory days the University had enjoyed under Sammy Woods and Gregor McGregor were things of the past. To follow in such illustrious footsteps would have seemed a daunting prospect to the average man.

Jackson, however, was not the average man.

He took the captaincy in his stride, making no attempt to imitate either of his predecessors. He had his own style of leadership: if he was less demonstrative than Woods or McGregor, it was simply because he was a different kind of man. Jackson could rag with the best of them, but he was not a man in the mould of Sammy Woods; he was at Cambridge to prepare himself for roles other than those of cricketing immortality. Cricket was his first love, but it was not allowed to undermine wholly the broader aims of his life. Sammy Woods was almost sent down for ignoring his studies; Jackson was always in control of his destiny.

In a funny sort of way, Jackson was an outsider.

He was a team man, yet he remained his own man. After a day's play his peers would dwell on events out in the middle, but Jackson would discuss politics and world affairs. Away from cricket his conversation rarely touched upon the game he loved. Cricket was for the playing; at close of play the playing ended. Jackson was not just an all-rounder in the cricketing sense; the summer game was only one part of his life for he was a man for all seasons. It was this quality that set him apart from his contemporaries at Trinity, and which in later years was to be his most enduring personal asset. However, from the moment he became the Cambridge captain it was his tenacity of purpose that impressed his friends and foes alike.

Captaincy under Woods and McGregor was an inspirational exercise, and opponents often found themselves swept aside. Jackson's captaincy was a calm, confident contrast to the highs and lows of the previous two years. Under Jackson Cambridge were a calmer, more businesslike side, less brittle, an XI markedly less inclined to snatch defeat from the jaws of victory. There were those who thought him a trifle aloof, somewhat distanced from his fellows, and his sense of humour, very dry, and occasionally a shade sardonic, was not to everybody's taste.

Jackson set the highest standards for himself and he expected his players to do no less. His appearance was always immaculate; no man's flannels were whiter than his, no man's pads or boots as clean. He could bat or bowl throughout a session and at the end of it he would still be well-groomed, unruffled, every inch the perfect gentleman, at peace with himself and the world.

It mattered how one played the game.

Attitude was everything.

When he batted he got into line and played with a straight bat, when he bowled he got side-on with a high arm and tried his best to make the batsman play at every delivery. As a batsman he never flinched and as a bowler he never bowled to hit a batsman. These were the unwritten laws, the code by which he judged others, and by which he expected others to judge him.

In the modern age such an approach to the game might seem somewhat naive, and perhaps it is, but Jackson played his cricket in an age different from our own and in a world now lost, a world in which the values of our times - our very modernity - would have been an abomination to the vast majority of Jackson's fellows. To Jackson it was precisely this old fashioned idea of cricket that made cricket the great national game of the golden age. To a man like Jackson 'playing the game' was everything. The game was nothing if it was not played in the right spirit.

Remember, cricket offered him no crock of gold, nor would he have accepted it, even if it had. Cricket was his recreation, and this was as true when he was twenty-one and captain of Cambridge, as it was when he was fifty-one and batting - with a faultlessly straight bat - for the Lords and Commons against Westminster School. Perhaps, it was because he believed so fervently in this idea of the game, that he was slow to recognise that in 1892 Cambridge had within its walls and available to its cause, a genius.

Kumar Shri Ranjitsinhji - later His Highness Shri Sir Ranjitsinhji Vibhaji, Jam Sahib of Nawanagar - was an authentic Indian prince, a genial potentate, deposed in his youth and then reinstated by successive palace coups; sometime heir apparent, sometime pretender, he eventually became lord of a fiefdom at the heart of the Bombay Presidency, but to cricket he was, and will always be, 'Ranji'. With the possible exception of his Sussex contemporary, C.B. Fry; Ranji was the most spectacularly successful, and the most remarkable English batsman of the golden age.

Many reasons have been advanced to explain why

Jackson overlooked Ranji in 1892, the year Ranji transferred from Fitzwilliam to Trinity, mostly out of a desire to further his cricket. Then, as now, Trinity was the more fashionable college, and rightly or wrongly, given the surfeit of cricketing talent at Cambridge in those days, it was widely held that to come from a fashionable college was of itself, a fillip.

Ranji's season began very early when he turned out over the Easter weekend for an XI of England against an XVIII of Kingston, at Kingston upon Thames.

He found himself in good company, batting tenth in the England XI's first innings in a list that included the likes of William Brockwell, Tom Hayward, William Lockwood, and the young Tom Richardson. He scored 15 in the first innings and 26, opening in the second. Though not tall, and physically frail, his medium-fast bowling claimed 5 for 26 in the Kingston innings, whilst the real carnage was being wrought by Lockwood with 11 for 56 and Richardson with a devastating second-innings spell of 9 wickets for 4 runs.

Early in May Ranji appeared in the Cambridge University Seniors' match at Fenner's, scoring 3 and 29 not out, and at the end of that month played for the Next XVI against the First XII, registering 0, and then a noteworthy 58.

His showing in the two trial matches was creditable, but several other batsmen had performed with equal aplomb; in the second trial T.N. Perkins (12 and 67), V.F. Leese (4 and 58) and E. Field (33 and 29), had all scored more runs for the Next XVI than Ranji.

That year he was second only to Jackson in the Trinity College batting averages, scoring three centuries in the process. In all, he hit eleven hundreds that season, including three for the Cassandra Club, two for Bassinettes, two for Cambridge Victoria, and one for Anchor. In August alone he reached three figures five times. In 1892 he hit over two thousand runs at an average in excess of 60, and not surprisingly he became something of a celebrity at Cambridge. It was not unusual for a sizeable crowd to gather when word got around that Ranji was batting; his disdain for orthodoxy and the recklessness of his stroke play made for compelling entertainment.

Jackson appeared only rarely for Trinity that season, but he recalled seeing Ranji bat on one occasion:

> On my way up to Fenner's I noticed a match in progress on Parker's Piece, and seeing a rather unusually large crowd of spectators I stopped to watch. As luck would have it Ranji was at the wicket. After a short exhibition of brilliant and certainly unorthodox strokes I thought Ranji was stumped, but much to the satisfaction of the crowd, the umpire decided in his favour. I left the scene not particularly impressed.

Jackson was aware of Ranji's feats, and had the evidence of the two trials in which he had played to substantiate his opinion, but that year the University side was particularly strong in batting. It was no exaggeration to say that the XI that faced Oxford batted all the way down the order. H.R. Bromley-Davenport who batted last in the first innings against Oxford at Lord's would later score 84 in one of his six subsequent innings in Test Matches. It would also be true to say that Jackson mistrusted unorthodoxy in a man whose claim to a blue rested solely on his batsmanship. To the end of his career in the first-class game he regarded unorthodoxy as the bedfellow of frivolity, as something not to be entirely trusted. In 1905 Gilbert Jessop was left out of the England side because Jackson felt he was a 'hundred or nothing' batsman, and he thought it was too much of a risk to play him in a game as important as a Test Match. It was one thing for Ranji to torment the bowling in a minor match with his improvisations, but it was another matter altogether to try and repeat the exhibition against top-line bowlers.

In any event, it would be wrong to suggest that Ranji was completely ignored. Although he did not win a place in the XI, his quicksilver fielding won him several appearances as a substitute fielder. Like so many other hopefuls, he waited in vain for the call that never came. If Jackson had a prejudice against Ranji, it arose from his suspicion of his batting technique. Ranji's method was eccentric and Jackson, with his growing experience in the first-class game, did not consider him to be a serious batsman - at least not then.

Moreover, Jackson had other preoccupations. The future of the University Ground, Fenner's, was in doubt. Since the mid-1870s Fenner's had been on lease from Caius College. In 1889 'the Orchard', a piece of land adjoining the ground where practice was possible (even during a match) had been reclaimed by the College, and been lost to cricket. Now, plans being formulated by Caius threatened the existence of Fenner's itself. Caius College was in the process of improving and expanding its facilities, and it was proposing to 'diminish the present area of the University Ground', depriving the Cambridge University Cricket Club of its practice grounds, and inevitably, impinging on gate receipts.

The problem was simple: the College's priority was the development of its properties, and Fenner's was a university rather than a college amenity. The Cambridge University Cricket Club decided on 26th October 1891 that in the circumstances there was only one course of action to be pursued, namely that the freehold of Fenner's be purchased from Caius. It was further determined that the President, Treasurer and Captain (Jackson), of the C.U.C.C., aided by the President and Treasurer of the Athletic Club, which shared Fenner's, should forthwith approach the Bursar of Caius and find out what terms might be acceptable to the College.

On 10th February 1892, the Bursar of Caius, informally outlined his terms. The College was prepared to sell Fenner's for £12,000, to be paid by Michaelmas 1894, providing the land be secured for ever as open space, and surrounded by a brick wall to be erected at the expense of the C.U.C.C.

The fund-raising operation began soon afterwards. The total amount required, including legal fees and other expenses was £12,800, of which some £6,000 would come from the savings of the C.U.C.C. and the C.U.A.C. The balance would have to be raised by voluntary subscriptions. By October 1892 donations and promises already totalled £2,739, and in December, when Caius confirmed the sale of Fenner's, £4,600 had been raised. The fund raising was so successful that by January 1893 it had exceeded the original target, allowing plans to be made to acquire further small plots of land adjoining Fenner's, and for the building of a small pavilion.

Jackson was the ideal figurehead. He was an accomplished public speaker, accustomed to the role of ambassador ever since his later days at Harrow. He was handsome, charming, virtually unflappable with none of the rough edges of a Sammy Woods. People trusted him. He was the perfect man for the job. Not only did he have the political skills required to enlist support, but he possessed the energy and the will to employ those skills. He was not alone in the campaign to purchase Fenner's - on the contrary, his involvement in the project was to lapse for several months in the winter of 1892-93 when he was on tour in India and Ceylon with Lord Hawke's team. There must have been many others who worked harder and longer to ensure the success of the venture than Jackson, but he was its public face, its popular impetus. In the press the myth was purveyed that he had bought Fenner's, that he was the sole mover behind the scheme. The reality was that he was the Cambridge captain, his name was already a name known the length and breadth of cricketing England, and he was, quite simply, the natural focus of the campaign.

Many men's cricket would have suffered; Jackson's cricket went from strength to strength.

The University's fixtures began with the visit of C.I. Thornton's XI to Fenner's at the end of the second week of May. On this occasion, the redoubtable Thornton was absent, and his XI was led by A.J. Webbe. The team, in batting order, was: C.E. de Trafford, H.T. Hewett, W.L. Murdoch, C.W. Wright, J. Briggs, A.J. Webbe, F. Vernon, P.J. de Paravicini, J.J. Ferris, S.M.J. Woods, and W.

Attewell. Cambridge fielded seven blues, three seniors (L.H. Gay, the wicket-keeper, N.C. Cooper, the old Brightonian who had done everything but win his blue the previous year, and H.R. Bromley-Davenport, whose fast left-arm bowling was the ideal foil to Streatfield's out-and-out pace in the opening attack) and one freshman J. Douglas, the younger brother of R.N. Douglas, a slow left-arm bowler and good-looking right-hand batsman.

The visitors were all out for 215 on the first afternoon, Jackson taking 4 for 44 after Streatfield, Bromley-Davenport and Wells had failed to make much of an impression on the early batting on a wicket that was distinctly fast. Cambridge struggled against the four-pronged attack of Sammy Woods, his Australian henchman, Ferris, and the two crafty professionals, Briggs and Attewell. In his first match as captain, Jackson played a captain's innings of 53, hitting out freely as the wickets tumbled. *Cricket* described the batting of the University as 'disappointing and, excepting the play of Messrs. Jackson and (G.J.V.) Weigall, was very tame'.

When Cambridge followed on Jackson's batsmen were unrecognisable as the timid boys they had seemed in the first innings. Jackson was a man who rarely needed to raise his voice; it was not his style. Whatever he said to his batsmen, it did the trick. R.N. Douglas and N.C. Cooper put on 115 for the first wicket, withstanding Ferris, Briggs and Attewell, and 'getting after' Sammy Woods. Only two of the nine subsequent batsmen failed to reach double figures and Jackson himself held the middle order together, sharing a seventh wicket partnership of 92 with J. Douglas. When he was out for 67, Bromley-Davenport launched himself into an assault on the bowling that had brought him 46 invaluable and undefeated runs by the time the last wicket fell, and the Cambridge total had reached 368. Thornton's XI were left 271 to win the match on a pitch that was becoming lower and slower all the while. The task proved beyond the visitors, Bromley-Davenport with 4 for 22 started the decline, J. Douglas, Streatfield and Jackson each chipped in with wickets, and C.I. Thornton's XI were beaten by a margin of 97 runs.

The match was a personal triumph for the new Cambridge captain. Jackson had scored 120 runs and taken 3 wickets for 60, but more than this, he had led the University out of the arms of defeat on the second morning, to a handsome victory and he never looked back.

In the next match Cambridge lost by 4 wickets to a strong Gentlemen of England side under the captaincy of A.J. Webbe. The Gentlemen included among their number, a canny and extremely able professional, J.T. Rawlin, and it was Rawlin, in league with Sammy Woods, whose bowling finally undid the University's cause. Jackson scored 5 and 19, and captured 4 wickets at the cost of 97 runs in the match, but on a placid third-day Fenner's wicket there was little he could do to defend the target of 229 runs Cambridge had set Webbe's XI.

At the end of the month the University entertained an under-strength M.C.C. team. Cambridge won at a canter by an innings and 61 runs, despite the absence, due to examinations, of R.N. Douglas, the opening bat, and Streatfield, the spearhead of the attack. Jackson led the way with a chanceless, dashing 84, an innings which included a six, 8 fours and 3 threes, the highest score in a total of 351. Picking up the ball he claimed 6 for 37 in the premier club's first innings, and 2 for 17 in the second as the visitors lurched towards defeat. As an aside, this was one of the matches in which Ranjitsinhji was called upon to act as a fielding substitute. Ranji's appearance on a cricket field inevitably provoked incident, and he recounted one event from the premier club's second innings in *The Cricket Field*:

> I was standing at mid-on, and C.W. Wright, who was the only man who was making a stand, hit a half-volley off Jackson very hard in my direction. I caught him with one hand high up. Wright, who thought it was well out of reach, started to run without looking, and just as he was returning for a second run Jackson said to him, 'Charles, I'm afraid that your energy is wasted'.

The Jackson sense of humour could be distinctly dry.

The omens were hardly set fair for Yorkshire's annual visit to Fenner's at the end of May so far as the University were concerned. Streatfield and R.N. Douglas were still unavailable for the XI due to the exigencies of the tripos, and an untimely sprain robbed Jackson of the services of C.M. Wells, a tried and tested batsman who was always liable to turn in a useful bowling performance. The Yorkshire side was in a transitional phase, Hall and Ulyett remained, but Lord Hawke had reinforced Peel, Wainwright and Hunter with two new names, those of John Tunnicliffe and George Hirst. Jackson, who knew more about the strengths and weaknesses of Yorkshire cricket than any of his team mates, must silently have bemoaned the absence of three key players.

For once Jackson's bowling was not decisive against his native county. He took 4 for 43 in the Tykes' first innings, removing both openers, Lord Hawke and Louis Hall, but in the second innings when Yorkshire were chasing 135 to win the match, his bowling was roughly handled, his 45 deliveries yielding 46 runs without reward. Opening the bowling he found himself on the wrong end of a Yorkshire opening partnership of 51 struck in 25 minutes. It was not a happy match for the 'Cantab' captain. With the bat he had managed 2 and 23 as Peel and Wainwright wrecked both Cambridge innings. Yorkshire won easily in the end by 7 wickets, and Jackson was left pondering the fates which had robbed him of Bromley-Davenport's bowling in the Tykes' second innings. The Old Etonian had damaged a hand stopping a hit from Lord Hawke on the first day, further eroding the University's slender bowling resources.

A captain's life is never dull, and, in the next match, at the Oval against mighty Surrey, he had Streatfield, Bromley-Davenport and R.N. Douglas restored to the XI, but was now without four other regulars, L.H. Gay who was injured, Wells, Weigall and Jephson, all virtual certainties to appear in the Oxford - Cambridge match.

One of the replacements drafted into the side was A.O. Jones, a future captain of England. Many captains would have despaired, but Jackson went out and led the University to an unlikely victory by the margin of 80 runs. Surrey, too, had their problems, but they were not as pressing as those of their visitors. George Lohmann had been unwell, and was rested, his place going to a young unknown who had cut a dash at Kingston that Easter in the company of Ranji, playing for an XI of England against an XVIII of Kingston: his name was Tom Richardson.

The county was also without their normal wicket-keeper, Henry Wood, the England stumper. If the Surrey attack was diminished by the absence of Lohmann, the University batsmen were still faced with an attack comprising Lockwood, Sharpe, Brockwell, Abel, and the raw hostility of young Tom Richardson.

Cambridge batted first. The pitch was fiery, but the batsmen found that if they could survive for any length of time, then the ball sped off the bat and runs came at a rush. The match lasted only two days; two days in which 938 runs were scored and 40 wickets fell. Jackson scored 12 in the first innings as the University hurried to 218 all out. His bowling removed four Surrey batsmen for 62 runs as the home side achieved a first innings lead of 49, then, with Lockwood in full flight he went in and scored 61, sharing in a 70-minute stand of 103 with P.H. Latham. His was the highest score of the innings. Surrey were set 243 to win, but Bromley-Davenport and Streatfield made deep inroads into their order before Jackson joined the attack. In a spell of 11 overs he took the last 5 wickets for 39 runs.

The University's worst showing of the season was reserved for the visit of H.T. Hewett's XII to Fenner's. After the heady wine of victory over Surrey in their citadel in Kennington, the 'Cantabs' fell into the trap of resting on their laurels. Hewett's XII was largely a Somerset team, with two guest players, N.C. Cooper and Gregor McGregor, both Cambridge men. The previous week Somerset had been roundly beaten at Oxford, where they had been unable to find an answer to C.B. Fry's batsmanship and G.F.H. Berkeley's fast bowling. Nevertheless, the county attack, which was heavily dependent upon Sammy Woods' pace, and Edwin Tyler's slow left-arm trickery, was not to be treated lightly. The University XII were bowled out for 97 and 106, Sammy Woods (6 for 108) and Tyler (14 for 80) taking all bar two of the wickets and bowling all bar five of the overs bowled by the county players in the match. H.T. Hewett's XII were dismissed for 81 in their first knock, but in their second Sammy Woods, after being dropped by the wicket-keeper standing back when on 12, struck 103 in 95 minutes before Jackson induced him to give another chance, which Jephson safely pouched. By then the damage had been done and the match was beyond the University's reach. The collapse of the Cambridge second innings was as abject as it was inevitable on a deteriorating wicket. It was insult heaped upon injury.

The match against H.T. Hewett's XII bruised a goodly number of young egos, and it was Sussex's misfortune to entertain Cambridge at Brighton the day after the defeat. Sussex were brushed aside inside two days on a wicket of variable bounce and pace on which the odd ball was always liable to lift awkwardly off a length. The honours were shared on the first day, Sussex making 170, and the University replying with 184, Jackson's contribution being 26 before he was adjudged run out. In the Sussex innings Jackson had been the most expensive of the University bowlers, his 2 wickets costing 67 runs. He atoned on the second day of the match, taking 5 for 25 after Streatfield made the initial breakthrough, to see the home side dismissed for 82. R.N. Douglas rediscovered his form with the bat and Cambridge got home easily with 6 wickets to spare. The result said much for the depth of Cambridge cricket, since the University had again been without the services of three stalwarts, Gay, Bromley-Davenport and

Jephson.

Jackson's bowling method had attained maturity; he had come to terms with the realisation that he would never be an out-and-out fast bowler. His high, fluent action and natural athleticism lent themselves to a brisk, rather than express, delivery, and from now on he would be content to bowl within himself, letting the virtues of line and length and the vagaries of bounce and movement off the wicket do his work for him. He could still send down a distinctly fast quicker ball, but it was a weapon he used sparingly, discriminatingly. His stock ball was a delivery pitched just short of a length that tended to break back into the right-handed batsman. Sammy Woods in *My Reminiscences* (1925) paid this tribute to Jackson's bowling:

> He had a lovely action and...great command of the ball. He had a ball that did three inches with his arm, mixed up with a good off-break. I saw him at Lord's on a grand wicket bowl Arthur Shrewsbury out, when well set, with his bat over his shoulder, with a ball that came back six inches and hit his off-stump.

The incident to which Woods referred actually occurred in the Gentlemen versus Players match at the Oval the previous year. Sammy Woods' eyes would have lit up at seeing Shrewsbury - the acknowledged master of defensive play, and possibly the most technically accomplished batsman of his day - undone in such a fashion.

Leaving Brighton behind, the University travelled up to London to meet sterner opposition in the form of a strong

M.C.C. team under the captaincy of W.G. Grace at Lord's, the last trial before the Varsity match. The first day was washed out, and not unnaturally, when W.G. won the toss he inserted the opposition on a damp wicket and unleashed J.T. Hearne, J.J. Ferris and A.D. Pougher. At one point Cambridge had been reduced to 62 for 7, but C.M. Wells (48) and Streatfield (46) fought a dogged rearguard action and saw the University to a total of 149. When the premier club batted the Cambridge score was passed for the loss of just 2 wickets, those of W.G. himself for a swift 36, and William Chatterton for 5, both sent back to the pavilion by the Cambridge captain. But after Jackson had W.L. Murdoch bowled for 57, and C.M. Wells had A. Hearne caught at the wicket for 61, the innings fell away, closing at 229. Jackson finished with 4 for 54, Wells with 5 for 55. Solid batting all down the order eventually put Cambridge into a position where they set M.C.C. 204 to win in a shade over two hours, a task just beyond W.G.'s XI, who lurched to 187 for 7 at the close, so leaving the match drawn.

The 58th Oxford - Cambridge Match at Lord's was one of the classic Varsity encounters. Over 30,000 people passed through the turnstiles - 10,051 on Thursday, 11,493 on Friday, and 8,794 on Saturday - and they witnessed an exciting contest of fluctuating fortunes. Within minutes of the start Oxford, who had won the toss and elected to bat, were reduced to 0 for 2 wickets, with both openers out. Jackson himself had induced Lionel Palairet to snick a catch to the wicket-keeper, and Streatfield had trapped R.T. Jones leg before wicket. At that stage Cambridge, who were generally acknowledged to be the stronger side, were rampant. However, there followed a remarkable Oxford revival, started by C.B. Fry with 44 in 85 minutes, and completed by M.R. Jardine and V.T. Hill who both made centuries. The key contribution was that of Malcolm Jardine. He was predominantly a leg-side player, scoring the majority of his 21 fours from deflections off his legs. His chanceless innings of 140 kept him at the crease for four and three-quarter hours.

Highly rated as a batsman by many good judges, he never seemed to realise his potential, this being the solitary century he logged in a first-class career of 46 matches between 1889 and 1897. Jardine entered the fray with openers back in the pavilion for no score; with Fry he shared in a stand of 75, then two further small, significant stands with F.A. Phillips and T.B. Case, before he was joined by V.T. Hill with whom he added 178 in just 100 minutes, Hill's share being 114 in an exhibition of free hitting that included 18 fours, blemished only by chances offered when he was on 64, 96 and 103. Oxford made 365 and in the short while before the close of play Cambridge were reduced to 34 for 2, R.N. Douglas baffled (and bowled) by one of J.B. Wood's seemingly harmless lobs, and his brother, J. Douglas, disconcerted by the pace of Berkeley, offering a sharp chance to Jardine, who gladly clung on to the catch.

On the second morning Jackson, who had been the best of the Cambridge bowlers in returning figures of 4 for 76 in forty five-ball overs, batted in his now customary style - redoubtable defence mingled with elegant cutting and crashing driving - until at 34 he was run out in a disastrous misunderstanding with G.J.V. Weigall. It was an event which so demoralised the lower order that the last 6 wickets went down for only 53 runs and Cambridge collapsed to 160 all out. With Jackson's dismissal went any chance of avoiding the follow on. (At this time any side dismissed for a total that was 80 or more in arrears of the score of the team batting first was obliged to bat again. The follow on was compulsory, whether the captain holding the initiative liked it or not.)

Cambridge made a better start to their second innings against the tiring Oxford attack, R.N. Douglas and Latham hit fifties, Jackson a solid 35 before he was beaten by Berkeley's pace, and Streatfield a belligerent 116 in a little over two hours to raise the Light Blue reply to 388, setting Oxford 184 to win on the third day. The Dark Blues won the day after a grim early struggle against Jackson and Streatfield. Streatfield bowled over after over at negligible cost, while Jackson snapped up the wickets of Phillips, Jardine, Berkeley and Fry. In the end it took a remarkable unbeaten innings of 71 in 90 minutes by Lionel Palairet, batting with an injured hand, to get Oxford home by 5 wickets.

Jackson was left to rue what might have been. He had taken 8 for 147, and scored 69 runs in the match, captaining his side astutely throughout. And yet he had lost. Cricket is a funny game. In defeat he was philosophical, voicing the opinion that victory 'rested with the team that played the better cricket'.

Directly after the defeat at Lord's he took Cambridge to Ireland to face Dublin University. In a match that was closely contested until the third day Cambridge ran out the winners by the deceptively comfortable margin of six wickets to round off the University season.

Jackson finished top of the Cambridge batting and bowling averages, scoring more runs and taking more wickets than anyone else.

Of his captaincy *Wisden* observed:

He proved himself a most capable and energetic captain, the season was for him personally one of almost unqualified success.

On his return to England, Jackson took up an invitation to play for the Gentlemen against the Players in the Oval match. Both sides were below strength, particularly the Gentlemen, who took the field without the services of W.G. Grace, Sammy Woods, J.J. Ferris, Lord Hawke, Gregor McGregor and several others. The Players trounced the Gentlemen by ten wickets. Arthur Shrewsbury carried his bat for 151, and the amateurs never got into the game. Jackson fell to Lockwood in both innings, scoring 0 and 4. With the ball he was the most penetrative of the Gentlemen's bowlers, recording match figures of 4 for 100. It was the mid-point of his season and for the remainder of July and August he turned out, when fit, for his native Yorkshire.

He was now a fully-fledged cricketer. The days when he would be asked to bat down the order, or expected to perform as a mere change bowler were gone. On a rain-ruined pitch at Headingley, in a match against Middlesex, he scored 23 out of the Yorkshire second innings total of 46, surviving two chances before being bowled by J.T. Hearne. Throughout July his form was moderate, although he struck a courageous 48, opening the second innings with Tom Wardall against Surrey at the Oval - after being dropped at mid-off from his first ball by Tom Richardson - as Yorkshire slid to defeat. In the first innings he had been run out for the fourth time that year in a fashion that was sufficiently odd to earn it a place in F.S. Ashley- Cooper's *Curiosities of First-Class Cricket (*1901):

> When Messrs. A. Sellars and F.S. Jackson were batting, the former hit a ball from W.H. Lockwood to third man. Jackson, thinking a run possible, made his way to the other wicket whilst his partner stood still. H. Wood, the Surrey wicket-keeper, ran to the wicket to collect the ball, which was sent in rather wide, and then rushed off full speed towards the wicket Jackson had left, with the result that Jackson was run out. The spectacle of the Surrey wicketkeeper at full speed for the bowler's end with no one in pursuit caused great amusement.

One rather doubts if Jackson shared in the general mirth. He was acquiring something of a reputation for his running between the wickets. The Reverend R.S. Holmes was moved to write in *Cricket*:

> What a crying shame it is the fates won't be as kindly to F.S. Jackson when he dons his flannels for his county, as they are for his rival - the Dark Blue Skipper - whenever he turns out for *his* county. Palairet plays even better for Somersetshire than for Oxford. Neither Ernest Smith nor F.S. Jackson has done himself complete justice when helping Yorkshire. Last year their only conspicuous failures were for the County of the Broad Acres.

At the close of the month an injury to his hand

prevented him batting at Bradford in the match with Gloucestershire, and kept him out of the side until the second week of August.

In August Yorkshire at last saw Jackson at his best.

Against Somerset, albeit in a losing cause, he took 5 for 20, and 4 for 71, and hit 31 and 14 in a low-scoring match that had been turned on its head by a whirlwind innings of 76 by Sammy Woods.

Then, later that month with Ernest Smith captaining the county in the absence of Lord Hawke, Jackson was promoted in the order to open the batting. By the time Jackson was fifth out, he had made 76 in 135 minutes. It was a significant milestone in his career; his highest score for the county, and his first championship half-century. At one stage in his innings he found himself taking guard with the Grace brothers crowding him in. E.M. stood a yard or so off the cut surface of the wicket at point, W.G. as close on the leg-side, and in their best style the brothers Grace carried on a continual conversation across the young batsman. At one point Lord Hawke became so concerned that he contrived a pretence to come onto the field to speak to Jackson.

'Are these old beggars trying to bustle you?' he asked.

'I don't know.' Jackson replied, grimly determined, 'but anyhow, they can't!'

On 24th August, Jackson made a brisk 59 for Scarborough against the touring Dutch XI, and picked up five cheap wickets as the visitors were dismissed for 57.

The next day he was in the thick of the more serious business of championship cricket. He opened against Somerset at Taunton, scoring 55 on a batsman's wicket. Yorkshire scored 299; Somerset in a game restricted to two days by rain on the third day, were all out at the end of the second day for 592, H.T. Hewett (201), Lionel Palairet (146) and W.C. Hedley (102) taking a terrible toll of a strong Yorkshire attack. The Somerset opening partnership of 346, struck in 210 minutes, was a new record, bettering the 283 of W.G. Grace and B.B. Cooper for the Gentlemen of the South against the Players of the South at the Oval, in 1869. The figures of the four principal bowlers make sobering reading: Jackson 2 for 148, Peel, the only man to exert any hold over the batsmen, 7 for 133, Wainwright 1 for 117, and Ernest Smith 0 for 97.

Opening for the county at Scarborough in a match against M.C.C. Jackson scored just 3, comprehensively bowled by F.R. 'Demon' Spofforth. Then, in what turned out to be his last appearance of the season, for the Gentlemen against the Players at Scarborough, he made 11, batting down the order at number seven - bowled by Bobby Peel before he got into his stride. He had been invited to play for the Gentlemen, and a North of England XI in matches during the Hastings and St Leonards Cricket Week, but a hand injury forced his withdrawal and cut short by two matches his third season in the first-class game. It was a season in which his batting had come on by leaps and bounds, and his bowling had continued to develop. He had scored 751 runs at an average of 24.22, including six fifties. With the ball he had captured 80 wickets at 18.68 apiece.

A new star was rising in English cricket.

6 | Lord Hawke's Team in India and Ceylon (1892-1893)

In October 1892 Stanley Jackson boarded the P. & O. steamer *Kaiser-I-Hind* to embark upon what was destined to be his only overseas tour. He was one of a party of 14 amateurs under the leadership of Lord Hawke, the Yorkshire captain. Ahead of Hawke and his intrepid 'gentlemen' lay a gruelling itinerary of 23 matches on the Indian sub-continent. The cost of the tour to each member of the party was the princely sum of £150, exclusive of any expenses incurred in the employment of personal servants.

Under Hawke's stewardship the tour was an adventure approached with evangelical zeal; cricket was not merely a game - a great and noble game - it was the embodiment of everything that was best in the British, it was something above politics, a bridge that crossed the divides separating the races. Hawke organised the tour single-handed. Taking cricket to the dominions was hardly his recreation, it was his duty. Cricket was a mighty power for good in the world and throughout his life he did his utmost to ensure that no man used it otherwise.

It was Hawke who had invited Jackson to join the Yorkshire XI in 1890, and now it was Hawke who prevailed upon the young 'Cantab' to join his tour to India. In later life the two men were to become staunch friends and allies, but in those days, Jackson was in Hawke's shadow. It is a popular myth that from their earliest acquaintance

Jackson and Hawke were friends.

Hawke was not Jackson's mentor; nor Jackson his protégé. Jackson the team man was, paradoxically, too much his own man to surrender any part of his individuality. They were men with much in common, but they were also men with singular personalities, neither of whom made lasting friendships at the drop of a hat. Hawke was that much older (ten years) than Jackson, and, not unnaturally, when Jackson first came into the Yorkshire team, he deferred to his county captain. In India the two men found themselves compatible tourists. They were not close. Hawke was already a considerable presence in English cricket, Jackson still an upstart 'Cantab' with a lot to prove.

The tour was Jackson's finishing school; it signalled the end of his cricketing apprenticeship, and broadened him as a cricketer and as a man. After the tour he emerged as an England player, assumed the mantle of Hawke's lieutenant at Yorkshire and came of age on the big stage of English cricket. In later years, Jackson might have succeeded Hawke in the Yorkshire captaincy, had he not been thwarted by circumstance. Yet even when Jackson was captain of England, he was still Hawke's loyal lieutenant at Yorkshire and nobody, least of all Jackson himself, thought it untoward.

Martin Bladen Hawke, 7th Baron Hawke, was a descendant of the famous Admiral Hawke who had superseded the wretched Byng, and later put the French fleet to the sword at Quiberon Bay. He shares a special place in the history of cricket - with Lord Harris and W.G. Grace - as one of the three men largely responsible for making cricket recognisably the game it is today. He was captain of Yorkshire for 28 years from 1883 to 1911, President of the Yorkshire Club for 40 years from 1898 to his death in 1938 and the architect of the dominance of Yorkshire cricket in the golden age.

As captain of Yorkshire he insisted on the highest standards of conduct on and off the field, gave his professionals a financial security that was unheard of elsewhere, put the club's affairs on a businesslike footing and ruled Yorkshire cricket with a rod of iron. He dismissed both Edmund Peate and his successor Bobby Peel, the former for his disruptiveness, the latter for coming onto the field drunk; both Peate and Peel were the finest slow left-arm bowlers of their day - but it made no difference. Robert Moorhouse was sacked for not trying. Hawke's law was rigid: a player was chosen to do his best for the team; if he let himself or Yorkshire down by dint of his personal conduct, or by the spirit in which he played the game, then he had no future in any team of Hawke's. The services of J.M. Preston and Saul Wade, both very able all-rounders, and those of Frederick Lee, a fine batsman, were abruptly dispensed with because they transgressed Hawke's law.

Hawke's methods were patrician, and unapologetically so. He was a benevolent autocrat who gave democracy short shrift in the affairs of Yorkshire cricket. When he spoke, Yorkshire spoke. His contribution to English cricket was to put it on a professional footing. Yorkshire's professionals received winter payments, the county scorer was retained on half pay out of season and two-thirds of the receipts from a player's benefit or testimonial match were held in trust to ensure that a man had something to fall back on when he retired. Yet there was an essential benevolence in his rule. His philosophy of man management was simple: 'The more players are respected, the more they will respect themselves.'

No county treated its professionals as well, or conversely, expected so much of its professionals as Hawke's Yorkshire. The success of the Yorkshire system was an object-lesson to the other first-class counties. Hawke blazed a trail in English cricket that transformed the lot of the county cricketer. Controversy raged over his treatment of Peel; his dictatorial ways offended many people; his inflexibility was legendary and his dislike of change (except in specific areas of the game) infuriated his friends and foes alike. Hawke broke the mould of English cricket and substantially remade the summer game in the modern image.

He was an old-fashioned man, a Victorian who fell out of step with a changing world between the two wars. He was god-fearing, decent to the core, a man who did what he believed was right and said what he thought, regardless of the consequences. If something was worth doing, it was worth doing, and that was that. His most famous *faux pas* came when he was responding to what he believed was unfair criticism of A.E.R. Gilligan's captaincy of England in Australia:

> 'Pray God, no professional shall ever captain England. I love and admire them all but we have always had an amateur skipper and when the day comes when we shall have no more amateurs captaining England it will be a thousand pities.'

It caused a storm at the time, and has tended to distort

perceptions of Hawke down the years. Cricket would have been the poorer without him, immeasurably the poorer. If the cause of Yorkshire cricket was his preoccupation, his horizons were never defined by the boundaries of the county of the broad acres. He organised tours to India, North and South America, the West Indies, and to South Africa.

'Plum' Warner said of Hawke 'He was the first to preach the gospel of cricket throughout the Empire.' Hawke always stressed that the social side of touring was as important as the cricket. The purpose of his tours was to win the hearts and minds of cricket-loving folk everywhere. In his vision, sport in general, and cricket in particular, was crucial in cementing the *Pax Britannica.*

As a cricketer Hawke was a better batsman then his figures would suggest. The motto of the Hawke family was 'Strike', and as a hard-hitting middle-order batsman his response to most situations was to strike out with a vigour that was frequently his undoing. An ideal man to have coming in fourth, fifth or sixth in the order, he could play straight (holding the middle order together until the bowlers tired) and was in fact technically competent in defence, whilst being quite capable of hitting out for quick runs, a batsman who always played for his side, a batsman who scorned his average, in short, a man any county side would love to have up its sleeve. A mark of his batting skills is that he and Bobby Peel still hold [at the time of writing, 1989] the record for the highest partnership for the eighth wicket in English cricket, 292 fiercely hit runs scored as long ago as 1896 against Warwickshire at Birmingham. His share of the stand was 166, the best score of his career, in which he scored 16,749 runs at the relatively modest average of 20.15, even though he was good enough to log 13 hundreds.

It was said at the time, and echoed by Hawke himself, that his batting was not of a standard to guarantee him a place in the Yorkshire XI. Perhaps not, but it should be remembered that because of Yorkshire's wealth of batting he often came in low in the order, down at eight, nine or even ten. If he batted higher it was usually in the interests of knocking off a few quick runs, or (in an era when declarations were not permitted until the afternoon of the last day) to throw away his wicket to set an example to the following batsmen; if he was not a great batsman nor was he a bad batsman.

His talent was for captaincy. Under his leadership Yorkshire became the premier English county. Whether batting or fielding, Yorkshire attacked. Hawke's captaincy engrained 'attack' into the psyche of Yorkshire cricket. He inherited the Yorkshire of Tom Emmett and George Ulyett and forged it into a legendary cricketing machine. However, back in the winter of 1892 Hawke's triumphs – and controversies – still awaited him in an unknown and unknowable future.

To spread the gospel of cricket Hawke had assembled a well- balanced party: Lord Hawke himself, G.F. Vernon, G.A. Foljambe, J.A. Gibbs, A.B.E. Gibson, C. Heseltine, A.J.L. Hill, J.H.J. Hornsby, F.S. Jackson, A.E. Leatham, M.F. MacLean, J.S. Robinson, C.W. Wright, and H.F. Wright.

Of the fourteen, four were batsmen (Hawke, Vernon, Gibbs, and MacLean), seven could lay claim to being all-rounders (Foljambe, Gibson, Hill, Hornsby, Jackson, Leatham, and H.F. Wright) one was a specialist bowler who was by no means a rabbit with the bat (Heseltine), and two (Robinson and C.W. Wright) were wicket-keeper batsmen who were more than capable in either role. Any eleven drawn from the fourteen would possess depth in its batting, and ample variety in its bowling. Vernon had already played for England, and Hawke, Jackson, Heseltine, Hill and C.W. Wright would follow in his footsteps in the years to come (with Hawke and Jackson going on to captain England).

Several of the fourteen were essentially very good club cricketers who played little or no regular first-class cricket; Gibson, for example, had appeared twice for Lancashire in 1887 before emigrating to the colonies, Hornsby played once for Middlesex and Foljambe and MacLean never turned out for a first-class county. H.F. Wright did not actually play for his native Derbyshire until 1904, his county career then spanning just nine matches, and Leatham, who managed no more than a handful of games for Gloucestershire must also fall into this group. The other two members of the party, Gibbs and Robinson were useful county performers.

The average age of the party was 26 its oldest member being Vernon at 36, its youngest Hill, at 21; four of its members were over 30, eight were 25 or younger. In the torrid heat of the Indian subcontinent youth would be at a premium. Given the quality of the opposition it was likely to encounter, Hawke's team was formidable, a combination that would have held its own against many of the English counties.

The tour did not get off to a particularly auspicious start. Only eleven of the party actually sailed on the *Kaiser-I-Hind,* which was due to berth in Colombo on Lord

Mayor's Day, Wednesday 9th November. Lord Hawke had suffered a chill, delaying his departure. In the company of Vernon and Gibson he followed the advance guard in the *S.S. Shannon* two weeks later. The tour was due to commence on 11th November with a two day fixture against the Colombo Club, the party's hosts in Ceylon. It was the first of three games scheduled in the colony, before moving on to the sub-continent proper, where the itinerary included no less than twenty matches, the last of which finished on 2nd March 1893.

In Ceylon before Lord Hawke's arrival.
F.S. Jackson (in the tope seated second in from the right).

The opening match was drawn. Hawke's team scored freely on the first day to reach 252, although Jackson was out for 4. The Colombo Club XI was a singularly European side, drawn from the expatriate community. Six of the team were soldiers, the rest were colonial civil servants or immigrants from the mother country. The occasions when Hawke's team was to join battle with essentially native opposition would be few and far between.

In the second match, against the Colombo Colts, rain disrupted proceedings and in a low-scoring match the touring side won easily. Jackson found his form, making a battling 37 on a ruined wicket in the second innings, by a long way the highest score of the match. With the ball he wrought havoc, taking 4 for 7 and 4 for 18 as the Colts were skittled out for 24 and 44. That evening the tourists were regally entertained by the Governor who had arranged a banquet and dance in their honour. After some sightseeing and much needed net practice, the team travelled to Radella to meet an 'Up Country Clubs XI'. Hawke's Team won by an innings, Jackson hitting a dashing 109 and capturing 4 first innings wickets for 14. Sterner tests lay ahead in India.

Fortified by the arrival of Hawke, Vernon and Gibson the party sailed for Madras. *Cricket* noted that the team's time in Ceylon had been 'marred by one disappointment at not meeting a representative team of the whole colony', but the tour had begun successfully. In Ceylon, as throughout the tour in India, the members of the party were taken into the homes of their hosts, welcomed into the arms of the expatriate community like prodigals returning to the fold.

Although each of the twenty fixtures scheduled to be played on the sub-continent was of two or three days' duration, the majority were not regarded as being worthy of first-class status. Only four of the matches were so designated; two against the Parsees at Bombay, the match against the Bombay Presidency, and the match against an All India XI at Allahabad. Except for those occasions when successive matches were scheduled for one venue, the itinerary - of necessity, given the distances to be covered - allowed relatively generous intervals between fixtures.

The matches were to be played in the provincial centres of the Raj: Madras, Bangalore, Poona, Bombay, Calcutta, Mozenfferpore, Allahabad, Lucknow, Agra, Umballa, Lahore, and Peshawar. There was no criss-crossing of the vast Indian plateau, no retracing of earlier steps, just a gradual progression from city to city at a pace dictated by the speed of a train. Touring in the 1890s was not the fraught, frantic affair it has become in the age of the jetliner. However, if the pace of life for a tourist in India in the 1890s was slower, altogether calmer, the sub-continent was not without its perils. The heat, the diet and the ever-present threat of sickness were problems that dogged every European. For a cricketer the conditions presented not so much a test of his skill, but of his character. Against opponents who were fully acclimatised to the wickets, the heat and the food, Hawke's team - for all its strength on paper - often made hard work of overcoming apparently modest opposition.

The Indian tour commenced on 28th November at Chepauk with a two-day drawn match against Madras. Hawke's team struggled. Had it not been for a steady 50 by Jackson the home side's first innings total of 184 might have proved decisive. On a flat wicket the bowling of the tourists was less than penetrative, although Jackson claimed 4 for 77 in the match in 35 exhausting five-ball overs. The tourists restored their morale in the second match at Chepauk which was finished inside a day. A 'Native XI', drawn from the schools and clubs in the

Madras area, was beaten by an innings.

Jackson, rested for the first time, was an interested spectator as the pace of Heseltine with 8 for 10 and 5 for 16, and the left-arm spin of Hornsby with 2 for 16 and 5 for 29, swept aside the demoralised natives for 29 and 46.

On 1st December Jackson returned to the XI for the match against the Madras Presidency. In an even game, interrupted by rain, the home side reached 15 for 2 at the end of the third day chasing a score of 116 to win. Jackson did little with the bat but captured 5 for 30 in the home XI's first innings. It was Hawke's forthright 47 (out of his side's second innings of 112) that saved the day.

From Madras the party travelled west to Bangalore where on 6th December they took the field against a much-changed Madras Presidency XI. On a fast wicket Jackson and Gibson reduced the home team to 79 for 7. Although the Madras Presidency made 203 in the end, the initiative always rested with Hawke's team. Even without the services of Jackson, the tourists ran out the victors by nine wickets; Jackson was one of the tour's early victims of sickness and was unable to participate in the next match against Bangalore and District (victory by an innings) or in the following match at Poona against Poona Gymkhana (drawn after the tourists had engineered a winning position).

Jackson was sufficiently recovered to take his place in the team that took on the Parsees in a three-day match starting on 22nd December at the Gymkhana Ground, Bombay. The Parsee population of Bombay - which numbered some 75,000 - was a bastion of Indian cricket. The Parsees had been the first Indians to play the game and amongst their number were several cricketers who could hold their own in the best company; B.C. Machliwala was acknowledged as a very dangerous batsman, so too D.E. Mody, who was also a superb cover-point, N.C. Bapasola, D.N. Writer, and M.B. Kanga were deceptively good bowlers, and M.E. Pavri was an all-rounder of no mean repute in Bombay, where in later years he earned the accolade of 'the Indian Tom Richardson', on account of his extremely quick quicker ball.

The Parsees outplayed Hawke's team, defeating the tourists by a margin of 109 runs. For anybody who doubted the potential of native cricket in India, it was a salutary experience. Hawke recounts in his *Recollections and Reminiscences* (1924), how the outcome of the match had taken him completely by surprise:

> At a dinner given to my team at the Yacht Club, Lord Harris, the Governor, as Chairman, told us he had prepared a speech for a winning team, to which I replied that, I, too, had prepared one without a thought that we could lose.

It was not a particularly happy match for Jackson. In what was his fiftieth first-class appearance, suffering from mild sunstroke, he scored 0 and 4, and when he bowled on a helpful pitch, his bowling lacked penetration. He bowled 95 deliveries in the match, a number exceeded only by Hornsby, taking 2 for 30.

Yet in defeat there were lessons to be learned; foremost among them the realisation that Indian cricket played by Indians, rather than by the expatriates, was no longer a thing to be mocked. The *Bombay Gazette* commented: 'The success which the Parsees achieved by their superior fielding and bowling was greeted with thunders of applause.'

The Englishmen had failed to treat Parsee cricket with the respect it deserved and had paid the price. Hawke had anticipated that the Parsees would give a good account of themselves; in fact he had spared Heseltine, his quickest bowler, in the matches leading up to the party's stay in Bombay. In the event the heat and the slowness of the wicket took the sting out of Heseltine's bowling, and the tourists never really found their best cricket.

The tourists were busy men during Christmas and New Year in Bombay. They were the guests of Lord Harris, entertained one day by the Parsees at a garden party, at a banquet by the European Gymkhana on another, and this in blazing heat in the middle of a spell of almost continuous cricket. On Boxing Day, Hawke's team took on the Bombay Presidency and won by 8 wickets. Jackson was rested, still not fully restored after his touch of the sun in the first match at Bombay.

He came back into the side on 29th December, when, on a day of torrid heat, the tourists commenced the return match with the Parsees on the Gymkhana Ground where they had been so soundly beaten the previous week. Hawke won the toss and decided to bat. The tourists were soon in trouble, and it took a determined innings of 39 from Jackson to hold the order together on an awkward wicket. Even so the innings closed with a meagre 139 on the board. Jackson's 39 was the highest innings of a low-scoring contest, and as the match progressed it became obvious that it was one of the most important innings he was to play on the tour. His bowling was sparingly employed and without success, and in the second innings he was dismissed for a duck. In the end, victory was by the slender margin of 7 runs, after the Parsees had been set a mere 98 to win.

Once more the Parsees had given the visitors a nasty shock. The result of the match had been in doubt until the death. D.N. Writer, who had played (but not bowled) for the Parsees in the first game, tormented the Englishmen throughout, capturing in all 12 wickets for just 51 runs. The hero of the hour was Hornsby who had taken 15 wickets in the match for 86 runs although, but for Jackson's innings on the first day, Hornsby's toil would have been for naught.

From Bombay there followed a long and wearying journey to Calcutta, where 35 years later Jackson would return as Governor of Bengal. At Eden Gardens on 5th January 1893 Hawke's team met the Calcutta Club and handed out a comprehensive innings defeat to their hosts. Jackson had a quiet match, scoring 8, and taking 1 for 8 with the ball.

After the Calcutta match there was a break of a week until the next fixture. Jackson and the majority of his fellows went by train to the foothills of the Himalayas, and from there - despite the cold, made worse by their recent exposure to the scorching sun and the debilitating humidity of the lowlands - on to Daarjeeling, where the braver spirits viewed the snow-clad majesty of Kinchinjunga and Everest.

Returning to earth on 13th January, Hawke's team came up against the Bengal Presidency. It was a strange match dominated almost until the end by the tourists, and then nearly lost. Jackson's form seemed to have deserted him, hitting 10 and 13, and failing to take a wicket with his

90 deliveries in the second innings. As was the case throughout the tour, large crowds watched the match, crowds not just made up of expatriates, but of Indians who came to watch the cricket in their thousands. In Bombay the Parsees had been massively and vociferously supported by Indians from their own and other communities, whereas in Calcutta the matches were the social highlights of the European calendar.

Moving on to Mozenfferpore, the tourists - who were without their captain due to a sprained ankle - generously lent Gibson to their opponents and were defeated by the Behar Wanderers who won by 68 runs. The defeat was largely attributable to the exertions of the excellent Gibson, who scored 33 and 55, captured 4 for 22 and 7 for 43, and held 3 catches in the match. Jackson registered only 18 and 20 with the bat, but rediscovered his bowling form with 5 first-innings wickets. The tourists narrowly avoided the follow on, but never threatened to reach a target of 196 to win the match.

Despite such mishaps it was a happy tour. Indeed Hawke insisted on having a happy tour; discord was banished. In defeat, as in victory, the tourists were gentlemen cricketers, Englishmen abroad and expected to behave accordingly.

Jackson's tour had thus far been a mixed affair. Illness had laid him low, sapped his stamina and led to a loss of his bowling form. But in the lost cause at Mozenfferpore his bowling had suddenly slipped back into gear. It seemed to revive his all-round game at the very moment when the rigours of a long and demanding tour ought to have been bearing down on him.

At Alfred Park, Allahabad, against Upper India,

Jackson bowled a long economical spell that brought him 5 for 35 and set the tourists on the road to victory. In his only innings he hit 22. Hawke's team had sufficient runs to play with, running out the victors by ten wickets.

In the 17th match of the tour against All India at the same ground, Hawke's team triumphed by an innings. All India were bowled out for 139 on the first day, then, taking advantage of a custom peculiar to the subcontinent, the tourists opted to use a new pitch and proceeded to carry their reply to 343, Jackson (34), Hill (132) and Vernon (50) cashing in on the staunch work of the opener Gibson (58), to put the match completely beyond the reach of the home XI. Jackson bowled long, mean spells in both Indian innings as others took the wickets, finishing with 2 for 61 from the 255 deliveries he sent down in the match.

Hawke's injury kept him out of this and the next match, against Oudh at Lucknow. To an Englishman, Lucknow was one of those faraway outposts of Empire that held both a mystical and strategic significance. Lucknow, once the city of the Nawabs of Oudh, was saturated with memories of the Indian Mutiny of 1857 and the city's relief by Campbell's column (to the skirl of his highlanders' pipes) was honoured by every true son of the Empire. However, when the match got under way on the last day of January, the resistance offered by the XI of the Oudh province bore no resemblance to that of the defenders of Lucknow in those desperate times of the mutiny. Oudh, who were fielding a side composed of Indian Army Officers, went down by an innings. Jackson opened the batting and scored a useful 23; later he polished off Oudh's second innings with a burst of 5 for 19.

In the first week of February the tourists left Lucknow

behind and went on to Agra, the ancient capital of India and site of the Taj Mahal. Hawke returned to the side, but in the absence of Heseltine, Hill, MacLean and H.F. Wright who were away on a shooting trip, two substitutes had to be obtained to make up the eleven that took the field against Agra on 6th February. Jackson, opening the bowling with Hornsby, took 7 for 52 as the home side declined to 108, but Hawke's team was unceremoniously bowled out for 61, at one point slumping to the ignominy of 19 for 7. Hornsby and Gibson retrieved the situation somewhat, bowling Agra out in their second innings for 67, leaving the tourists 115 for victory. Jackson led the way with 47, aided and abetted by C.W. Wright (27), and the match was won by 4 wickets.

The tour moved from one military centre to another, this time to Umballa, where the team had the opportunity to get in some big-game hunting, and visit Cawnpore and Delhi. The tour was beginning to take its toll, and now that its end was in sight, thoughts were turning to the voyage home, and the English season to come.

The match against Umballa was drawn. Jackson scored 15 and 13, and took 1 for 19. When the rain-affected contest ended the tourists still had two wickets to fall in their second innings and were 183 runs ahead. The large crowds that had attended the match were content with the entertainment that they had seen. For the crowd the main thing was to see a side from England playing cricket; the result was academic. Everywhere they went, Hawke's team brought a breath of English air with them; that was the magic of the first tours, now quite lost with the advent of television and the jet.

In Lahore at the end of the third week of February the

tourists defeated the Punjab by an innings, winning at a canter after Jackson's 95, including 16 fours had thoroughly undermined the resolve of the home side.

A match against Sindh was set to begin the next day but rain prevented any play; in fact play was not possible until the second afternoon. The Sindh side had travelled 800 miles across the Rajputana Desert to fulfil the fixture, and they went down with honour by seven wickets. Jackson, again, was the destroyer with the bat. After Hawke elected to bat first on a wet pitch it fell to Jackson, coming in at the fall of the third wicket when the score was 47, to carry the innings to its final 138 runs, his share being 62 not out. On a rain-ruined wicket 138 was a big score, and thereafter Sindh were always fighting a losing battle. Jackson took 3 for 33 in the match as Sindh were skittled out for 50 and 112.

The tour ended with a match against Peshawar and District at Peshawar. The local side were overwhelmed, trounced by an innings and 303 runs. Jackson only bowled 20 deliveries in the match, claiming 1 for 7, his services were hardly needed. He scored 57 as Hawke's team piled up a total of 483. The victory was crushing, the perfect conclusion to the tour. Of the twenty-three matches they had played, the tourists had won fifteen, including eight by at least an innings, drawn six, and lost two.

On the day after the match at Peshawar the touring party was escorted by a detachment of Bengal Lancers on a visit to the Khyber Pass. Standing at the foot of the Pass, looking north into the foothills of the Hindu Kush at the very frontier of the Empire, no true Englishman could fail to be stirred.

Jackson was second in the batting averages to his Cambridge team-mate Hill, scoring 697 runs at an average of 30.30, and third in the bowling lists, behind Heseltine and Hill, taking 69 wickets at 10.39 apiece. No man finished the tour as strongly as Jackson.

At the end of the tour the party split up to make their way home as they thought fit. While several of the party remained in India to get in some shooting in Nepal, Jackson departed for home without delay.

7 | From Parker's Piece to Lord's (1893)

In March Stanley Jackson had stood at the Khyber Pass, at the frontier of the Raj; in April he was batting in the nets on Parker's Piece, adjoining Fenner's.

Outwardly, Jackson was the same man who had embarked on the *Kaiser-I-Hind* six months before. Inwardly, India had marked him indelibly. His student days were almost over, his education complete. The sun had burnished his face, India had touched his soul. Re-elected to the Cambridge captaincy he was the master of Fenner's.

A string of leading professionals had been engaged to sharpen the skills of the Cambridge batsmen as they prepared for the coming season on Parker's Piece. Pre-season net practice at Fenner's was a deadly serious business, many an aspiring batsman found his technique, and indeed his courage, tested to breaking point. It was a hard school, a trial by fire. That year the battery of bowlers toiling in the nets of the University Ground included W.H. Lockwood, T. Richardson, J.W. Sharpe, T. Hayward, J.T. Hearne, W. Mead and H. Carpenter.

Towards the end of April, Jackson turned out in a two-day match for Leighton against an XI captained by his Oxford counterpart, L.C.H. Palairet at W.H. Laverton's Ground, Westbury. Jackson departed for 3 when he opened the Leighton first innings, but soon had his revenge, snapping up five wickets. The Palairet brothers,

Lionel and Richard, were amongst his victims, both bowled. On the second day of the match, Saturday 21st April, Jackson hit an imperious 111.

Jackson the batsman had, hitherto, enjoyed a reputation for being a stylish, pleasingly orthodox bat who often flattered to deceive. At Westbury he began to show at last that he was a great deal more than just a good-looking batsman. In India his controlled hitting had demoralised his opponents. Now an English side, albeit not one of first-class standing, saw the 'new' Jackson in full flow. It was an innings that left its imprint in English cricket.

G.L. Wilson, an Australian blue who had played against Cambridge at Lord's in 1890 and 1891, a capable batsman and useful fast-medium bowler who made nearly fifty appearances for Sussex, ruefully recounted his experience of bowling to Jackson in this match to *The Cricket Field*:

> I always used to be a bit of a bowler, but I'm afraid I spoiled what reputation I had gained by a

performance at the beginning of the season... When F.S. Jackson was pretty well set I was put on to see what I could do in the way of getting him out. In the first over he hit me for 4 sixes out of the ground.

Undaunted, the redoubtable Wilson prepared to send down his next over, getting so far as to begin to set his field - spreading his men far and wide - before Lionel Palairet intervened: 'Twenty-four an over is quite sufficient for the time being,' commented a less than ecstatic Oxford captain, as he peremptorily removed Wilson from the firing line.

On 27th April, Jackson serenely proceeded to his B.A. degree in the Senate House.

Scarcely had the papers finished applauding his century at Westbury before they were praising his leadership of the Cambridge side and his part in the purchase of the University Ground. The notoriety did not go to his head. As everything he touched turned to gold, he accepted it all with charm and grace, to the manner born. If he was a trifle vain, as most young men are wont, nothing really ruffled him. A student magazine, called *The K.P.*, chided him gently and in good heart:

He has not bought Fenner's as some tardy subscribers seem to imagine, though his name is on the subscription list. He is very proud of his hair, and there are some who say that he wishes he had more of it. His moustache is all that could be desired. He plays cricket better than the piano...

Stanley Jackson's feet were firmly rooted to the ground. He was an older and wiser man in April 1893 than he had been when he set out for India the previous autumn. Bit by bit the arrogance he had displayed at Harrow had been stripped from him; very little now survived.

He recanted his error of the previous year in denying Ranjitsinhji his first-class debut. In a year when the batting resources available to the University seemed without limit, Jackson set aside his mistrust of unorthodoxy and included Ranji in the team for the opening match of the season against C.I. Thornton's XII at Fenner's.

His travels on the subcontinent had given him much food for thought about the merits of Indian cricket as played by Indians; but what clinched Ranji's place in Jackson's Cambridge team was his single-minded application in the pre-season nets on Parker's Piece. One day Jackson arrived to practice and found Ranji already hard at it. Later when he had finished he noticed that Ranji was still batting. Jackson thought that perhaps he was rather overdoing things, and suggested as much.

'I find I am all right for half an hour,' Ranji told him, 'but I cannot last. Now I must master endurance.'

Their friendship dated from about this time. Occasional teammates in the Trinity side of the year before, they had not been close. Now, with Cambridge cricket and India in common, they soon became natural allies and later lifetime friends. When Jackson went to Calcutta as Governor of Bengal, no advice was more willingly accepted than the counsel of his old friend, the Jam Sahib of Nawanagar. Both Ranji and Jackson were men to whom cricket was an enjoyable interlude, a fascinating distraction, and no more.

Cambridge began the season with a comprehensive 7 wicket win over C.I. Thornton's XII. In the University's first innings Jackson opened the batting - as he would throughout the season - and struck 80 handsome runs against an attack led by J.J. Ferris, and the fearsome Arthur Mold. Ranji, coming in at the fall of the seventh wicket, scored 18 in his introduction to first-class cricket, whereupon Mold bowled him. The depth of the Cambridge batting that year was remarkable; in the University Match at Lord's, A.O. Jones who scored four double centuries in his career, batted at number ten in the list; and was included principally for the variety his leg-spinners lent to the attack.

Leading Trinity College against Jesus College later that same week Jackson scored 146, struck in his best style; and against a Gentlemen of England side under the captainship of A.J. Webbe, Jackson hit a useful 43 to follow up the havoc he had wrought with his bowling. He had taken 8 for 54 in 130 deliveries to dismiss a powerful batting line-up for 165 on a blameless pitch. The visitors, who included Sammy Woods and J.T. Hearne, the Middlesex professional, fought every step of the way to get back into the contest, and in the end it was only the depth of Cambridge batting which won the day, Jackson and Ranji being at the wicket at the finish to see the University home by a margin of 4 wickets.

The weather played a major part in the University's low-scoring match with Yorkshire. Heavy rain the day before meant a drying pitch when the match got under way on Thursday 18th May. Cambridge had first use of the wicket and after 50 minutes had stumbled to 26 for 5, with

Jackson caught at slip by John Tunnicliffe off Bobby Peel for a single. When eventually the University were dismissed for 121, Yorkshire once again found themselves put to the sword by one of their own. The match was over in two days, Cambridge the victors by 27 runs. Jackson's command of length and line on a rain-affected wicket removed Tom Wardall, Tunnicliffe, Peel, George Ulyett and Johnny Brown at a cost of 25 runs and the Tykes were all out for a sad 83 in under two hours. Tunnicliffe's dismissal, caught at short slip by Ranji, was another demonstration of the Indian prince's quicksilver reflexes in the field. Percy Cross Standing, in *F.S. Jackson* (1906), describes the incident thus:

> (Tunnicliffe) had made one of his favourite late cuts, which Ranji grabbed in such a lightning-like manner that nobody knew what had happened - especially as the fieldsman quietly pocketed the ball. 'What are you doing, Ranji?' asked Mr. Leslie Gay, who was keeping wicket. 'Run after the ball - it's gone to the boundary!' Ranji didn't stir. 'Where *is* the ball?' asked Jackson. The fieldsman then quietly produced it - and poor Tunnicliffe had to go. 'Well,' said he, as he passed Ranji on his way to the pavilion, 'you *are* a conjurer, sir! *I suppose it's the same ball?'*

'Long John' Tunnicliffe had his revenge a little later when for the second time in the match it was he who caught Jackson off the bowling of Peel when the Cantab skipper had made 12.

If Jackson's bowling had tormented his Yorkshire

fellows in each of the four encounters at Fenner's, his batting had been a disappointment. In the four meetings between Cambridge and his native county, he scored 45 runs with a highest score of 23, at an average of 6.42, whereas, with the ball he had taken 33 wickets at 9.63 apiece, capturing at least 5 wickets in an innings five times. His bowling figures in these matches had been: 1890, 12 for 114; 1891, 10 for 65; 1892, 4 for 90; and 1893, 7 for 50.

In the last week of May, Cambridge crushed a below-strength M.C.C. XI by 10 wickets. As a cricketing contest the match was significant only in that it was the fourth successive Cantab victory that season. In the cricketing career of the Cambridge captain it marked a personal milestone.

It was his 56th first-class match, and when he went out to bat it was to commence his 98th innings. The premier club had compiled 268, a moderate total on a flat, rather benign pitch. The M.C.C.'s bowling was in the capable hands of three respected professionals: Francis Shacklock, Nottinghamshire's New Zealand-born fast bowler whose name, legend has it, was the inspiration for Conan Doyle's somewhat better-known fictional detective; George Davidson, one of the earliest of Derbyshire's renowned line of fast-medium bowlers; and Walter Mead, later of Essex, a purveyor of an awkward form of 'slow-medium orthodox right-arm spin' mixed up with an occasional leg-break. Backing up the trio was J.H.J. Hornsby, who had been one of the most penetrating of the bowlers in India that winter, and G.A. Foljambe, another of Jackson's recent touring companions. On a good wicket it was not perhaps an attack that held too many terrors for an in-form batsman of the highest class, but it was certainly an attack which demanded respect.

Jackson hit 102 as Cambridge romped to 352 in 4 hours 40 minutes, a scoring rate of about 80 runs an hour. Jackson's maiden first-class century came up in 125 minutes.

There was a festival atmosphere at Fenner's in June. The talk was of the purchase of the University Ground, the triumphs of the previous month, the batting of the Cantab captain, and the two specially arranged fixtures against Surrey and the visiting Australians.

Surrey had not played at Fenner's for many years and to commemorate the event the county XI were the guests at a dinner held in their honour by the Cambridge University Cricket Club. Jackson toasted his adversaries one evening, and plundered a dashing, chanceless 123 off the bowling of Lockwood, Richardson, Hayward, Walter Read and William Brockwell over the next two days, in an innings lasting just 3 hours. Jackson took 5 for 61 in the county's second innings in a match of fluctuating fortunes that could have gone either way until Lockwood, at his inspirational best, ripped through the Cambridge batting in the last innings. Cambridge went down, overwhelmed in the end by the all-round cricket of their opponents. It was defeat with honour. A week later the University lost to the Australians, again after securing a big first innings advantage. This time the visitors were compelled to follow on and as a result enjoyed the best of the wicket in the latter part of the match. Jackson hit 49 in the first innings but was run out for 3 in the second, a misfortune that undermined the whole innings and probably cost the University what slim chance it had of making the 226 runs needed for victory.

In the last two trial games before the Lord's match, Cambridge lost to Sussex in a close contest, and overran M.C.C. by an innings and 155 runs. Jackson registered scores of 24 and 34 against Sussex, and 37 against the premier club. His bowling had fallen away a little after the Surrey match, but he bowled enough to keep his arm supple and his figure trim.

Oxford came to the Lord's match without a victory in their trial matches; Cambridge were regarded by most as by far the stronger side. Oxford could field several players of immense promise, the Palairet brothers, C.B. Fry, J.B. Wood, and Berkeley, the fast bowler, but they lacked the strength in depth of their opponents. Cambridge ran out the victors by 266 runs, in a match that was closer for the first two days than the final result would suggest.

Jackson won the toss and thereafter Cambridge never surrendered the initiative. He made the highest score in each innings with 38 and 57, including 10 fours. His relatively modest bowling returns of 1 for 35 and 3 for 22, disguise the fact that he took wickets at important stages of the Oxford innings.

The match was not without controversy. Against the Australians at Fenner's, Cambridge had had the worst of the conditions after their visitors had followed on. Something similar almost happened against Oxford. When, in the Dark Blues' first innings the ninth wicket fell with 95 on the board, C.M. Wells deliberately bowled wides to the boundary to prevent Oxford following on. There was a furore in the press which could not help but reflect on the Cambridge captain, who, by his own admission, unreservedly sanctioned his bowler's action. Had Oxford been inserted again with the wicket playing easily, and his bowlers weary, Cambridge would, he argued, have lost whatever advantage they had earned through bowling out the Dark Blues cheaply, and then had to bat last on a wearing wicket. All very well, the papers chorused, but hardly sporting.

Hardly cricket?

It must have stung Jackson. Many other men in his position would have vented the kind of bitter retort that turns a debate into a shouting match, souring the air for years to come. He held his peace, listened politely to the criticism, and replied to it with unfailing good humour.

The situation eased with the intervention of W.G. Grace. 'The Doctor' thought it was something of a storm in a tea cup:

> Eight runs were wanted to save the follow-on, and when three more were added the batsmen were seen to consult together between the wickets. It was at once assumed by all that Oxford meant to throw away a wicket so that (they) might bat again. Cambridge, however, had everything to lose by a compulsory follow-on, and C.M. Wells, who was bowling, took measures to frustrate it... Personally, if I believed a batsman meant to sacrifice his wicket in order to secure a follow-on for his side, I should throw away runs to frustrate his purpose; but if on the other hand, if I saw that a bowler was bent on preventing a follow-on I should knock my wickets down without hesitation.

It seemed the Cambridge captain had powerful friends.

W.G. had as good as come down on Jackson's side and in so doing, dared lesser mortals to defy him. It was a brave man indeed who stood up to W.G., and the public debate moved on. The incident itself was in many ways the most important of a series of episodes which eventually led to a long overdue change in the follow-on law.

Jackson had been captain of a vintage Cambridge XI, six of whom were destined to represent England: Jackson himself, Ranji, A.J.L. Hill, L.H. Gay, A.O. Jones, and H.R. Bromley-Davenport. The victory was the crowning moment of his young life although it would be another twelve years before he was given the opportunity to captain a side for a whole season. It was a wise man who said that 'cricket is a strange game.'

He appeared for the Gentlemen in the Lord's match, scored 19 and 10 not out, and took just one wicket, albeit the prized 'castle' of Arthur Shrewsbury, bowled out before he was set.

Stanley Jackson's form had been irresistible and his selection for the England side scheduled to meet the Australians in the First Test Match at Lord's was anticipated long before it was confirmed by the M.C.C.

After the controversy of the Oxford - Cambridge match, and the inevitable speculation about the forthcoming Test Match, it was probably a merciful relief to go up to Trent Bridge to play in his first match of the season for the county of the broad acres. Bobby Peel was indisposed and in his absence Jackson captured 5 wickets for 42 runs in 27 mean five-ball overs. Then, on a slow, awkward pitch, he scored 59 of Yorkshire's first 77 runs in 80 minutes. The visitors made 182, and won by an innings.

Jackson's debut for England at Lord's, was upon him

almost before he realised it.

The Australians were a solid, workmanlike side whose bowling lacked the cutting edge that has always been at a premium in international cricket. C.T.B. Turner was still a very fine bowler, but his pace was not what it had been, George Giffen needed more bounce than most English wickets usually provided to be effective against the best batsmen, and Hugh Trumble was not yet the thorn in England's side he would become in later years. The side the Australians put in the field against the might of England in that third week of July 1893 was not one of the great Australian sides.

England, were for the first time on home territory against the Australians without W.G. Grace, who had sprained his hand in a match at Bristol. In his absence A.E. Stoddart assumed the captaincy. The team he led was roundly criticised for the names that were missing rather than for those actually in it. In batting order the side was:

A. Shrewsbury (Nottinghamshire), A.E. Stoddart (Middlesex), W. Gunn (Nottinghamshire), F.S. Jackson (Yorkshire), J.M. Read (Surrey), R. Peel (Yorkshire), W. Flowers (Nottinghamshire), E. Wainwright (Yorkshire), W.H. Lockwood (Surrey), G. McGregor (Middlesex), A. Mold (Lancashire).

Jackson was one of four debutants, the others being Lockwood, Mold and Wainwright. Whatever doubts its critics harboured, it was a powerful and balanced side. There were four specialist batsmen, Shrewsbury, Stoddart, Gunn and Read; five all-rounders, Jackson, Peel, Flowers,

Wainwright and Lockwood; a wicket-keeper batsman, McGregor; and an out-and-out bowler, Mold. There was a surfeit of batting and no shortage of variety or penetration in the bowling.

Test Matches in 1893 were not the affairs they are today. In England they were played out over three days, the Lord's match being scheduled to commence on Monday 17th and end on Wednesday 19th July. The England side was selected by a committee set up by the authorities of the ground staging the match: thus, at Lord's, M.C.C. selected the England eleven; at the Kennington Oval, the venue for the second Test, the Surrey committee chose the side; and at Old Trafford, for the third Test, the task fell to the Lancashire committee. Moreover, the counties could, and often did, refuse to release players if a Test Match clashed with a vital Championship fixture. It was a recipe for anarchy, only Englishmen could have tolerated such a system, and – probably - only Englishmen could have made it work, in a fashion, for as long as it did.

Test Matches in England in the early 1890s had yet to attain the status they are now accorded; a Test Match was on a par with the Gentlemen - Players match at Lord's or the Kennington Oval. It would all change in a very few years. Test Matches in 1893 were still novel events, restricted to spasmodic encounters with the Australians. If Test Match cricket was still undervalued when Jackson came onto its stage, its very 'specialness' would soon see it grow in stature to its rightful place atop the commanding heights of the summer game.

It had rained on the Sunday and it was thought that the wicket would be on the slow side, and possibly, awkward when play began on Monday morning. Stoddart was therefore posed an immediate problem when he won the toss. However, coming to the conclusion that a captain of England at Lord's could do no more than elect to take first use of the pitch, he decided to bat. He and Gunn were soon back in the pavilion, the score just 31. The fall of another wicket might easily have precipitated a crisis when Jackson walked down the steps and out onto the hallowed turf to join Arthur Shrewsbury. Later, Jackson was to say that he learned more that day batting with the little Nottinghamshire master batsman than he could have learned in years of normal cricket.

Shrewsbury put down anchor.

Jackson flowed into the attack.

It was apparent from the moment the Cambridge captain arrived in the middle that he was gifted with a temperament that was equal to the occasion. He played himself in, gathering momentum the longer he batted. He hit 13 fours in scoring 91 out of 137 while he was at the wicket. He gave a sharp chance when he had raised his fifty and another later, before he departed to a catch at the wicket off Turner, the pick of the Australian bowlers. Shrewsbury went on to score 106 in four hours, but his contribution was put into the shade by the debutant's batting.

On that Monday, either side of luncheon, Jackson became a national hero.

The match was drawn, a deluge on Wednesday terminating proceedings, after Stoddart had declared England's second innings closed; the first declaration in a Test Match in England. Jackson had failed in his second knock, scoring only 5. He had had scant opportunity to show his worth with the ball, something he would have to get used to throughout his international career. It went without saying that he was an automatic selection for the second Test, due to be played at the Kennington Oval, on 14th, 15th, and 16th August.

He appeared three times for Yorkshire between the Tests, against Gloucestershire, Kent and the old enemy, Lancashire. His batting was less than inspired, his best score in four innings being 17. His failures were not wholly of his making. In an era of uncovered wickets the weather was always the joker in the pack, no more so than in the Roses Match at Old Trafford. In A.A. Thomson's famous words: 'No Act of Parliament or Order in Council can prevent the rain at Old Trafford.' On a wet wicket the match was over in a day and a half, Lancashire scoring 64 and 50, Yorkshire 58 and 51 in front of a Bank Holiday crowd of 12,554 on the first day, and 9,599 on the second.

Opening with Sellars in the visitors' second innings as Yorkshire went in search of a winning total of 57, Jackson had made 12 of a stand worth 24 when he was involved in an infamous run out. It began when a ball from William Oakley, the Lancastrian left-arm medium pacer hit Jackson on the pad. The story is taken up in a letter written to *Cricket*, by two ladies who observed the incident from the relative calm of the Ladies Enclosure:

> The bowler appealed for L.B.W., the umpire said 'out', and then, correcting himself, 'not out', whereupon Mr. Jackson ran for a leg-bye. But Mr. Sellars refused to move, so that the only thing for Mr. Jackson was to get back as fast as possible. Before he could do so his wicket was thrown down by Tinsley.

Jackson seemed destined to exhaust his share of misfortune outside the Test Match arena. He had been dogged for a long time by the myth that he was a less than safe runner between the wickets, and well-publicised misunderstandings such as the one at Manchester, tended to add insult to injury. That year he was run out only three times in his 36 innings, hardly a disastrous record.

There were four changes in the England team that faced the Australians at the Oval. Wainwright was not released by Yorkshire, Peel and Maurice Read were dropped, and Flowers was unwell. Into the side came W.G. Grace, who resumed the captaincy, Johnny Briggs and Albert Ward of Lancashire, and Walter Read of Surrey. The Surrey Committee had decided that the match would be for Maurice Read's Benefit. With a paying crowd over the three days totalling 28,252, each paying a shilling, and the proceeds being split two ways with the tourists, Read's share of the gate receipts alone was over £700, a figure swelled to £1,200 by donations and subscriptions.

W.G. Grace took Jackson aside before the match.

'With all these batsmen I don't know where to put you,' confessed the Doctor.

'Anywhere will do,' Jackson returned.

'Then number seven.'

'That's my lucky number,' said the younger man, 'I was the seventh child.'

Batting at number seven, Jackson scored his first century for England. In glorious sunshine and 'tropical heat' he scored 103 in 135 minutes after the early batsmen had beaten the heart out of the Australian attack. When Jackson was last out, 483 runs had been scored in less than seven hours.

His century had not been without its moments, as Jackson was to recollect in the *Daily Graphic*:

> When Mold, the last man, came in, I was still just short of the hundred. Now Mold was an awful batter...but somehow he managed to stop the four balls left in the over. Then I got my turn, and played the first up to third man. Well, if you please, Mold shouted 'Come on!' and came pounding up the pitch. So he had four more balls to face, and was almost out to each of them. However, after Giffen had nearly finished me, I got hold of one and lifted it over the ring, and there was my coveted century.

It was the first time a hundred had been reached with a hit over the boundary in a Test Match in England (in Jackson's day hits over the ring counted as four runs, only blows out of the ground counting for six). The excitement was too much for the wretched Mold, who promptly ran out Jackson.

Jackson was invited to play in the third and last Test Match at Manchester, but the game clashed with a county fixture against Sussex at Brighton and Yorkshire were on the verge of clinching the County Championship, so Jackson declined the invitation. He was at the crease, undefeated on 35 when victory over Sussex was secured by a margin of 8 wickets. Yorkshire were champion county, Lord Hawke's men were on the march. The third Test was drawn, and the Ashes safe in England's hands.

Jackson's season ended with a dramatic flourish

during the Scarborough Festival, which was the most successful to date, making a profit of £640. Since coming down from Cambridge his bowling form had been eclipsed by his batting feats and so it continued as his season finished in a flurry of runs. He scored 0 and 111 not out for Yorkshire against M.C.C. and Ground, 20 and 38 for the county against the South of England, and 62 and 68 for C.I. Thornton's England XI against the Australians.

Hawke recalls Jackson's remarkable century against the premier club with marked affection in his *Recollections and Reminiscences* (1924):

> There, against M.C.C., who had F.R. Spofforth, J.T. Hearne, Rawlin and A.E. Stoddart to bowl, we had, on fourth hands, to get 195 on one of the most kicking and vile wickets I recollect. Somebody said it was a hundred pounds to a Ribston Pippin we were beaten. But that was just the time when 'Jacker' had to be reckoned with...he batted as though the wicket were perfect and the bowling tosh. He accounted for 50 runs of the first 70 in an hour, and completed his century only forty minutes later; whilst Ernest Smith and he gave us victory by terrific hitting, actually knocking off the last 66 runs in eighteen minutes, the Old Cliftonian's share being 40 of them. It was all the more effective because the Club had twelve men in the field.

Jackson's wicket was now a great prize: a bowler who claimed Jacker's castle was a hero for a day. In the second innings of the penultimate match of the season, against the South of England, Walter Humphreys - a seasoned county performer whose 150 wickets at 17.32 apiece that year, set a record for 'lob-bowling' that has never been surpassed - captured Jackson's wicket. He told his tale to *The Cricket Field:*

> I have a habit of following up the ball a long way, and though I try to be careful when a hard hitter is in, I sometimes forget, and go as far up as to a steady player...I did this when Mr Jackson was in, and he came out to, and sent the ball back straight to me. By one of those freaks...the ball stuck in my hands, and I tried to look as though it were quite the ordinary thing to make a catch of that sort. Mr Jackson hardly seemed to realise he was out, and we stood looking at each other for an appreciable time.

The Cambridge captain concluded his season with a regal flourish against the Australians, who, by then, must have been sick and tired of the sight of him. *Cricket* picks up the story:

> Jackson and Stoddart, the first two batsmen, soon got the measure of the Australian bowling, and runs came fast from the first. The Middlesex amateur was in particularly fine form, and though his partner, as a rule, scores at a good pace, in this case a greater proportion of the runs came from Stoddart. The hundred went up after an hour and a quarter's batting, and at the luncheon interval both batsmen were still in with the total 170, of which Stoddart's share was 104. On resuming,

Jackson added four, and was then well caught at long on. At the time of his retirement 176 runs had been made in a few minutes under two hours, and of these he had contributed 62 without anything like a chance.

It was festival cricket in a truly golden age; 170 for 0 in a 105-minute session before lunch on the first day! And not easy runs, but runs taken off the strongest attack the tourists could muster, with Australian tourists out to avenge the iniquities - real and imagined - of a recently lost Test Match series.

J.M. Blackham, the Australian captain, told the *Scarborough Post* that he thought Jackson was 'as good as any of them', and that 'some of his off strokes are magnificent, and his driving and cutting are as good as anything I have seen.' He included Jackson with Gunn, Shrewsbury, Stoddart and W.G., as the best English batsmen he had seen, and put the young Yorkshireman in the same company as Peel and Briggs, as his pick of the all-rounders he had faced that season.

Jackson finished third in the national batting averages, behind Gunn and Stoddart, and twenty-ninth in the bowling lists. *The Cricket Field* declared that 'unquestionably the most promising of the younger players is F.S. Jackson...as brilliant a batsman as anyone in England, besides being very safe.'

1893 was the first of Jackson's great years.

8 | The County of the Broad Acres (1894-1895)

While Stanley Jackson's batting was gracing the big stage of English cricket, his cricketing twin, Joe Darling was finally emerging from his years of exile in the country.

At the age of nineteen Joe Darling received an invitation to visit Melbourne and Sydney as a member of the touring South Australian XI, but his father had refused to grant him leave, sending him instead to the outback to manage one of his farms. Many young men in Joe Darling's position would have quietly settled in the country and set aside their dreams. Not Joe Darling. His batting prospered 'on the mat' and he bided his time.

On 3 May 1893 he married Alice Minna Blanche Francis at Mundoora, South Australia. Soon afterwards the couple moved to Adelaide, where Joe opened a sports store, in Rundle Street. It seems that the Honourable John Darling accepted his son's wish to live his own life, although his disapproval of cricket was undiminished.

Joe Darling's schoolboy deeds and reputation on the mat ensured his swift promotion to the state side, and he soon made his mark. Representing South Australia in interstate matches his scores that season were 5 and 32, 4 and 1 against New South Wales, 63 not out and 0, 87 and 24 against Victoria. His batting in the second match against Victoria was instrumental in securing a 58-run victory which ensured that South Australia, under George Giffen's captaincy, won the Sheffield Shield.

Stanley Jackson's feats against Blackham's side had attracted a great deal of interest back in Australia. English cricket had found a new knight to carry the fight to the colonial foe, and Jackson's inclusion in the England team due to tour the Antipodes in the Australian summer of 1894-95 was eagerly anticipated. Joe Darling's name was as yet unknown in the old country to all but the most assiduous of *Cricket*'s readers, who might have noted the arrival of a new name in the South Australian side when perusing the scorecards of the handful of interstate matches.

Much was expected of Jackson when the English season of 1894 began; the previous season had been blessed with glorious weather for the most part, but, in contrast, the summer of 1894 was destined to be wet and dismal as only British summers can be.

He appeared for C.I. Thornton's XI against Cambridge University at his old stamping ground, Fenner's, in the second week of May, scoring 40 in good style in a match spoiled by the weather. At Old Trafford later in the week he was clean bowled in the Roses Match by one of Arthur Mold's thunderbolts when he had made 7. This was Johnny Briggs' rain-interrupted benefit, completed in a little over a day's actual playing time. The match was won by Yorkshire by an innings, with Peel, Hirst and Wainwright at their irresistible best on a ruined wicket.

In the middle of the month Jackson returned to Fenner's, scoring 72 and 37 for A.J. Webbe's side against the University, and bowling creditably for match figures of 4 for 74. Webbe's side moved on to Oxford after vanquishing Cambridge. Oxford, however, were sterner opponents; Jackson recorded a duck in his only innings, although he could take heart from his four cheap wickets in the drawn game.

He caught up with the Yorkshire XI at Brighton in the last week of May. Sussex batted first and were soon dismissed for 114. Then, opening the county's batting with Lord Hawke, Jackson blazed a brilliant, chanceless 131 - his highest score to date - in 140 minutes. When the hosts batted again Jackson and Peel made short work of a Sussex line-up depleted by injury, Jackson's share of the spoils being 3 for 28. The match was over within two days, the home side crushed by an innings and 36 runs. May ended with the fixture against Nottinghamshire at Trent Bridge, in which Jackson's fighting 42 out of a first innings total of 94, in a narrow win, was worth a hundred in any other context.

June was a barren month. In eleven innings he scored 7, 22 and 10, 0 and 25, 8 and 10, 5 and 1, 7 and 0 not out. With the ball he did little better, taking only 3 wickets. Uncovered wickets had much to do with his singular lack of success with the bat in June 1894, and, ironically, he was denied the opportunity of bowling on the same rain-affected pitches by the strength of the Yorkshire attack.

At the beginning of July, Jackson went up to Leeds, where he captained Yorkshire against Nottinghamshire. He scored 43 in the first innings and in the second, in a little over two and a half hours, he struck a faultless 145, improving upon his career-best score for the second time in five weeks. Declaring the Yorkshire innings closed at 330 for 7, and setting the visitors 353 to win, Jackson claimed 5 for 37 as the Nottinghamshire reply crumbled and Yorkshire ran out the victors by 201 runs.

As so often happens, one good performance leads on to a string of others. Invited to play in both the Oval, and Lord's matches for the Gentlemen against the Players, Jackson travelled south to write his name in the record books. The first match, at the Oval, was an unequal struggle, the Gentlemen going down by an innings. Jackson made 41 and 3, and took 1 for 55 in the match.

Then came the Lord's match.

The Gentlemen, fielding a much strengthened side, won the toss and W.G. Grace decided to bat. Against an attack which included J.T. Hearne, Lockwood, Flowers, Briggs and Wainwright, Jackson's flawless 63 in 105 minutes out of the 127 scored while he was at the wicket, was the main reason the Gentlemen eventually reached the dizzy heights of 254. When the Players batted, W.G. put Sammy Woods and Jackson on to open the bowling; together they were to bowl unchanged throughout both innings of the Players, bowling 91 five-ball overs and one ball, and taking 18 for 201. The full figures were:

Bowler	First Innings				Second Innings			
	O	M	R	W	O	M	R	W
S.M.J. Woods	24.2	8	61	4	21.4	6	63	2
F.S. Jackson	24	8	36	5	21	7	41	7

It was a mighty achievement, as *Cricket* commented:

With all the outcry about the weakness of amateur bowling at the present time, it is a little singular that Messrs Woods and Jackson should have been able to perform a feat at Lord's this week which has only three times before been recorded in the history of the contest between Gentlemen and Players. Altogether on only four occasions have two bowlers been able to keep up their ends without a change during this most important of matches.

Sammy Woods had bowled his heart out, but it was Jackson's match. Jackson himself always regarded this as the finest all-round performance of his whole career. His 12 wickets for 77 runs was the best return he achieved in a first-class match. A fond memory was the manner of William Gunn's dismissal in the first innings, bowled by Jackson's infamous 'arm ball' as he shouldered arms, no doubt convinced - as his great Nottinghamshire and England team-mate Arthur Shrewsbury had been before him - that the ball was going away down the slope at Lord's.

In this modem age it is hard to appreciate what such a performance meant to an amateur. In today's cricket with its surfeit of Test Matches and its remorseless one-day competitions which have tended to put the rest of the first-class game in the shade, it is all too easy to forget that in Jackson's age the focus of the English season was not necessarily the outcome of a Test Match series, nor even the result of the County Championship. For a man like Jackson, to whom cricket was his joy rather than his livelihood, the season revolved around the three traditional fixtures played at Lord's at the end of June and the beginning of July; Eton against Harrow, Oxford against Cambridge, and the Gentlemen against the Players. Test Matches were infrequent events, the matches at Lord's in midsummer were annual institutions, intrinsically social as well as sporting occasions. In later years - whilst at the height of his powers - Jackson would drop out of the Yorkshire team and travel to London to watch the Eton - Harrow, and the Oxford - Cambridge encounters, meet with old friends, and practise in the nets of the nursery ground in preparation for the great test of the Gentlemen and Players match that followed.

Nowadays, the very concept of the Gentlemen - Players match is alien to English cricket. To contemporary ears the match has about it the ring of the 'haves' against the 'have nots'. Victorian England was a land where inequality was rife, where economic and social injustice were taken for granted, institutionalised, and the Gentlemen - Players Match had a symbolism that has largely been lost from the game in recent times. Yet the significance and the general appeal of the fixture owed little to either the social climate in which it was played, or the legitimate political grievances of the disadvantaged masses of Victorian England. It was proof positive of the unifying influence of sport. When the Gentlemen met the Players at Lord's the best cricketers in England were in opposition, and it made for cricket of the most compelling sort. In many ways the fixture was the ultimate test of an English cricketer, a trial by fire that has been replaced by the cauldron of the Test Match arena. In Jackson's day there were two, three, or sometimes four, Gentlemen versus Players contests every year (annually at Lord's and the Oval, and less frequently as part of festivals such as Hastings Week, or Scarborough) whereas home Test Matches were only played every few years and always against Australia. Until the Edwardian era Test Match cricket had more or less the same status as the Gentlemen - Players matches.

The Reverend R.S. Holmes put his valedictory seal on Jackson's deeds in the Lord's Match of 1894 when he wrote in his 'Cricket Notches', in *Cricket:*

> I don't think enough has been made of Jackson's wonderful bowling against the Players at Lord's. It would have been considered worthy of the boldest type had a bowler like Briggs or Richardson scored a similar triumph.

Jackson left the best of his season behind him when he departed from Lord's. His batting form slumped, and his bowling suffered as it had during the latter part of the previous season from underemployment. As a bowler he maintained his form, and his fitness, by bowling in anger. As time went by he practised his batting as keenly as ever in the nets, other commitments permitting, but his bowling needed continual match practice to keep it in good order. In the Roses Match at Bradford - Bobby Peel's benefit - he scored 2 and 34, and captured 2 for 39 and 4 for 14 as Yorkshire defeated Lancashire by 117 runs. But in the last six matches of the season he took just nine wickets, and in nine innings passed fifty only once.

It was the hallmark of the man that his one sizeable score as the season drew to a close was in a low-scoring encounter with Middlesex on a rain-affected pitch. He scored 91 out of Yorkshire's first innings total of 184 against the bowling of J.T. Hearne and J.T. Rawlin, bowlers who routinely destroyed sides under the conditions prevailing that day at Bramall Lane, Sheffield. *Cricket* described Rawlin's bowling as being 'unplayable'. The next best score in the match was Peel's hard-hit 39, nobody else got into the thirties. With Peel claiming 6 for 33 in the Middlesex first innings, and Wainwright 9 for 66 in the second, Jackson, who had mesmerised the Players at Lord's, hardly got a look in with his seamers.

It was in this match, indeed with his first scoring stroke, that Jackson scored his 5,000th run in first-class cricket.

In the aftermath of his triumphs of 1893, the season of 1894 had its mundane moments. Appointed vice-captain to Lord Hawke at Yorkshire, Jackson had frequently captained the side in a Championship campaign which ultimately ended in failure. He was becoming more involved with his father's business concerns, contemplating a future role in local politics in Leeds and, not unnaturally, there were times when his concentration wandered. He had batted well enough to maintain the reputation he had earned in 1893, and throughout, he had bowled meanly and sometimes destructively. The Gentlemen - Players Match at Lord's had been the focus of the summer, and after it was over, his season had fallen away.

When Jackson played for Yorkshire he was employed essentially as a specialist batsman; his bowling was a bonus by dint of the simple fact that by the time Wainwright, Peel and Hirst had done their worst, it was usually time for Yorkshire to bat again. Yorkshire's three-pronged attack took over 400 wickets that season; between them they left precious few pickings. Jackson enjoyed his cricket for Yorkshire, but there were times when he found it nigh impossible to summon the application required to excel consistently in county cricket. He was, and, to a lesser degree, always had been, the man for the big occasion, the man for a crisis. The normal round of Championship cricket simply did not provide the stimulus he needed to give of his best day in, day out.

In the absence of Test Match cricket, the Gentlemen - Players matches became the commanding heights of his season, and these he had conquered.

Two major overseas tours were in the offing that winter: one under A.E. Stoddart to Australia to defend the Ashes; and another under Lord Hawke, to North America. Jackson would have been welcome in either, although had he gone abroad that winter, it would surely have been with Stoddart s England XI. In the event, he went on neither. He had commitments in England, not least to Messrs W.L. Jackson and Co. He felt that a break from cricket would not be amiss, and besides, he was only twenty-four, and there would be many other opportunities to tour Australia.

While Jackson's education in the ways of business and commerce in the West Riding continued, Joe Darling's pugnacious batting carried him into the Australian team that faced England at Sydney in the opening Test Match of the first ever five-match Test series. He had collared the tourists' bowling for 117 at the Adelaide Oval earlier in the tour; and it had been more than enough to earn him his first Test Match cap.

Like many debutants whose later careers have blossomed at the highest level, Darling was dismissed for a duck in his first innings in international cricket, bowled by Tom Richardson, the third Australian wicket to fall with the score just 21. It must have seemed an awfully long way back to the dressing room that morning at the Sydney Cricket Ground. Australia, however, recovered from 21 for 3 to amass a total of 586 runs, and in a remarkable contest, in which a record 1,514 runs were scored, England, after following on 261 runs behind, eventually set the home side 177 to win on a rain-affected pitch. Darling redeemed his first innings failure with a fighting 53 against the bowling of Bobby Peel and Johnny Briggs on a drying wicket.

It was to no avail as Australia slumped to defeat by 10 runs on the sixth day, but Joe Darling [pictured *left*] had arrived in international cricket. He was one of nine debutants in the match, five Australian, four English, notable amongst whom was Ernest Jones, his fellow South Australian, shortly to become the most terrifying of shock bowlers, Jack (J.T.) Brown, Jackson's Yorkshire team mate, and a certain Archibald Campbell MacLaren, formerly of Harrow School, latterly of Lancashire.

MacLaren scored 4 and 20 on his introduction to the Test Match arena. It was not until the Fifth Test at Melbourne, with the rubber undecided that MacLaren found his true form. In the first innings he blazed a majestic century and everything that had gone before was forgotten. In the same match J.T. Brown hit 140 to see England home by 6 wickets, his hundred coming up in 95 minutes. MacLaren was headed towards immortality; another fate awaited Jack Brown. For a moment they were the uncrowned princes of English batsmanship, then the wheel of history turned and they went their separate ways to their different destinies.

Back in England Jackson briefly stole back the limelight with a sparkling innings of 122 in his first knock of the season of 1895, opening for C.I. Thornton's XI against Cambridge at Fenner's, in mid-May. Missed before he had scored, he made the University pay dearly, hitting 16 fours in an innings lasting just 135 minutes.

It was to be the only time he reached three figures that season, although he averaged better than thirty with the bat in logging his thousand runs for the year.

He appeared for England against Surrey at the Oval, in Walter Read's benefit match. The old fixture had lapsed for some thirty years and its revival was well-received. Jackson hit a sound 57 as England overwhelmed the county side in two days. He failed with the bat in the Roses Match at Sheffield in early June, scoring 3 and 1, running into Arthur Mold at his most ferocious. His four previous innings for Yorkshire had been 11 and 1, 0 and 22. It was a disheartening start to the county programme.

Jackson was the last man to mope overlong about these things. As June went by he rediscovered some batting form and he shook the cobwebs out of his bowling. In the three Championship fixtures following the Roses Match, against Middlesex at Lord's, Hampshire at Southampton, and Surrey at Bradford, he registered scores of 30 and 26, 55 and 36, 50 and 46. At Lord's he captured 6 wickets for 47 in the match, and 4 for 48 at Southampton.

It was a run which put him in good fettle for his trip to

Lord's in the third week of June where he turned out for I Zingari against the Gentlemen of England in the jubilee match of the famous wandering club. Opening with H.T. Hewett he scored 34 and 23. In the second innings he was caught by W.G. Grace (senior), off the bowling of W.G. Grace (junior).

Returning to the Championship round he participated in 9-wicket victories over Nottinghamshire and Sussex before taking his place in the Gentlemen's XI in the Lord's match. This was a desperately close contest in which Jackson, with 6 for 166 in the match, was the pick of the amateur bowlers, but disappointed with the bat, making 11 and 8 at number three in the list.

Jackson's bowling tended to prosper the harder it was worked. He had bowled 67 five-ball overs against the Players, and the next day he was in the field for Yorkshire at Dewsbury, setting the Kent batsmen problems a-plenty as he claimed 5 for 32 in the visitors' first innings, and 8 wickets in the match. His batting flourished against the Kentish bowlers as he and David Denton chased a winning score of 247 with time running out. Jackson was missed at 25 and 26, and went on to make 81. Denton was 44 not out at the close, but victory eluded the team.

At York later that month Jackson opened for the Gentlemen of Yorkshire against the Players of Yorkshire. The amateurs included F. Mitchell, A. Sellars, Ernest Smith, Lord Hawke and F. W. Milligan, but were soundly drubbed by the professionals who were by far the stronger all-round side, with J.T. Brown, Wainwright, Tunnicliffe and Denton occupying the first four places in a batting line-up which had Bobby Peel entering the fray at the fall of the seventh wicket. Jackson scored 18 and 0, and took 3 for 57 in the Players' only innings.

The Yorkshire team that contested the Roses Match at Old Trafford at the beginning of August had the distinctive look of the great Yorkshire sides of the golden age. In batting order the county of the broad acres put into the field: F.S. Jackson, F. Mitchell, J. Tunnicliffe, J.T. Brown, D. Denton, E. Wainwright, R. Moorhouse, Lord Hawke, R. Peel, G.H. Hirst and D. Hunter. Ernest Smith was absent having got married on the Saturday before the match. Substitute Wilfred Rhodes for Bobby Peel, and Schofield Haigh for Moorhouse and the legendary Yorkshire side of the golden age is there before one's eyes. The signs of what was to come were writ plain: in first-class cricket that season, Jackson, Moorhouse, Hawke, Tunnicliffe, Brown and Denton all topped a thousand runs, Peel and Hirst each took over one hundred and fifty wickets, Wainwright over eighty, and Jackson sixty-seven. There was endless batting, variety and penetration in the bowling, and under Hawke's stern gaze, both vigour and efficiency in the field.

The Roses Match was drawn, in Yorkshire's favour, Jackson top-scoring in the match with a handsome 76, struck in a little over two hours after Lancashire had been dismissed for 103 on a slow, awkward pitch. Later he prised out four batsmen as the home side struggled to avoid defeat. The next day he was bowling out Kent at Canterbury, capturing 5 for 28 as Yorkshire's hosts slumped to 135. Indeed, the sight of Kentish men seemed to provoke Jackson, for when Kent batted again he claimed 7 for 63, making a nonsense of Canterbury Week. Set just 50 to win, Yorkshire made rather hard work of their task, losing Jackson, Mitchell and Brown in securing victory. Moving on to the Oval for Bobby Abel's benefit match against Surrey, Jackson scored a valuable 35 in a low-scoring contest which the Tykes won by an innings.

That Yorkshire could so easily sweep aside the might of Surrey must have worried the rest of the English first-class game. The years of Yorkshire domination were not yet, but every now and then Hawke's men were wont to serve notice of their intent.

A week later against Middlesex at Leeds, a battling partnership of 130 in 150 minutes between Jackson and John Tunnicliffe saw off the southern county's challenge. Jackson, dropped when he had made 33, was at his most dogged, hitting only a single four in his stay at the wicket. Set 262 for the match Middlesex were routed by Hirst and Peel for just 57. Kent, Surrey and Middlesex had fallen to the Tykes in a fortnight.

In the end it was unfashionable Somerset who, in the last week of August, stopped Yorkshire in their tracks and dashed any hopes of the Championship. Lionel Palairet hit 165, Tyler took 14 wickets for 247 runs in the match, and together they sank Yorkshire. Jackson, who had not planned to play in the match, came in for the injured Moorhouse and scored 46 in an hour in the first innings.

Jackson's last appearance of the season was for Yorkshire against a moderately strong England XI at Scarborough. His bowling finished with a flourish, taking 6 for 24 in the visitors' first innings, but with scores of 9 and 8, his batting concluded with a whimper rather than a bang.

Jackson was second in the Yorkshire batting averages, and first in the bowling lists in 1895. It was the season Archie MacLaren's star outshone that of his old school captain, the year Lancashire's Old Harrovian scored 424 at

Taunton and became a cricketing legend. It was the season W.G. Grace - now in his forty-seventh year - scored a thousand runs in May. And it was the season when the runs began to flow from Ranjitsinhji's bat.

The period that A.A. Thomson designated as the 'diamond decade' of English cricket had begun.

9 | The Return of the Australians (1896)

In 1896 Stanley Jackson and Joe Darling met for the first time on a cricket field, and England defended the Ashes retained so valiantly by Stoddart's side in the winter of 1894-95.

Under the captaincy of G.H.S. Trott the 1896 Australians were an entirely different proposition to the side of 1893, a fact that was to be quickly, and painfully, impressed upon Jackson and his England fellows in the first month of the new season.

The shock of the new Australians was still a week away when Yorkshire travelled to Old Trafford on 4th May to face Lancashire. The two committees of the 'Roses' counties, unable to fit matches against the tourists into their crowded fixture lists, had determined that the only way out of their difficulties was to play the first of the Roses matches at the beginning of the season, rather than over the Whitsuntide weekend. So it was that Yorkshire opened the campaign of 1896 against the old enemy on a grey May morning in front of a 'disappointing' first-day crowd of some eight thousand.

On an underprepared, soft wicket the batsmen struggled throughout. Jackson recorded scores of 21 and 41, and took 2 for 21 and 4 for 30 in the match, but others, in need of a deal more practice than someone of his particular natural gifts, found it harder to find their touch. Yorkshire won by the narrow margin of 2 wickets.

On 7th May Yorkshire went to Edgbaston to meet Warwickshire, who had been routed by Surrey earlier in the week. Lord Hawke won the toss, and on a cold day, elected to bat on what looked like a perfect pitch. Jackson opened with Tunnicliffe, and together they put on 63 for the first wicket. Jackson was at his most fluent, playing with grace and timing, combating the initial movement off the pitch - as the effects of the roller wore off - with an air of complete command. J.T. Brown batted brightly and breezily, Denton never got in, and 3 wickets were down for 141. Jackson's century came up in a shade over two hours, and when he was out for 117 Yorkshire had compiled 211 runs for the loss of 4 wickets in just 150 minutes.

Yorkshire went on batting until the close of the second day and when Hawke's men had finished the record books were in urgent need of amendment. Reaching 452 for 7 on the first day, Yorkshire thrashed 887 runs before the close of their innings. It was the highest total achieved in first-class cricket, the first time four batsmen - Jackson (117), Wainwright (126), Peel (210 not out) and Lord Hawke (166) - had scored centuries in one innings. The

Yorkshire total has only once been exceeded in a match in England. In 1938 a son of the county of the broad acres, Leonard Hutton, hit 364 of England's 903 for 7 declared against Australia. Hawke and Peel's stand of 292 for the eighth wicket remains at the time of writing (1989) the English record.

In normal circumstances Lord Hawke would have instructed his batsmen to throw away their wickets on the second morning of the match, so as to let his bowlers get their teeth into the Warwickshire batting, but on this occasion, the temptation to bat on and on was irresistible. The Yorkshire captain thought that the law preventing a declaration until the last afternoon of a match was nonsensical, and letting his batsmen run riot was his chosen way of drawing attention to the problem. He and Jackson shared the view that high-scoring matches were not necessarily the most interesting of contests, and that the balance between bat and ball had to be maintained to ensure really interesting cricket. On the second day of the onslaught at Edgbaston the Warwickshire bowling and fielding became ragged, and runs came with almost offensive ease. It was not Hawke's idea of how the game ought to be played.

Needing to bowl out the home side twice in a day to force a win, Yorkshire had to settle for a draw, capturing only eleven of the twenty wickets they needed by the time stumps were drawn.

From the batsman's paradise at Edgbaston, Stanley Jackson took the train south to Sheffield Park in Sussex, where he and W.G. Grace were to open the batting for Lord Sheffield's XI in the first match of the Australian tour. The tourists had first use of the wicket, and Arthur Mold made life more than somewhat uncomfortable for the early batsmen. The Australians battled all day to make 241 for 5, Joe Darling's 67 leading the way, with another left-hander new to England, Clem Hill, showing flashes of genius late in the proceedings when he made a handy 32. It had been very dry in the south of England that spring, the wicket was hard, fast and true, but liable to reward genuine pace with excessive lift off a good length. Mold quickly mopped up the Australian tail the following morning, and facing a total of 257, W.G. Grace and Jackson walked out to bat. Mold had struck several of the Australians about the body, now the tourists had their revenge.

The Australians had brought two fast bowlers to England. One was Ernest Jones, a giant of a man whose pace had more than once disconcerted Stoddart's side a year before, and T.R. McKibbin, a bowler with a dubious action who, though not capable of matching his partner's sustained hostility, was a most unpleasant proposition on a wicket that offered him the least encouragement.

Ernest Jones' first ball whistled through W.G.'s beard, others thudded into his broad chest. McKibbin dealt out more of the same, although he tended to pitch shorter than Jones, and this gave the batsmen more time to take either evasive or retaliatory action.

The openers fought it out gamely, with W.G. striking back, hitting both Jones and McKibbin for boundaries in front of the wicket. The opening stand was worth 56 when Jackson was finally undone by Jones' pace and lift, offering a catch to Clem Hill; he had scored 17. Jackson was acknowledged as one of the best players of fast bowling in England, but Jones had hit him repeatedly, and at no time had he ever really settled. Later, when the livid weals about his torso subsided, two cracked ribs were diagnosed. For the while, he nursed his sore chest, and pondered how to deal with Jones.

Meanwhile, Lord Sheffield's XI crumbled before the barrage. W.G. went for 49, taking on Jones once too often, Arthur Shrewsbury and William Gunn touched catches to the waiting slips and departed the scene without regret and C.B. Fry was bowled for a duck. Only Ranjitsinhji carried the fight to the tourists, relying on his lightning reflexes for survival and scoring 79 as the scratch side were bowled out for 195. According to P.C. Standing in *F.S. Jackson* (1906):

> Poor Shrewsbury was heard to remark that people with families dependent upon them couldn't afford to throw their lives away!

The Australians set Lord Sheffield's XI 257 to win on the third afternoon. The pitch was scarcely any easier; it was beginning to wear and the bounce was less predictable. It was a question of playing out time and saving the match. W.G., Jackson and even Ranji had taken something of a battering in the first innings, Gunn and Shrewsbury had shown a marked disinclination to get into the firing line, and Fry was 'on a pair'. The omens were not favourable.

Both W.G. and Jackson survived loud and concerted appeals for catches behind in the first over - to the eternal chagrin of the Australians, who felt that several English umpires were rather too much in awe of the Doctor and his 'heir apparent'. Joe Darling, for one, formed the early opinion that Jackson had a hold over some of the English umpires, and was incensed when the Yorkshireman stood his ground in the face of the appeal. W.G. soon departed to a catch by George Giffen off Jones, but Jackson fought it out. The longer he stayed at the crease the better he played; at stumps he was 95 not out. Restricted in his stroke play by the discomfort of his damaged ribs, he had mastered Jones for a day and the match had been saved.

Despite his injuries Jackson joined the Yorkshire team at Bristol and played his full part in the 9 wicket win over Gloucestershire, scoring 25 and 28 not out, and taking 3 Gloucestershire wickets for 29 runs on the second day of the match. It was only after this that Jackson heeded medical advice, and conceded that he had sustained more than just a few bruises against Jones and McKibbin the previous week at Sheffield Park.

He was prevailed upon to rest but with the first Test Match less than three weeks away he returned to the Yorkshire side at the start of June after just fifteen days. He opened the batting scoring 38, and, to prove his fitness, bowled 80 five-ball overs in the match for figures of 7 for 143. He was less successful in the following matches against Cambridge University at Fenner's and Surrey at Bradford. Both matches were rain-affected; one lost, and one drawn. He took 6 wickets against Surrey, but did little with the bat in either match, scoring 10 and 14, 2 and 27. Lord Hawke, in his *Recollections and Reminiscences* (1924), recalled the final throes of the Surrey match:

> I declared, leaving Surrey 123 to get to win on a slow pitch in two hours. Bobby Abel and Brockwell started at a run a minute, and it began to look pretty dubious, therefore I put on Jackson, because of his unimpeachable length. At once, as I expected, he checked the pace of the scoring, but presently he bowled some ball which he did not think right for the way he had carefully placed his field. He came over to me on purpose to say: 'I am awfully sorry.' I have never known anyone else do that, but to fall from the standard he set himself, in Jackson's opinion, needed an apology.

The match was drawn, Surrey having reached 75 for 6 at the close, Jackson's analysis being 3 for 24 off 22 five-ball overs.

He was invited to play for M.C.C. against the tourists at Lord's in the second week of June. Ernest Jones was absent but Jackson, batting at four, took 51 off Trumble, Giffen, McKibben and Trott. The wicket deteriorated rapidly as the day went on, and by the time the Australians batted, it was at its worst. This was the day J.T. Hearne and A.D. Pougher bowled out the tourists for 18, Hearne claiming 4 for 4, and Pougher, the Leicestershire medium pacer, 5 wickets for no runs. Giffen was unable to bat, but the last seven Australian batsmen failed to put a single run on the board, the last six wickets falling without a run being added to the total. The tourists lost by an innings, despite a defiant second innings 76 from Joe Darling.

Rain disrupted the Australians' visit to Leeds in the aftermath of the defeat at Lord's. Jackson scored 20; Joe Darling scored 0 in the tourists' first innings, bowled out by Bobby Peel, and 21, caught at slip by Tunnicliffe off Wainwright, as the match ended in a tame draw. Shortly afterwards, Yorkshire compiled another vast total, 660 against Leicestershire at Leicester, Jackson's share being 77. He batted at number three in the list, J.T. Brown and John Tunnicliffe opening. Unlike Warwickshire the previous month, Leicestershire could not hold out against the relentless Yorkshire attack. The Tykes won by an innings and 302 runs, Jackson picking up 6 for 76 as the wickets tumbled.

For a long time Lord Hawke had been concerned about Jackson and Brown's running between the wickets. Many years later he wrote, in his *Recollections and Reminiscences* (1924):

> Again and again they seemed unwittingly to baffle each other, so much so that I never felt comfortable when they were partners. Indeed, after one mishap Jacker declared: 'I'll be shot if I go within ten of him again. I never know with him whether I'm to run or be run out.'

Yorkshire needed a regular opening pair. That season Brown, Tunnicliffe and Jackson shared the opening role between them, although Jackson would increasingly find himself coming into the fray at the fall of the first wicket. There was no sudden decision, no new policy, it simply happened over the space of two to three seasons that Brown and Tunnicliffe became the county's established opening pair, and a Yorkshire legend was born.

The England side that faced the Australians at Lord's in the First Test comprised three amateurs and eight professionals. In batting order it was:

W.G. Grace (Gloucestershire), A.E. Stoddart (Middlesex), R. Abel (Surrey), J.T. Brown (Yorkshire), W. Gunn (Nottinghamshire), F.S. Jackson (Yorkshire), T.W. Hayward (Surrey), A.F.A. Lilley (Warwickshire), G.A. Lohmann (Surrey), J.T. Hearne (Middlesex), T. Richardson (Surrey).

There were murmurs of discontent when Ranjitsinhji was omitted, but otherwise the XI selected was broadly supported in the Press. Lord Harris had observed that Ranji was no Englishman, and therefore could hardly be selected to represent England. And that was that. Such things did not in 1896 provoke the outrage they might now occasion.

Australia won the toss and batted on a wicket that looked full of runs. Joe Darling opened with Henry Donnan; Richardson and Lohmann shared the new ball. Three runs were on the board when disaster struck. Donnan drove hard to cover where Johnny Brown half-stopped the shot. Donnan ran, Joe Darling, seeing that the ball had deflected to Jackson, wisely stood his ground. The throw came in over the top of the bails and Lilley, the wicket-keeper, did the rest. Donnan had no hope of regaining the crease and was gone for a single. Australia never recovered. Richardson's pace and

Lohmann's trickery bowled them out before lunch for 53 in front of a vast crowd. Over 30,000 were at Lord's, many spilling onto the playing area.

England's score had progressed to 197 for 4 as Jackson walked to the wicket in the final session of the day's play. Stoddart, Brown and Gunn had gone relatively cheaply and the credit for England's substantial lead lay with the captain who had made 66, and a limping Bobby Abel, who had gamely battled away for his fifty at the other end as wickets fell. From the start Jackson batted freely, pressing home the advantage. Then, with the close of play near, and 40 runs against his name, he stepped out to Giffen and hit him down the ground to where Joe Darling was fielding. He sprinted for the catch. It was a high, swirling ball, a desperately difficult chance at any time, let alone at the end of a long, frustrating day. Darling might even have caught it, but for the fact he was impeded by several members of the crowd who had been sitting well inside the rope. A boundary was signalled. *Cricket* reported the strange, almost quixotic, events that ensued:

> Jackson appeared to be walking away towards the pavilion, but returned to his wicket after a few words with Trott. He hit the next ball not quite so hard, and was caught; it almost seemed as if it were done intentionally.

The catcher out in the deep was Joe Darling.

Jackson later denied that he had deliberately offered another chance as if to atone for the behaviour of the crowd. England won the match easily, and nobody doubted Jackson's word; the incident was forgotten. Had England lost, one is bound to wonder whether he would have been given the benefit of the doubt. But England won.

Stanley Jackson would have played the same stroke regardless of the situation of the match, which he would have considered peripheral. It was his idea of cricket, not his conscience that made him play *that* shot into Joe Darling's waiting hands. 'Walking' when one was out was part of cricket, intrinsic to everything he loved in the game. When the crowd denied Darling a chance to take the catch, Jackson simply put up another.

The first and second Test Matches were three weeks apart, and Jackson played in five first-class matches in the interval. He batted serenely, scoring 51 against Derbyshire at Derby, 45 and 22 against the tourists at Bradford, 5 against Warwickshire at Leeds, 0 and 59 against Nottinghamshire at Huddersfield, and then 57 and 40 not out at Lord's against the Players. His bowling in this period, as it was for much of the season, was ordinary. He was often asked to break partnerships, sometimes employed as a stock bowler, rarely as the spearhead of an attack.

Although he opened the bowling for the Gentlemen in the Lord's match in mid-July, it was the last time he was entrusted with the new ball in 1896.

Jackson failed in the second Test at Old Trafford. He ran himself out for 18 when he was batting with Johnny Brown in the first innings, and he went for just a single in his second knock as England were beaten by 3 wickets in a remarkable contest. It was Ranjitsinhji's first match for England, an event he celebrated with scores of 62, and a brilliant, undefeated second-innings 154, during which he notched 113 runs in the pre-lunch session on the third day, which remains to this day an 'Ashes' record. The match was also Tom Richardson's finest hour; following up his 9 wickets in the first Test, he took 7 for 168, and 6 for 76 in the course of 110 lion-hearted five- ball overs. In taking 2 for 89 on that same Manchester wicket Ernest Jones bowled but a fifth of the balls Richardson had sent down. Yet not even the deeds of the Indian prince and the yeoman Surrey professional could stave off the inevitable: Australia levelled the series.

The deciding Test was to be played at the Oval, and the encounter was eagerly awaited, but before the vital match Jackson was to play a couple of games for his native county. He warmed up with a freely hit 91 against Gloucestershire at Sheffield as Yorkshire overwhelmed W.G. Grace's side and then, at the end of July, travelled south with the Yorkshire team to face Surrey at the Oval in George Lohmann's benefit match. The third Test was a little less than a fortnight away. Surrey dominated from the start, with Tom Hayward's big hundred carrying the home county to a total of 439. It was Jackson who broke the major stand of the innings, inducing Charles Baldwin to snick a catch behind to David Hunter for 84. Shortly afterwards, in attempting to field a fierce drive by Lockwood, the new batsman, Jackson damaged a finger. He completed the over, bowling the three remaining deliveries standing at the crease, and retired to the pavilion to take stock of the injury. When Yorkshire batted Jackson came in at the fall of the sixth wicket. Hardly able to hold a bat, he had made 10 by the time Richardson speared a ball through his defences. Faced with the likes of Lohmann, Richardson, Lockwood, Hayward and Brockwell, a batsman needed every faculty at his disposal and Jackson's fellows had difficulties a-plenty, batting two-handed. In the second innings Hayward broke

Jackson's wicket almost as soon as he had got off the mark.

Jackson shrugged off the injury, rested his damaged hand, satisfied himself that he could grip a bat and declared himself fit for the forthcoming Test Match.

England's preparations for the contest were hardly ideal. In the days before the start several professionals demanded a doubling of the normal Test Match fee of £10. It was a demand that was robustly refused by the Surrey committee, even when the professionals concerned threatened to strike. The dispute was blown up out of all proportion by the press, and split the ranks of the professionals. Eventually, a compromise was found, and a strike averted. The controversy highlighted the pitfalls that awaited any county committee charged with the selection of an England team, and the staging of a Test Match. It was a fiasco that hastened the M.C.C. towards taking sole responsibility for Test Match cricket in England.

On the eve of the match, Stoddart was forced to withdraw due to injury, and Jackson, less than fully fit, was promoted in the order to open with W.G. Grace. England won the toss and elected to bat, but as the umpires were walking out to the middle the heavens burst and drenched the Oval. The ground was saturated, and by modern standards, unplayable. When play eventually commenced at around five o'clock the conditions underfoot kept Jones and McKibbin out of the attack, and the two spinners, Giffen and Trumble were unable to put any real work on a sodden ball. Jackson, opening for his country for the first time, and his captain batted carefully and suspiciously, then with growing assurance in murky light.

Against a turning ball that was liable to come through at wildly varying heights, the bat briefly held sway over the ball. The partnership was worth 54 when W.G. was caught at point by his counterpart, G.H.S. Trott, off the bowling of George Giffen, for 24. At stumps after some 90 minutes' cricket Jackson had progressed to 39, and England had reached the dizzy heights of 69 for 1 on that already ruined wicket. In the morning as the pitch dried England were soon dismissed for 145. Jackson was one of Hugh Trumble's 6 victims, as the tall, Victorian off-spinner made the ball turn and stop.

Joe Darling opened the Australian reply, and with Frank Iredale struck up a stand of 75 in good time, mixing sound defence with measured aggression, hitting out at every opportunity. At the very point when it seemed the match was slipping from England's grasp a quicksilver pick-up and throw from Ranji ran out Iredale. It broke the spell, J.T. Hearne sent Darling back to the pavilion for 47, the highest score in the match, and Australia rapidly declined to a total of 119.

More rain overnight made the wicket a batsman's nightmare, and there was a sad predictability about the third day's play. Trumble took another 6 wickets when England batted again, including Jackson's for 2, as the home side reeled to 84 all out, setting Australia 111 to win back the Ashes. On that mud-heap of a wicket they might as well have been set 1,011, for against Bobby Peel and J.T. Hearne on such an evil surface, they were without hope. At one stage Australia were reduced to the ignominy of 19 for 8, and only a slog by McKibbin, the number eleven, lifted their total to 44. The Ashes had been retained.

Jackson had scored 110 runs at the apparently moderate average of 22.00 in the three Test Matches, but his runs had been made when they were most needed and his reputation was enhanced. His innings of 45 at the Oval had been the corner-stone of England's victory.

A week later at Bradford, when Yorkshire played host to Middlesex, Jackson celebrated in style, taking 115 and 83 off the visitors' attack, which in addition to J.T. Hearne, boasted J.T. Rawlin, A.E. Stoddart, and H.R. Bromley-Davenport. In his next innings, against Sussex at Brighton, he plundered 102 as the Tykes piled up a total of 407. For once, though, he was over-shadowed, but only by Ranji's peerless feat of scoring two separate centuries on the last day of the match, 100 in the first innings, and an undefeated 125 in the second. Nonetheless the Championship was Yorkshire's.

Jackson was one of five Yorkshiremen to score over a thousand runs in the Championship, the others being J.T. Brown, Peel, George Hirst, and Tunnicliffe. It was also the year that Tunnicliffe took 46 catches, and that four Tykes each took more than seventy wickets, Peel (97), Wainwright (90), Hirst (80) and Haigh (71).

Jackson's bat struck a rich seam of runs as the season drew to a close at Scarborough. He struck 67 for C.I. Thornton's XI against the Australians, sharing, with Lionel Palairet, in an opening partnership of 119 in 90 minutes on the first morning of the match. The season finished with Jackson taking 70 off M.C.C., again at Scarborough, in Yorkshire's last match of the season. F.R. Spofforth caused all sorts of problems for the county's batsmen, but Jackson, playing with his customary calm assurance, scored his runs in 110 minutes, despite the inconvenience of a slow outfield. The match ended in a draw, the rain having had the last word.

That autumn Jackson embarked on his career in politics. His first steps were humble ones, no more than a cautious testing of the waters. He stood for Leeds Council and was duly elected. There were many in the county of the broad acres who had mixed feelings about Jackson's aspirations, realising that the time would come when cricket would be the loser. George Hirst, albeit somewhat tongue in cheek, articulated the feelings of the majority at a meeting in Leeds during Jackson's campaign:

> Mr. Jackson is a good man and a fine cricketer, and the finest gentleman I ever met, on or off the field, but if he gets on the council it'll cut down his cricket, a thoroughly bad thing for Yorkshire, England and everybody. So don't vote for him, whatever you do.

Stanley Jackson had not yet sacrificed his cricket career to business, soldiery and politics, but his intentions were nothing if not clear.

10 | Yorkshire Pride (1897-1898)

There were times when Stanley Jackson's appetite for the summer game waned. He needed the stimulus of the big occasion, and was born to grace the great stages of English cricket; the county game did not always fire his imagination. He cautioned others against the malaise that sometimes afflicted his Championship batting, and which he called carelessness, but it went deeper than that, much deeper. His position in Yorkshire might have driven another man to despair; for so many years he was the man who would be king, but was somehow destined never to be crowned. Stanley Jackson aspired to the Yorkshire captaincy, and in any other age it would have been his for the asking. A lesser man than Stanley Jackson might have contemplated a palace coup, but not he. He saw the situation for what it was, and awaited the unfolding of events. If the captaincy was to come to him, then it would come to him by natural succession.

He knew no other way. He was an ambitious man, but his ambition was never an obsession, and perhaps this, more than anything else, denied him the highest political offices in later life. It mattered to him how a thing was achieved, not merely that it was achieved. His loyalty to Lord Hawke never wavered.

Cricket in Yorkshire is not as it is elsewhere. It never has been. The club has always been a battleground between warring factions. Civil war is never far below the surface of Yorkshire cricket. Cricket is in the blood of every true Tyke. Cricket in Yorkshire is hardly a pastime, more a way of life. There is a myth that when Yorkshire cricket prospers, peace breaks out in the county of the broad acres; but history shows that Yorkshire cricket has to be at peace with itself for it to prosper. Hawke understood as much, and so did Stanley Jackson. Hawke ruled Yorkshire like some latter-day Cromwell, impervious to the infighting.

Hawke's law prevailed and Yorkshire were triumphant: the interests of Yorkshire cricket were paramount. With a lieutenant of Stanley Jackson's stature at his side, nobody dared challenge Hawke's law.

Yorkshire were unable to retain the Championship in 1897. It was a season in which the Tykes showed flashes of irresistible form, yet were strangely vulnerable. It was an 'in and out' sort of year, and Stanley Jackson's cricket tended to reflect the ups and downs of the county. His season began at Fenner's, when he turned out for C.I. Thornton's XI against his old university. He scored 28 and 4, dismissed in both innings by Gilbert Jessop, as the scratch side went down to a crushing defeat by an innings and 334 runs, mainly due to the exertions of N.F. Druce, the 'Cantab' captain, who hit an unbeaten 227.

Jackson was in the Yorkshire team that took the field against Gloucestershire at Bristol the next day. He scored 68 at the top of the list as Yorkshire sailed to a 10 wicket win. After the weekend Yorkshire took on Somerset at Taunton, and ran up 385 on the first day, Jackson with 124 in 165 minutes, and David Denton with 112 in two hours, sharing in a punishing stand. By the third morning, the home side seemed to be stumbling towards an inevitable defeat. Set 115 to win, Brown and Tunnicliffe put on 49 for the first wicket. At this juncture

Jackson, captain in Hawke's absence, determined that there was very little cricket left in the match and departed for London with Frank Milligan to prepare for the next day's cricket, against Essex at Leyton.

As the train pulled out of Taunton station and past the county ground, the two amateurs were horrified to see that five wickets had fallen and the last two fit Yorkshire batsmen, George Hirst and Schofield Haigh were at the wicket with twenty or so runs still to get. When some men err the world falls about their heads. Stanley Jackson's greatest gift was that he was a man who could err, and survive. Haigh and Hirst were equal to their task; Yorkshire won by 5 wickets, but the hours of waiting as the two amateurs travelled to London taught Jackson once and for all that no match is ever won until the final ball.

In Hawke's continuing absence Jackson was captain again at Leyton when Yorkshire lost by 3 wickets inside two days. On a bowler's pitch he played the innings of the match in Yorkshire's second knock, scoring 57. Yet whilst his batting won high praise, there was a question mark over his captaincy. *Cricket* posed the relevant questions in its 'Pavilion Gossip' column:

> It would be interesting to know how many captains of first-class county teams agree with the policy of Mr. Jackson in allowing the match with Essex to be finished on Friday night. Essex had still to make 17 runs at half-past six with three wickets to fall, two men, Mr. Kortright and Mead, being well set at the time. It is, even as the novice knows well enough, a very different thing to begin an innings from continuing it when well set, and as the bowlers

had the best of it on the whole throughout the match, Essex would have had a very hard time if the game had been adjourned until the Saturday morning. It is necessary to refer in 'Gossip' to the action of the Yorkshire captain because it may be said to have created a precedent. That it was sportsmanlike will not be denied by anybody.

The following week Jackson led Yorkshire to a crushing innings victory over Leicestershire at Headingley. He made only 31 as the first three Yorkshire wickets fell cheaply, then Moorhouse (91), Peel (115) and Hirst (89) carried the total to 435. It was the last century Bobby Peel scored for Yorkshire. George Hirst opened the bowling with Schofield Haigh, the pair for whom the future was so bright.

On a bowler's wicket at Fenner's at the end of the month Yorkshire lost out in a low-scoring contest with Cambridge University. Jackson's innings of 61 and 59 not out were the best scores of the match, the next best being 31, by N.F. Druce. Yorkshire's downfall had much to do with a fiery spell of 5 for 19 by Gilbert Jessop, who concluded the match with a quick-fire innings of 25 when it seemed the visitors might steal the verdict. It was not the last time Jessop would be a thorn in Yorkshire's side.

Lord Hawke was still unable to take the field as May turned to June, a combination of lumbago, committee work, and business matters conspiring to give Jackson an extended period in command.

Hampshire were brushed aside at Bradford, Jackson's opening partnership with Tunnicliffe of 70 in an hour setting Yorkshire on the winning road. His 57 in that innings was hit up in 75 minutes. At Bramall Lane in the second week in June, Jackson (81) and Tunnicliffe (96) put on 175 for the first wicket against Warwickshire. With the Yorkshire score at 337 for 5 at the close of play, the hard-pressed visitors must have been dreading the days to come, but it rained for two days and they were spared further misery. Yorkshire marched on, visions of a second successive Championship already burning bright on the horizon. Kent were seen off by an innings at Halifax. At Derby, the home side would have halted the Tykes but for a dogged last wicket stand between George Hirst and David Hunter that snatched victory from the very jaws of defeat. Such was the strength and depth of Yorkshire cricket; there was no better number eleven in the land than Hunter.

Lord Hawke rejoined the side in time for the match with Middlesex at Lord's, a contest drawn after Yorkshire, largely due to Wainwright's 171, had amassed 439. Hawke's return was short-lived, and Jackson resumed the captaincy for the visit of Surrey to Headingley in the fourth week of June.

On a drying pitch both sides were bowled out on the first day, Yorkshire for 90 with Tom Richardson taking 7 for 55, Surrey for 75 with Schofield Haigh claiming 7 for 17. On the second day Jackson and Tunnicliffe put on 70 for the first wicket before they were parted, Jackson going on to make 92. By the time Richardson had bowled out Yorkshire for a second time, returning figures of 8 for 99, Surrey needed 272 to win, a task that was beyond them on a rain-damaged wicket. In the end they were dismissed a hundred runs short of their target.

Jackson dropped out of the side to face

Nottinghamshire at Trent Bridge, but appeared in the weather-disrupted fixture against the touring Philadelphians at Sheffield at the end of the month. John Barton King, one of the most destructive of the many fast bowlers to emerge from the New World, bowled him for 4. It was hardly ideal preparation for the return match with Surrey at the Oval at the beginning of July. As Hawke was again unable to play, Jackson led Yorkshire. The wicket was at its liveliest on the first morning and he was struck repeatedly during his innings of 29, which ended when he was caught by Tom Hayward running in from third man off the bowling of Richardson. The pitch was easier in the second innings, and although Tom Richardson took 12 wickets in the match, Yorkshire had slightly the better of the draw.

Jackson's style of captaincy had altered little from his Cambridge days. There was never any doubt about who was in charge when Stanley Jackson captained a side. What had changed since those heady seasons at Fenner's was that in his own mind at least, he no longer regarded himself as a strike bowler on a good wicket. He tended to under bowl himself, witnessed by the fact that in the first two months of the season he bowled only 168 five-ball overs in 14 matches, from which he had conceded 355 runs and taken just 9 wickets at an average of 39.44 apiece. His defence was that he had Peel, Hirst, Wainwright and Haigh, so his services as a bowler were often superfluous.

His county captain thought otherwise. Restored to fitness Lord Hawke returned to lead Yorkshire for the second half of the season, and he soon had Jackson back at his bowling mark. In the past Hawke had employed his lieutenant's bowling sparingly and had kept it up his sleeve to break an important partnership or to keep down the runs. Now, as Yorkshire struggled to retain the Championship and the storm clouds gathered over the head of Bobby Peel, he looked to Jackson to bolster an attack that, inexplicably, was failing to carry all before it.

Jackson responded in characteristic fashion; he took 56 wickets in 11 Championship matches. Against Hampshire at Southampton he took 6 for 19 and 6 for 61 as Yorkshire cruised to a 10 wicket win. In the same fixture he surrendered his place at the top of the order to J.T. Brown. Henceforth, Hawke decreed, he would bat - all things being equal - at number three in the Yorkshire list. He failed in the Gentlemen and Players match at Lord's with both bat and ball, and while he was away in London, Brown (311) and Tunnicliffe (147) were rewriting the record books with a first wicket stand of 378 in 4 hours 35 minutes against Sussex at Sheffield. Yorkshire - without Hawke, Jackson and Hirst who were engaged in the Lord's match - ran up 681 for 5 and trounced the visitors by a margin of an innings and 307 runs. The Yorkshire captaincy passed on this occasion to Frank Mitchell, the Cambridge blue, who was later to win Test caps for both England and South Africa, and lead the Springboks in England in 1904 and 1912.

Jackson took over the captaincy when he returned to the side at Dewsbury for the match with Nottinghamshire. He bowled meanly, and acquitted himself honourably with the bat. In the first innings he was unwell, but coming out to bat at the fall of the seventh wicket, he scored 10 before he ran out of partners. In the second innings as Yorkshire followed on some 121 runs behind, Jackson's

77, scored at a time when defeat seemed almost inevitable, had much to do with the saving of the match.

The Roses Match at Bradford was drawn. At one stage Yorkshire had seemed well-placed to press home their advantage, but a regal 152 from the bat of Archie MacLaren - playing in his first match of the season - turned the tables, and in the end the Tykes did well to hold out for the draw. The match was David Hunter's benefit and realised £1,950 for the wicket-keeper, two-thirds of which was immediately put into trust for him by Lord Hawke, as was the practice at Yorkshire. Hawke's law touched every facet of Yorkshire cricket. If it was dictatorial, it was also paternal.

Yorkshire's Championship aspirations were slipping away now. Bobby Peel had fallen ill during the Roses Match, and his bowling was to be sadly missed in the coming weeks. A defeat by a single run by Essex at Huddersfield was followed by a convincing win over lowly Somerset at Headingley, then by a drubbing from Gloucestershire at Harrogate. This last defeat was a body blow, not because it was a match lost, but because of the manner of defeat.

Gilbert Jessop mercilessly savaged the Yorkshire attack early on the first day, hammering 101 in just 40 explosive minutes at the wicket before Jackson put an end to the Tykes' suffering and bowled him with his arm ball. At the time it was the quickest hundred ever scored in first-class cricket, and has been bettered on but three occasions in the ninety years since, and never against an attack that included bowlers of the calibre of George Hirst, Edward Wainwright and Stanley Jackson. When the whirlwind was spent and Jessop was on his way back to the pavilion

W.G. Grace turned to Lord Hawke with unashamed glee and was heard to remark:

'Eh, what, he gave you some, didn't he?'

Later that day C.L. Townsend scored another hundred, albeit more sedately, to raise the Gloucestershire total to 370, with Jackson claiming 5 for 73. Yorkshire had no chance to win the match but, with the wicket playing easily, they ought to have been able to force the draw. It was a chastening defeat, a test of Yorkshire pride, a beating that would have thoroughly demoralised a lesser team.

Victories over Warwickshire and Kent restored morale in the county of the broad acres. Against Kent at Canterbury Jackson once again ruined Canterbury Week, taking 7 for 78 and 4 for 44 as the home side were swept to defeat. But at Brighton in the next match the Tykes faltered, losing to Sussex by 6 wickets. Jackson's batting had fallen away as he filled the gap left in the Yorkshire attack by Peel's absence. Since the Oval match against Surrey at the beginning of July his scores had been 6, 6 and 1, 10 not out and 77, 34 and 2, 20 and 0, 44, 7 and 4, 30 and 11, 3, 9 and 1. In the same 10 matches he had taken 50 wickets. At Manchester, in the meeting of the Roses counties, he played a flawless innings of 59 that marked the beginning of an end of season batting revival. Yorkshire lost by an innings in a contest disrupted, and ultimately decided, by the vagaries of the English summer, the Tykes having much the worst of the conditions.

Jackson scored his second century of the season in the next match, 101 against Middlesex at Bramall Lane in a drawn match that owes its particular place in the history of English cricket, not to his feat of batsmanship, but because it was Bobby Peel's last match for Yorkshire.

Bobby Peel was the second of the four great slow left-arm bowlers who graced Yorkshire cricket from the 1880s to the outbreak of the Second War in 1939. Before him Edmund Peate had been the acknowledged master of the left-armer's craft, and had, in fact, kept Peel out of the Yorkshire side for many years. After Peel came Wilfred Rhodes, and then Hedley Verity. All four were very much 'their own men'. Peate had fallen foul of Hawke's law, and had been dismissed for being a man 'with too many friends', a disruptive influence, a rebel by any other name.

Peel was a taciturn man who rarely showed emotion on the field, whether his bowling was being hit into the deep or he was running through a side. He took the good with the bad, and no bowler was steadier under fire than he. He bowled with a loop that always made the ball pitch that fraction shorter than the batsman anticipated, and had the uncanny knack of inducing the best batsman to play forward into the unknown, while others waved their bats forlornly at thin air, thoroughly bamboozled. At the height of his glory days at Cambridge Jackson had found even his own unquenchable confidence shaken to the core by the little Tyke magician. Peel was a remorseless opponent, impossible to hit off a good line, unplayable on a wicket giving him the least assistance. Yet he had an Achilles' heel, and it was his downfall. Bobby Peel liked his ale.

In an age when a professional either brought his own sandwiches to a match, or took his chances with the public in the beer tent at the luncheon and tea intervals, Peel's tipple was a fairly harmless failing, found in countless of his fellows. From time to time he drank to excess, an easy enough thing to do, for in Yorkshire there was scarcely a man alive who would have turned up a chance to buy Bobby Peel a pint, or two…or five.

There were rumours that Hawke had given Peel a final warning during the Middlesex match at Bramall Lane, and doubts were voiced about the nature of the 'illness' that had prevented Peel from batting in the Yorkshire second innings. The following day, Thursday 19th August, Yorkshire were due to commence a Championship match with Derbyshire at Bradford.

It was the day the axe fell.

On the morning of the match George Hirst found Peel still drunk from the night before, and like the friend he was, put his team-mate back to bed. When he arrived at the ground he reported to Hawke that Peel was ill, and would not be able to play. Hirst's well-meaning endeavours were a lost cause. As Yorkshire took the field after losing the toss, Bobby Peel shambled to the bowling crease, red-faced and drunker than ever as he took the ball. Hawke saw the condition he was in.

'Leave the field at once, Peel.'

'Not at all, my Lord,' returned the professional, full of the joys of life, 'I'm in fine form this morning.'

Some say Peel proceeded to urinate on the wicket; tamer-hearted folk say he bowled a ball to the sightscreen, quite oblivious to the poverty of his aim. It matters not, for all the legends share a common conclusion: Lord Hawke took Bobby Peel by the arm and gently led him off the field and out of Yorkshire cricket. At first it was announced that Peel had been suspended by the Yorkshire Committee, but there was no coming back, his career at Yorkshire was over.

There were many who thought Hawke's action overly harsh. Hawke admitted in later years that it probably cost Yorkshire the Championship that season. But what angered his critics was the manner in which the Yorkshire captain set out to justify Peel's dismissal. Stanley Jackson had not been playing in the match at Bradford; had he been in Hawke's place, he might have acted as Hawke had done, but unlike his captain he was not a man given to public self-justification. Moreover, Hawke could have acted sooner and pre-empted matters.

When he discovered Peel on the field in a 'proper state,' his behaviour was irreproachable; it was only afterwards, when he spoke of Peel's going as if it were unavoidable, and done for the good of Yorkshire cricket, that he cut the ground from under his own feet. When Hawke declared: 'Peel never bore me any malice,' the veil slipped. Hawke was wont to speak of the pain it caused him to censure and dismiss Bobby Peel, and no doubt he was sincere, but to other ears it all sounded rather feeble. The departure of Bobby Peel brought about the final schism between the old Yorkshire that Hawke had inherited a decade before, and the county he was now leading. As with any such split, it left Yorkshire cricket with deep and lasting scars.

Had Stanley Jackson been captain of Yorkshire, the Bobby Peel saga may have had another ending. Yet if he harboured any reservations he kept them to himself: publicly he stood shoulder to shoulder with his captain for all the world to see, and as the season drew to its close his batting at Scarborough helped to distract the committed and the uncommitted alike. He hit a match-winning 72 - including 9 fours and a drive out of the ground off 'Demon' Spofforth - for the Tykes against the M.C.C. Then, for the

Gentlemen against the Players, he shone with innings of 59 and 23, his wicket falling to fellow Yorkshiremen in both innings, bowled out respectively by George Hirst and Edward Wainwright.

In the winter of 1897-98 an England team under the captaincy of A.E. Stoddart travelled to Australia to defend the Ashes. Jackson remained at home. Unlike many amateurs he was never beset by financial worries and money worries never kept him from his cricket but there were always other calls on his time, and increasingly as the years went by it was inevitable that cricket would be the loser. Indeed it is unlikely that he ever seriously considered joining Stoddart's campaign for his business commitments in the West Riding called, and his fledgling career in local politics in Leeds could not be neglected.

England won the first Test at Sydney, but thereafter Australia ruled the roost, winning the other four matches by handsome margins. Stoddart fell ill before the Test Matches began, and Archie MacLaren found the captaincy thrust upon him in three of the five matches. It was under MacLaren's captaincy at Sydney that England won a famous victory in a match overshadowed by later events. MacLaren scored 109 and 50 not out in the match, opening the batting with J.R. Mason in both innings. In the same match Ranji hit 175 in what was his first Test in Australia, repeating his feat of the previous year at Old Trafford when he had scored a century in his debut against Australia in England. But perhaps the most notable batting milestone was achieved by an Australian, Joe Darling, whose second-innings century was the first ever scored by a left-hander in Test Match cricket.

It was to be Joe Darling's series. His scores of 7 and

101, 36, 178, 12 and 29, 14 and 160 did more than rewrite the record books, they established the young South Australian opener as the heir apparent to the Australian captaincy, then in the capable hands of G.H.S. Trott. It was not just the weight of runs he scored, but the way in which he scored them. At Adelaide in the third Test, when he made 178, he went to his hundred with a six - which in 1898 required the ball to be struck out of the ground - for the first time in a Test Match; indeed it was the first occasion a six had been recorded in international cricket without the aid of overthrows. In the same innings he became the first batsman to hit twenty or more fours in a Test Match innings. In the fifth Test at Sydney his 160 in the last innings of the match snatched victory from the jaws of defeat; set 275 to win (with both C.E. McLeod and Clem Hill back in the pavilion with 40 on the board) Darling tore into the bowling and raced to his century in 91 minutes, to this day the fastest by an Australian against England. Before then, no one had scored three hundreds in a Test Match rubber.

During the series Archie MacLaren became Australia's favourite Englishman. He never did anything by halves, whether he thrashed the ball to the boundary or was comprehensively bowled, he played his stroke with a majestic flourish, and Australia took him to its heart. His finest hour was in the third Test at Adelaide when in the second innings he hit a defiant 124, including 26 fours as England slid to defeat by an innings.

It was at Adelaide, too, that Joe Darling had prevailed upon his father, John Darling, to watch him bat. The old man was present when his wayward sixth son hit what was destined to be the highest score of his Test Match career.

It seems that Darling senior was overwhelmed by the experience, and from that day onwards recanted his former prejudice against cricket.

Archie MacLaren had stolen a march on Jackson in the matter of the succession to the England captaincy and Joe Darling had become the man most likely to lead the Australian team when it toured England in 1899. However, as Jackson emerged from the English winter and set about sweeping the cobwebs from his game in the pre-season nets at Headingley, he had other things on his mind. In the absence of Bobby Peel much was going to depend upon him, if Yorkshire were to challenge for the Championship that year.

He turned out for C.I. Thornton's XI, captained by Lord Hawke, against Cambridge University at Fenner's in the second week of May, before joining Yorkshire's southern tour. The scratch side, which included eight Test players, was altogether too strong for the University. Tom Richardson ran through the Cantabs' batting in the first innings, and Jackson with 5 for 27 repeated the medicine in the students' second knock.

Hawke and Jackson travelled down to Lord's to play in Yorkshire's opening first-class fixture of the new season, against an M.C.C. side under the captaincy of W.G. Grace. The county had brought two slow left-arm bowlers on the tour. It was the intention of the Committee that they should appear in alternate matches so that the merits of each man could be properly assessed. Bobby Peel had been Edmund Peate's natural successor, but there was nobody on the Yorkshire staff waiting to step into Peel's boots. For the two aspirants the county's southern tour was a once-in-a-lifetime chance.

The twenty-sixth birthday of the elder of the two colts, Albert Cordingley, fell on the second day of the Lord's match. His rival was a twenty-year-old who had played in the same Kirkheaton village side as George Hirst. His name was Wilfred Rhodes.

The vagaries of the weather meant that only one trial match had been possible before Yorkshire journeyed south. Played over two days at Bedale in the first week of May, the county side had taken on an XVIII of Bedale and district. Cordingley had returned figures of 2 for 39 and 3 for 36 for the local side, Rhodes 3 for 16 and 3 for 21 playing for the senior XI. Of the two, Cordingley's showing against what was (allowing for the absence of Jackson and Hirst) a representative Yorkshire team, had been the more impressive.

Hawke was undecided as to which man to play at Lord's against the premier club. Cordingley had taken the Yorkshire captain's wicket at Bedale, as he had those of J.T. Brown, Denton, Moorhouse and Milligan, but Rhodes had hardly disgraced himself as Haigh and Wainwright tormented the local batsmen. On the evidence of the trial Hawke was inclined towards Cordingley, but he had his doubts. He turned to Stanley Jackson and asked his lieutenant to test out Cordingley and Rhodes in the nets.

It seems that Cordingley was nervous, and perhaps a little off colour that day. Upon such quirks of fate great careers often hang. Wilfred Rhodes bowled steadily and won Jackson's vote.

If Lord Hawke had hoped that Jackson's verdict would confirm his own tentative support for the claims of Albert Cordingley, he was to be rudely, and somewhat abruptly, disabused of the notion. Jackson told him that Rhodes was the better bowler and ought to be in the side that took on the M.C.C. Hawke, who had actually seen Cordingley bowl under match conditions, argued the opposite case.

Jackson stood his ground and the debate became more than a little heated. It is unlikely that any other Yorkshireman would have dared to question the judgement of the Yorkshire captain, least of all on the subject of cricket, or the composition of the Yorkshire side. But Jackson's position at Yorkshire was singular. The events of the previous season had marked a subtle change in his relations with Hawke, and the two men were closer now. Hawke had come to realise that in Jackson he had a friend and ally second to none, and, moreover, one who had the courage to warn him when he was about to err.

Hawke was not the ogre he sometimes seemed, but for too long he had been judge and jury in the court of Yorkshire cricket. The departure of Bobby Peel, or a similar debacle, had been waiting to happen for years. Wilfred Rhodes was named in the Yorkshire side, allegedly on the toss of a coin, but named he was, and there he stayed until his retirement 32 years later.

On a bowler's wicket he took 4 for 24 in the M.C.C.'s second innings, bowling unchanged with Jackson who captured 6 for 45 to give the Tykes victory by 99 runs. In the days that followed Rhodes put Somerset to the sword at Bath, taking 7 for 24 in the first innings, and then, on a drying wicket, 6 for 21 as he and Schofield Haigh skittled out the home side for just 35 to see Yorkshire home by 108 runs.

History bypassed Albert Cordingley. He played against Worcestershire in July in a non-first-class fixture played over two days at Worcester, took 0 for 24, scored 2 not out batting at number eleven, and bowed out of Yorkshire cricket. Wilfred Rhodes, who at one stage had gone north to Galashiels in search of a living from cricket, captured 154 wickets at an average of 14.60 apiece in his first season, and went on to take over four thousand first-class wickets. In time he would go on to open both the batting and the bowling for England. Cordingley went to Sussex in despair, played a handful of matches between 1901 and 1905 without much success and eventually became the professional at Lytham Cricket Club.

Jackson's batting form was elusive in the early part of the season. Although he hit one or two useful scores (45 in the second innings against Somerset and 67 in the next match at Bristol against Gloucestershire) the weather ruled in favour of the ball throughout May and early June. He captured 5 for 46 at Leyton as Essex put up a valiant fight before the Tykes got home by 3 wickets.

His scores up until 15th June were 3, 3, and 11, 10 and 45, 67, 9, 38 not out, 13, 3, 3, 46 and 31. Then, against Middlesex at Lord's, he suddenly struck the richest seam of runs he would ever know. Between 16th June and 25th July he scored 979 runs at an average of 75.30, scoring five centuries. At Lord's on the first day of the Middlesex match he hit 133 in three hours as Yorkshire defeated the home side by an innings. At Headingley against Nottinghamshire he briefly faltered, scoring 13 and 0 in a low-scoring contest played on a bowler's wicket, in which he returned bowling figures of 5 for 59 and 3 for 27. His fourth wicket in the Nottinghamshire first innings was his 500th in first-class cricket, captured in his 186th match.

At Leicester later that same week he took 147 off the Leicestershire attack in 160 minutes. Then, with Rhodes, he twice bowled out his hosts, taking 5 for 20 and 3 for 34, the Kirkheaton man returning match figures of 9 for 67 as Yorkshire triumphed by an innings and 266 runs.

Against Essex at Bradford, Jackson scored a useful 33 after Hawke (62) and Brown (42) had set Yorkshire on the way in a match in which Rhodes and he were again to bowl out the home side twice. On this occasion, Rhodes' share of the spoils was by far the greater, 11 for 92 in the match as opposed to Jackson's 6 for 74. Jackson had a quieter match against Sussex at Bradford at the beginning of July, scoring 13 and 49 not out. The match was decisively swung in the Tykes' favour by a remarkable spell of 6 for 52 by J.T. Brown - a very occasional bowler who dabbled with slow right-arm spinners, mostly of the orthodox, off-spin variety - after the visitors had withstood the wiles of Jackson, Rhodes, Haigh, Wainwright, and a strangely out-of-sorts George Hirst, who was still suffering from the debilitating effects of a long, and personally disappointing, tour of Australia.

Jackson came to the Roses Match in fine fettle. The sun smiled on Sheffield throughout the contest which was nominated as Edward Wainwright's benefit. Jackson scored 38 on the first day, playing second fiddle to J.T. Brown who followed his unlikely exploits against Sussex with a battling 144. In the second innings Jackson (134 not out) and John Tunnicliffe (102) put on 206 runs for the second wicket. It was Jackson's first, and, as it turned out, last hundred in a Roses Match, and it enabled Hawke to set Lancashire 271 to win in 3 hours. The challenge was never taken up, Jackson's 3 for 28 reducing the visitors to 140 for 5 at the close. In the next match, at Maidstone against Kent, Jackson hit 38 and 1, and took 4 for 87 as the Tykes slumped to their first defeat of the season.

In the Gentlemen - Players match at Lord's, which was arranged to commence on W.G. Grace's birthday, Jackson acquitted himself honourably, scoring 48 on a drying wicket on the second day as Lockwood, J.T. Hearne and Haigh did their worst, and 33 in the last innings of the match as defeat beckoned. The glory, however, belonged to W.G. when the great man, batting down the list with an injured foot, was joined by the last man, C.J. Kortright in a legendary stand. Kortright and W.G. had not spoken to each other for some years, a situation resulting from a contretemps during one of their earliest confrontations. W.G. had not taken kindly to being beaten repeatedly by Kortright's excessive pace, and worse, had been rather knocked about as he attempted to see off the fast bowler. Kortright struck out as W.G. defended stoutly and it almost seemed as though the amateurs might save the match. With W.G.'s own connivance - even though there was no way the amateurs could possibly win the match - the contest continued after half-past six, the scheduled close of play. It was Lockwood who eventually induced Kortright to hole out to Haigh for 46, but by then the greatest batsman in the land and the man reputed to be the fastest bowler were well and truly, and very publicly, reconciled. They left the field wreathed in smiles, W.G.'s arm about his team-mate's shoulder.

At Scarborough, luck was with Jackson in the match with Somerset. He was dropped three times as he buccaneered his way to 139 in three hours, hitting all around the wicket and sharing in a stand of 140 with Frank Milligan (60) in under 90 minutes. In 1896

Jackson had hit his thousandth run of the season on 23rd July, in 1897 on 26 July and now in 1898 he achieved the feat on 22nd July.

Every purple patch comes to an end sooner or later. Jackson's ended after the match against Gloucestershire at Sheffield in the last week of July, which Yorkshire won by an innings and 17 runs. His 160 struck in 220 minutes out of a Yorkshire total of 331 was to be the highest score of his career.

He sustained a damaged hand against Surrey at the Oval at the end of the first week of August, and, not surprisingly, his batting form suffered. The glut of runs had, in any case, rather sated his appetite. Now he looked to another target, a hundred wickets, and the prized 'double' of a thousand runs and a hundred wickets in a season. He required 30 wickets as July turned to August. He took 6 for 52 in the Roses Match at Manchester, 8 for 61 (including 7 for 42 in the first innings) against Middlesex at Leeds, 7 for 78 against Derbyshire in the match in which J.T. Brown (300) and Tunnicliffe (243) lifted the record stand in first-class cricket to 554, went wicketless against Sussex at Brighton, and claimed 4 for 82 for Yorkshire against M.C.C. at Scarborough.

He was a tired, and rather jaded, cricketer as he approached what was the penultimate match of his season and the highlight of the Scarborough Week, the meeting of the Gentlemen and the Players. His wicket tally stood at 97 when the contest began and by the afternoon he had added another six victims. He had 'done the double', and along the way helped Yorkshire to regain the Championship. The double was a bonus, something that he greeted at the time with relief, not elation. He was not a man who cared overly for his average, and the quest for the double had taken a good deal of the fun out of his cricket.

The decline in Jackson's batting form in August is illustrated by his scores after his century against Gloucestershire: 23 and 39, 14, 10, 3 and 1, 14, 50 and 9, 23 and 12 not out, 8 and 32 not out, 31 and 36. At one stage, after managing just 3 and 1 in the low-scoring defeat by Middlesex at Headingley, he indicated he would like to drop out of the side, but Hawke would have none of it and told him he could bat down the order and play as a bowler in the next match, at Derby against Derbyshire, if that was the way he felt about it.

Ironically, this was the match in which J.T. Brown and Tunnicliffe put on 554 for the first wicket, and Hawke, who had decided to bat at number three instead of Jackson, spent eight hours waiting to bat only to have to throw away his wicket in the interests of getting a result. (In 1898 declarations were still not permitted until the third afternoon of a match, so Yorkshire declined from 554 without loss to 662 all out as the batsmen slogged willy-nilly to complete the innings as soon as possible. J.T. Brown showed his fellows the way by knocking down his own wicket as soon as he had raised his triple century. Jackson, entering the mayhem at the fall of the fourth wicket, clouting 14 before he edged a ball into the wicket-keeper's gloves.

He was a tired man at the end of the 1898 season. Contented also.

11 | The End of an Era (1899-1901)

On 12 July 1898, the President of the Yorkshire County Cricket Club, M J. Ellison died. A founding father of the Yorkshire club, he had served as its President for thirty-five years. Lord Hawke once described him as 'a jolly old autocrat' and it was Ellison who had decreed that only men born in the county could play for Yorkshire, although in the case of Hawke, who was by birth a Lincolnshire man, he had turned a 'Nelsonian blind eye'.

Before Hawke's arrival, Ellison and J.B. Wostinholme, the club's Secretary, had run Yorkshire cricket virtually unchallenged, with Ellison acting as Treasurer until as late as 1894, when his son relieved him of the burden. The *Daily Telegraph* suggested that Ellison's death might have an unfortunate effect on Yorkshire cricket, 'the danger lying in local rivalries'. It was a sentiment echoed throughout the English game, but was, in the end, wholly confounded by events.

Lord Hawke assumed the Yorkshire Presidency, and Stanley Jackson, in his turn, became ever more involved in the administration of the club. In December, J.B. Wostinholme and Jackson represented Yorkshire at the annual meeting of county delegates at Lord's, when the vexed question of cricketers' residential qualifications dominated the agenda. In May 1899 Jackson was elected to the Committee of the M.C.C.

That year, the Board of Control bowed to Hawke's insistence that there should be a single, unified England selection committee. Hitherto the committee responsible for the ground staging a Test Match had chosen what was, in effect its own England team. The first Selection Committee included both W.G. Grace and Hawke. Jackson was one of two leading amateurs - the other was C.B. Fry - co-opted to assist the committee in its deliberations. Stanley Jackson's days as a simple cricketer were long gone.

The season of 1899 held in store the visit of the Australians and, for the first time in England, a five-match Test series. Jackson's preparations for the season were rudely disrupted by a damaged shoulder sustained in a fall whilst out riding with the Bramham Moor Pack. He shrugged off the injury and was soon in the runs and bowling out well-set batsmen.

Jackson did not excel in Yorkshire's first match of the season, at Lord's against M.C.C., but the same week, against an under-strength Somerset side at Bath he scored a cavalier 91 as the Tykes piled up a big score and went on to win by an innings and 301 runs. Jackson's share of the bowling spoils was 6 for 45. At Bristol against Gloucestershire he was dismissed without troubling the scorers, but Yorkshire won by an innings and 196 runs, regardless, with Jackson the bowler capturing 5 for 44 in a supporting role to Wilfred Rhodes, who took 9 for 31 in the match.

Yorkshire's southern tour concluded with a visit to Fenner's, where a certain G.L. Jessop eagerly awaited Hawke's men. Fortunately for Yorkshire, not even Gilbert Jessop could defeat the combined talents of the county of the broad acres single-handed.

Jessop's undefeated 171, scored out of 206 while he was at the wicket on the first day of the match, ranks as one of *the* great innings, not just of the golden age, but of *any* age of cricket. He batted for 105 minutes, hit 27 fours, 6 threes, 14 twos and 17 singles, and, although according to Cricket, he offered two chances, he treated the bowling of Hirst, Rhodes and Jackson 'as if they were hardly up to the standard of third-rate London club bowlers'. The assault was irresistible and the only way the despairing Yorkshire attack could put an end to the mayhem was to bowl out the rest of the University side, a task duly achieved by the time 246 runs had been put on the board. Stanley Jackson was to have his revenge. In league with J.T. Brown (168), he shared in a second-wicket stand of 194, going on to make 133 in 3 hours and 50 minutes, exercising his cutting to good advantage on a flat, true Fenner's pitch.

It was in this innings that he passed the milestone of 10,000 runs in first-class cricket

When the University batted a second time, some 183 runs in arrears of the Yorkshire score, abetted by Rhodes (4 for 18), he ran through the Cambridge batting, taking 6 for 51, including the wicket of the troublesome Jessop, caught by Edward Wainwright when his score was 2.

In the three matches before the First Test at Nottingham at the beginning of June, Jackson went into his shell, scoring 38 not out against the tourists at Sheffield, 28 and 23 against Essex at Leyton, and 21 and 5 against Middlesex at Lord's. Rain ruined the match against the Australians, and his bowling was little used at Leyton as Rhodes wreaked havoc and returned match figures of 15 for 56. In the Middlesex match Yorkshire were beaten by an innings, Plum Warner (150) and Albert Trott (164) punishing all the bowlers alike. Warner later recalled having hit Jackson for 3 fours in his first over after lunch on the second day, much to the exasperation of the bowler, who, unaccustomed to such treatment, exclaimed: 'Look here, what the devil are you doing, Plummy?'

Jackson was not alone in his frustration that day. Only Rhodes, with 7 for 147, had any joy from the wicket as Middlesex ran up 488 runs, Hirst, Haigh, Wainwright and Jackson coming alike to the batsmen.

In the days before England took on Australia, now under the captaincy of Joe Darling, at Trent Bridge, Bobby Abel scored 357 not out for Surrey against Somerset at the Oval, and W.G. Grace 175 not out for his London County side against Worcestershire at Worcester. There was no place in the England XI for Bobby Abel and W.G.'s England days were almost over.

The England team lacked fast bowling, as, by dint of injury, personality, or a dubious bowling action, none of the obvious fast-bowling candidates were included in the side, which otherwise drew little adverse comment. In batting order, England fielded:

W.G. Grace (Gloucestershire and London County), C.B. Fry (Sussex), F.S. Jackson (Yorkshire), W. Gunn (Nottinghamshire), K.S. Ranjitsinhji (Sussex), T. Hayward (Surrey), J.T. Tyldesley (Lancashire), W. Storer (Derbyshire), G.H. Hirst (Yorkshire), W. Rhodes (Yorkshire), J.T. Hearne (Middlesex).

There was one debutant in the England side; Wilfred Rhodes. Australia included two newcomers, one of whom was a certain Victor Thomas Trumper.

The match was drawn, very much in Australia's favour. Darling's side might have won but for a brilliant undefeated 93 by Ranji as England batted out time. Jackson failed with the bat, scoring 8 and 0, redeeming himself with the wickets of Clem Hill, Trumper and Frank Laver in the Australian second innings at the cost of 57 runs. Fry had scored 50 in the first innings after being bowled by a no-ball from Jones before he had scored, but apart from Ranji the English batsmen had hardly covered themselves in glory.

It was the last match W.G. Grace played for his country. In his fifty-first year his batting powers remained formidable, but in the field he was stiff and leaden-footed. He fielded at point, the position every first-class side put its weakest fielder in his age, but even so the barrackers seized on his slowness and mocked as too many balls beat his despairing clutch. W.G. knew it was time for him to step down. On the train after the match he turned to Jackson and said: 'It's all over, Jacker. I shan't play again.' It was a sad day for English cricket, the end of an era.

Jackson returned to the Yorkshire fold and scored

freely. He hit 97 and 8 against Essex at Sheffield, and 82 against Derbyshire at Dewsbury. The Tykes won both matches with ease.

The second Test was at Lord's in the middle of June. By the time the Selection Committee met at the Sports Club on the Sunday before the Lord's Test, it seems that W.G.'s resolve to stand down had weakened. He asked his colleagues if he should resign the England captaincy. When it was put to the vote, still no decision emerged. Stanley Jackson was absent from the fateful meeting, and the casting vote fell to C.B. Fry, who had been delayed and arrived some minutes late. As soon as the Sussex amateur walked through the door W.G. turned to him and asked:

'Do you think MacLaren should play at Lord's?'

Fry said he did, not realising until later that it was W.G.'s place that MacLaren would be filling. When Fry became aware of the hidden meaning of W.G.'s question, he was ill at ease. Fry had every right to feel he was being dealt with in a less than straightforward fashion.

It was an odd sort of a meeting. Once it had been settled that W.G. would stand down, everything else must have seemed rather petty, almost unreal. Only six of the England side that played at Nottingham were retained for the Lord's match; Jackson, Fry, Ranji, Hayward, Tyldesley and Rhodes. In came A.F.A. Lilley (Warwickshire) behind the stumps, and three debutants, G.L. Jessop and C.L. Townsend (Gloucestershire), and Walter Mead (Essex). As if such wholesale changes were not sufficient, the Committee compounded its folly by appointing Archibald Campbell MacLaren captain of England. In so doing the Committee, which included W.G. and Lord Hawke, passed over the senior amateur in the England side, Stanley Jackson.

MacLaren had captained England in Australia, he knew the strengths and weakness of the Australian players, he was an established county captain, he was without doubt a tactician of the first order, a man who liked nothing better than a back-to-the-wall fight, and there was no batsman in England more feared by the Australians. He had the credentials to be a successful England captain, but he was still the wrong man for the job.

Stanley Jackson must have greeted the news with a mixture of disbelief and horror. There was no outcry in the Press. W.G. had stepped down, English cricket was reeling, and Jackson was not a man given to venting a private grievance in public. He took MacLaren's promotion with good grace, accepted the invitation to play in the Lord's match and contemplated his future. He almost pulled out of the third Test at Leeds, tempted to rest a nagging injury, but in the end he played. He swallowed his pride, and battled on. Inevitably, Lord Hawke's part in the affair had its effect. It was no coincidence that 1899 was the last season in which Jackson wholly committed himself to the Yorkshire cause in the County Championship. He had been deeply wounded and afterwards, his attitudes to many things were subtly altered.

The news was probably as great a bombshell to Archie MacLaren as it had been to his old captain at Harrow. He had not appeared in first-class cricket in England that season, and his hold on the Lancashire captaincy was tenuous. MacLaren deserves better than to be cast in the role of the villain of the piece, for villain he was not. In

Australia, on Stoddart's second tour he had found the England captaincy thrust upon him, and now it had happened again. In the public eye he was a popular choice. Cardus called him 'the noblest Roman' and aptly so, for he was the epitome of the golden age, a batsman whose uncompromising style was one of the hallmarks of the period. The sight of Archie MacLaren with bat lifted high over his shoulder as the bowler reached the crease thrilled every man, woman and child who saw it. Yet there was more to MacLaren than his batting.

He was a complicated man, a man of moods, moods that his Lancashire team-mates understood, but others less familiar with his ways often found contrary. At Lancashire they knew his ways, fathomed his dry, sometimes sardonic, humour; his jokes went over the heads of strangers, his outbursts offended and discouraged the unwitting. If MacLaren did not like the team his selectors had given him, he said so and in public for all to hear. When he was down in the dumps he made no secret of the fact. He was a difficult man, a man quite capable of inspirational acts of leadership. He was a fighter. A born gambler. He was a much misunderstood man.

Between 1897 and 1909 MacLaren captained England in five separate series against Australia, three at home, and two away. He lost all five rubbers, winning just four out of the 22 Test Matches in which he led his country against the old enemy. In 1899 it was his misfortune to inherit the captaincy when England were confronted with perhaps the strongest Australian side that had ever come to the British Isles.

The 1899 Australians were strong in every department

of the game: the batting was in the formidable hands of Joe Darling, Clem Hill, Victor Trumper, Sydney Gregory and the all-rounder, Montague Noble, who, in league with Ernest Jones and Hugh Trumble, spearheaded an attack that had both hostility and trickery in abundance. These were men who would vie for places in any Australian side in any age.

England were roundly beaten by the Australians in the Lord's match. At one time on the first day Ernest Jones had reduced England to 66 for 6, but Jackson (73) and Gilbert Jessop (51) counter-attacked, scoring 95 runs in 65 minutes to avert a complete debacle. MacLaren, opening with Fry, had been bowled out by Jones for 4, and although he was to hit a dogged undefeated 88 batting at number six in the list in the second innings, by then the damage had been done. When Australia batted Clem Hill (135) and Victor Trumper (135 not out) carried the tourists to a total of 421. Apart from MacLaren only Hayward (77) and Jackson (37) offered any real resistance as Australia took the match by a margin of 10 wickets.

Jackson went up to Leeds where Yorkshire were playing Surrey, scoring 23 and 31, and taking 5 for 98 in a drawn match. It was his only appearance between the second and third Test, which was staged at Headingley at the end of June. There were more changes in the England team; in came J.T. Brown, who had scored 84 and 166 against the tourists at Bradford earlier in the month, W.G. Quaife the Warwickshire batsman, H.I. Young the Essex left-arm medium-pacer, Johnny Briggs and J.T. Hearne. Out went Townsend, Tyldesley, Jessop, Mead and Rhodes.

Rain washed out the second day's play and the match fizzled to a tame draw. Jackson scored just 9, but took consolation from having Trumper caught by Ranji off his bowling in the Australian second innings. The proceedings were marred by an incident off the field that saddened every cricket lover.

Johnny Briggs suffered a violent fit on the first night of the match, and was taken into the Cheadle Asylum. He had been plagued by a rare form of epilepsy since 1889, and he played no further cricket that year. In 1900 he returned and bowled with all his old skill, but after a series of severe attacks he went back into the Cheadle Asylum where he died in January 1902. He was thirty-nine.

Jackson scored 44 for the Gentlemen against the Players in the Lord's match as a powerful amateur XI piled up a total of 480 and defeated the professionals by an innings and 59 runs. Then he was Manchester-bound where the fourth Test was scheduled for mid-July. Walter Bradley, the Kent fast bowler who had taken a hatful of wickets for the Gentlemen at Lord's filled Briggs' place, and Surrey's William Brockwell came in for an indisposed J.T. Brown, but otherwise the England XI was unchanged. England compiled 372 in their first innings, largely due to Tom Hayward (130) and some spirited batting by the tail-enders after another early collapse had been repaired by Jackson's resolute 44. In reply the Australians scored 196, and as the follow-on law required, batted again. Against weary bowlers on a pitch offering little assistance the Australians amassed 346 for the loss of 7 wickets before Darling declared the innings closed, so as to give the English batsmen a nasty couple of hours batting at the end of the match. England had reached 94 for 3 at the close, with Ranji (49) and Jackson (14) at the wicket. The absurdity of the follow-on law had been demonstrated once too often, and the law-makers at Lord's soon acted to make the follow-on optional, at the discretion of the bowling side's captain; but the Australians had successfully defended the Ashes.

At Bradford later that same week Jackson plundered 155 off Middlesex, as he and David Denton hit up 219 for the second Yorkshire wicket in 2 hours 40 minutes. It was Jackson's fourth Championship century against Middlesex, struck in 4 hours. Yorkshire declared at 575 for 7, both Denton (113) and Frank Mitchell (121) also scoring hundreds. The rain came and saved Middlesex at 87 for 3 in their second innings, when they were still 300 adrift of the Yorkshire total. Jackson took 65 off the Kent attack at Headingley, then 20 and 68 off Gloucestershire at Huddersfield in matches won easily by the Tykes. In a high-scoring draw against Nottinghamshire at Bradford at the beginning of August he hit 114 in 135 minutes, but the centre-piece of the game was a long, defensive innings of 175 played by Arthur Shrewsbury. In the Roses match at Old Trafford, Jackson batted in his best style for scores of 68 and 43. At the Oval against Surrey he experienced a rare failure, out for 18, but as the Tykes ran up a total of 704, including contributions of 228 from Wainwright and 186 from Hirst, it was not exactly a catastrophic lapse. On a perfect batting wicket, Surrey played out time, reaching 551 for 7 at stumps on the third day, Abel (193) and Hayward (273) sharing in a fourth wicket stand of 448. Jackson was the best of the Yorkshire bowlers with 4 for 101, dismissing - albeit belatedly - both Abel and Hayward.

MacLaren promoted Jackson to open the England innings with Tom Hayward in the fifth Test at the Oval. England needed to win the match to level the series, and made four changes from the previous match, bringing in Townsend, Rhodes, W.H. Lockwood and A.O. Jones in place of Brockwell, Quaife, J.T. Hearne and Young.

MacLaren won the toss and England batted. Jackson and Hayward began cautiously. It was a bright, sunny day and the wicket was flat and true. Nine of the first ten overs were maidens but then Jackson began to take charge of matters. At lunch he had made 95 to Hayward's 50 and after the interval he soon put up his century, his second against Australia. When the stand passed 170 it bettered the thirteen-year-old first-wicket Test Match record partnership of W.G. Grace and W.H. Scotton, and when Jackson was bowled by Ernest Jones at 185 (with his own score on 118, made in 173 minutes) it was the highest score made for any wicket in international cricket by two Englishmen. England ended the day at 435 for 4, with Tom Hayward scoring his second century in successive Tests. On the second day England were all out for 576 and the Australians were left with the task of batting for ten hours to save the match, and to win the rubber. In the end the tourists held out with relative ease; bowled out for 352 in their first innings, they had reached 254 for 5 in their second when the stumps were drawn on the third day. Joe Darling had won his first Ashes series.

Just after the final Test Yorkshire's Championship aspirations were briefly revived by a convincing innings victory over Nottinghamshire at Trent Bridge. Jackson batted at four and scored 20. His bowling was sparingly used as Wilfred Rhodes caught the home side on a crumbling wicket, taking 8 second innings wickets for 38 runs. A defeat at the hands of Kent at Tonbridge followed, before a draw with Sussex at Brighton finally extinguished

Yorkshire's Championship challenge. Jackson had contributed scores of 1 and 33, 88 and 32, keeping up his form as the closing festivities of the season at Scarborough drew nigh.

He scored 13 and 9 for the Tykes against M.C.C., then in the first week of September captained C.I. Thornton's XI against the Australians. The match itself was drawn after rain had disrupted the proceedings and made batting a lottery, enabling Rhodes to record figures of 9 for 24 in the tourists' second innings. The rain provoked what became known as the 'sawdust incident', which brought Jackson and Darling, meeting as opposing captains for the first time, into a cricketing conflict of an unusual kind. *Cricket* described the roots of the controversy thus:

> When the storm came which put an end to further play on Saturday at Scarborough, the Australian captain, instead of rushing to the pavilion with the rest of the team, stayed behind to fill up with sawdust the holes made by Jones in bowling. Louis Hall, one of the umpires, and F.S. Jackson, the captain of Mr. Thornton's team, protested against this proceeding. Darling justified his action by stating that Richardson had done the same thing in the Surrey match, and was, moreover, assisted by one of the umpires. Jackson then withdrew his protest. It is stated that the M.C.C. is to be asked for a ruling on this point.

If it was a storm in a teacup, it served to demonstrate the sporting antagonism that already existed between Joe Darling and Stanley Jackson. Darling had formed the opinion on his previous visit to England in 1896 that too many of Jackson's fellows were in awe of him, and that members of the umpiring brethren were not immune to the malady.

Darling was an intensely combative man who had been chosen by his team-mates to be their captain on the 1899 tour. Jackson's aristocratic bearing and manners were like a red rag to a bull to Darling, even if he always had the highest regard for Jackson's courage and skill as a cricketer.

Jackson concluded the season with a masterly display of batting for Yorkshire against C.I. Thornton's XI, his second innings 101 coming up in 135 minutes. This turned out to be Stanley Jackson's last innings for Yorkshire for more than two years, for events in faraway Transvaal intervened.

The rebellion of the Boer Republics in October 1899 touched a raw nerve in the national psyche. What was happening in southern Africa was not just another colonial insurrection, not simply another tribal revolt, but the utter repudiation of the *Pax Britannica* by what was essentially an ethnically European population.

With a profound sense of anger, not to say shock, the British Army set out to put down the uprising. Military operations commenced in a blaze of patriotic fervour quite inappropriate to the sort of war needed to be waged if the Boers were to be defeated. The terrain and the climate dictated a war of attrition; the Boers had to live off the land, to fight a war of movement - or perish. The generals understood none of this until it was almost too late. In the end, the British Army waged war on women and children, and pursued what amounted to a scorched earth policy. It was not a glorious war; typhus, dysentery, malaria, and cholera killed more British soldiers than Boer riflemen. The British Army was equipped and trained to fight Waterloo or Balaclava; Magersfontein, Colenso, Spion Kop and Vaal Kranz were tragic awakenings.

Ladysmith and Mafeking were under siege when Stanley Jackson was commissioned as a Captain in the 3rd (Militia) Battalion of the King's Own (Royal Lancaster) Regiment on 16 January 1900 at Lichfield. Shortly afterwards, he embarked with his regiment for Cape Town.

On 26 April 1900, *Cricket* published a list of 61 cricketers who were either at the front or on their way to South Africa. Some of the men on the list were professional soldiers, like Major R.M. Poore, the Hampshire batsman who had scored 1,551 runs in 1899 at an average of 91.23 and Captain W.C. 'Chucker' Hedley of Somerset. The majority, however, were volunteers like Jackson and his fellow Tyke, Frank Milligan, who died of his wounds at Ramathelabama whilst serving with Plumer's column in the attempt to relieve Mafeking in March 1900.

Frank Mitchell, another of Jackson's Yorkshire team-mates who served in South Africa, fell in love with the country and returned to live there after the war, later captaining the Springboks in England. Others were less fortunate: J.J. Ferris, who had appeared for both Australia and England, died of enteric fever in November 1900 while serving with Colonel Byng's South African Light Horse; Prince Christian Victor, a grandson of Queen Victoria, serving in Pretoria as one of General Buller's aides-de-camp, and who had played most of his cricket in India, was another victim of enteric fever. H.T. Stanley, the Somerset amateur, George Strachan the Gloucestershire, Middlesex and Surrey slow bowler, and D.H. Forbes, the Oxford blue, all succumbed to fever.

Stanley Jackson, too, was struck down by enteric fever in the summer of 1900, and was swiftly invalided home on the *Avondale Castle*. Arriving in England at the beginning of August, he went to the Oval to watch Surrey and Nottinghamshire, where he met R.P. Lewis, the former Oxford University wicket-keeper who had also been recently invalided home from the Transvaal.

The long voyage home had done much to restore Jackson's strength, although the debilitating effects of his illness were plain to see. His return was greeted with acclaim, nowhere more than in his native Yorkshire where, at the end of August, his acceptance of an invitation to play for the Gentlemen against the Players at Scarborough filled the seaside ground. The hoardings proclaimed: 'JACKSON WILL PLAY!' And play he did, as only he could.

He batted at number three in the order, survived while the early batting crumbled away, and was joined by his old Cambridge skipper Sammy Woods at the fall of the fifth wicket with a mere 34 runs on the board. The bowling was in the hands of Wilfred Rhodes, Schofield Haigh, H.I. Young and John Gunn, with George Hirst waiting to pick up any morsels the others left behind. H.D.G. Leveson-Gower, W.L. Foster, T.L. Taylor (the Cambridge blue who had stepped into Jackson's shoes as vice-captain at Yorkshire), Lord Hawke and Gilbert Jessop were already back in the pavilion.

After a year without holding a bat in anger, and no more than a couple of gentle nets, Stanley Jackson proceeded to play one of the great innings of his career. He batted in all for 2 hours 50 minutes, and when he was out, caught by John Tunnicliffe off the bowling of Schofield Haigh, he had scored 134. He was tired by then, desperately tired, but he and Woods (52), had saved the day. It was the stuff of which legends are made.

The Players ran up a score of 457 and caught the amateurs on a drying wicket on the last day, Jackson batting one and a half hours for 42, the highest score of the innings, as the Gentlemen went down to defeat by an innings and 22 runs.

At the annual meeting of the Yorkshire County Cricket Club, Jackson and Frank Mitchell, who had also recently returned to England, were present to hear Lord Hawke announce that the Milligan Memorial Fund had realised £442, and propose that this sum, together with that raised at the Low Moor Iron Works where he had worked, should be donated to the Bradford Infirmary for the endowment of a bed in a children's ward. Frank Milligan had been an aggressive, impetuous and talented batsman (and a somewhat erratic fast bowler) always looking to score quick runs, or snatch a wicket. His death saddened all who had known him. The meeting was a moment of reflection after a season of unbroken Yorkshire triumph. No county had defeated Yorkshire throughout the 1900 season and the Championship had been regained.

When Jackson returned to South Africa in the spring of 1901 the nature of the war had changed. There were no major engagements and few skirmishes. It had become a guerrilla war, a bitter, brutal struggle for control of the veldt. The Boers struck here and there, shrank away into the wilderness; the Army searched and destroyed, uprooted whole communities, destroyed crops, watched the Boer heartland wither and die.

The previous year the Royal Lancasters had operated in the Orange River Colony and now the 3rd Battalion guarded the lines of communication. Jackson found himself first a Railway Staff Officer at the Vet Station, then a Staff Officer at Virginia, and finally the Commanding Officer at Landsberg.

During his second tour of duty in South Africa, at the end of March 1901, Jackson's mother died. She was buried at Chapel Allerton, mourned by the whole community; the *Yorkshire Post* reported that 'there was hardly a house in the neighbourhood that had not its blinds drawn, and most of the shops were closed for a time.'

War, the death of his mother, and MacLaren's assumption of the England captaincy had conspired to make Jackson's life a rather more serious business than it had seemed in earlier years. Yet in a very real sense his years of trial were over, and when he returned to cricket in 1902 it was with an inner strength born of having overcome grief, disappointment and illness. Jackson rarely spoke of his experiences in the Transvaal; the most that could usually be drawn from him was a variation on a favourite anecdote, an anecdote best told in fun, not anger.

One night in 1901 as Jackson was going the rounds of the sentries, one of them approached him: 'Beg pardon, sir,' he was asked in a broad Tyke accent, 'but it ain't true as Somerset have beated Yorkshire, is it? I 'ave betted a chum 'arf-a-crown that it ain't true, and I know as you can tell me.'

Jackson was somewhat taken aback that a sentry on duty should speak out of turn and wantonly flout every accepted tenet of proper military discipline, but recognising another true Yorkshireman, he took pity on the soldier and told him that Somerset had indeed defeated Yorkshire.

Then he severely reprimanded the sentry!

12 | The Return of the Soldier (1902)

Stanley Jackson left Cape Town on 30 January 1902, homeward-bound on the *Tintagel Castle*. The Transvaal had been turned into a desert, and a flawed peace was going to be inflicted on the Boers.

For Jackson it was a time for reflection, and for assessing anew the future course of his life.

The voyage home must have seemed interminable as he looked forward to picking up the threads of his life.

Jackson was planning marriage to Julia Henrietta Harrison-Broadley, the eldest daughter of Colonel H.B. Harrison-Broadley, MP for Brough in the East Riding. It was a match which was welcomed unreservedly by both families, a union between two of the most influential and respected Tory clans of Yorkshire.

Behind the scenes William Lawies Jackson was gently prompting and guiding his son's career; a directorship of the *Yorkshire Post* was offered and accepted, and he was soon back at work in the Unionist camp in Leeds. It was a period of adjustment, of rethinking old values. On Thursday 24th April he opened a bazaar on behalf of the Ilkley Cricket Club, and, in a rather tongue-in-cheek speech, confessed that despite the representations of his many friends, he had not yet decided whether he would be able to play regularly for Yorkshire in the Championship.

After his return from South Africa Jackson's attitude to the game he loved was a little ambivalent; perhaps cricket had come to seem a shade trite when viewed in the bleak perspectives of the war in the Transvaal.

Yorkshire had won the Championship in 1900 and 1901 without him; Archie MacLaren had led England in Australia the previous winter, and despite failing to regain the Ashes, MacLaren remained the man most likely to captain England against Darling's touring Australians that season. Jackson knew that he had a lot to prove - as much to himself as to the world at large - and he would have been less than human not to wonder if his best years were behind him. He was thirty-one years old and had yet to settle on a career; he had dabbled in many things, given his life and soul to none. The worlds of commerce and politics beckoned, he retained his commission in the Territorial Force, and was still young enough to challenge again for the England captaincy. If he was more fortunate than the majority of his amateur contemporaries, in that financial considerations rarely impinged upon him, it was also the case that at an early age he had assumed duties and responsibilities far beyond the experience of almost all his peers.

He turned out for Yorkshire against Essex at Leyton in

the second week of May. The first two days were lost to rain, and when the match began Essex were swiftly bowled out for 89, Schofield Haigh (5 for 32) and Wilfred Rhodes (4 for 44) finding the conditions much to their liking. Yorkshire reached 171 for 3 at the close, Jackson finishing on 101 not out, scored in 140 minutes. The soldier had returned.

Cricket observed:

> Few cricketers...could have returned to first-class cricket after a lengthened absence, and have played a three-figure innings at the first attempt.

Jackson had now achieved the feat twice. In fact, he had scored centuries in his last three first-class matches, three hundreds in four innings: 101 for Yorkshire against C.I. Thornton's XI at Scarborough in 1899, 134 and 42 for the Gentlemen against the Players, also at Scarborough, in 1900, and 101 not out for Yorkshire against Essex in the match at Leyton.

In the four fixtures in which he appeared before the first Test Jackson registered scores of 5 and 2, 19, 33 and 7, but he had done enough with the bat in the match at Leyton, and with the ball in subsequent games, to walk back into the England side. At Sheffield in the Roses match Jackson's bowling decimated Lancashire. He took 3 for 5 in the first innings, then 5 for 8 in the second for match figures of 8 for 13 as the visitors were dismissed for 72 and 54 to lose by an innings and 22 runs. Jackson's own knock of 33 on a wretched pitch in the presence of the otherwise unplayable Sidney Barnes was a minor classic of its kind. Lord Hawke said of Jackson's bowling in this match: 'What more could one ask?' Nor was it a flash in the pan, for at Bradford in the next match against Kent, he claimed 6 second innings wickets for 30 runs as the Tykes strolled to another handsome victory. In two Championship matches he had taken 14 wickets at a cost of 3.07 apiece.

The England side named to face the Australians at Edgbaston has been called the 'golden eleven', for it was, perhaps, the strongest batting combination England has ever put into the field. The team was:

C. MacLaren (Lancashire), C.B. Fry (Sussex), K.S. Ranjitsinhji (Sussex), F.S. Jackson (Yorkshire), J.T. Tyldesley (Lancashire), A.F.A. Lilley (Warwickshire), G.H. Hirst (Yorkshire), G.L. Jessop (Gloucestershire), L.C. Braund (Somerset), W.H. Lockwood (Surrey), W. Rhodes (Yorkshire).

MacLaren, Fry, Ranji, and Tyldesley were specialist batsmen, Lilley a wicket-keeper-batsman of no little renown, and the other six, Jackson, Hirst, Jessop, Braund, Lockwood and Rhodes were all-rounders. It was a batting side without a weak link; Rhodes, who batted at number eleven, later scored hundreds for England as an opening batsman.

Needless to say, when Archie MacLaren won the toss and England took first use of the wicket at Birmingham, there was an early collapse. At 35 for 3, with MacLaren (9), Fry (0) and Ranji (13) back in the pavilion Stanley Jackson and J. T. Tyldesley began to rebuild the innings. Tyldesley, the Lancashire professional, batted in a manner as expansive as any amateur, was as fine an exponent of the cut as Jackson, and every bit as much a fighter. Together they took the score to 99 at lunch. Jackson departed for 53 with 112 on the board, bowled by Jones, but Tyldesley (138) held the order together, until an unbroken last wicket stand of 81 between Lockwood and Rhodes carried the England total to 376 for 9. As the rain swept across the ground MacLaren declared and waited to get to grips with the Australians on a drying wicket.

Caught on an impossible pitch by Rhodes (7 for 17) and Hirst (3 for 15), Darling's men were bowled out for 36 runs, whereupon the tourists were invited to follow on. More rain fell, no play being possible until a quarter past five on the third and final afternoon and the Australians battled grimly to 46 for 2 at the close, living to fight another day.

When looking to the averages of the leading figures of the golden age, it is as well to remember that this was cricket played on uncovered wickets. The side that Rhodes and Hirst had routinely demolished on a drying wicket at Edgbaston included the likes of Trumper, Darling, Noble, Hill, Gregory and Warwick Armstrong, men whose batting exploits in Australia the previous winter had seen England beaten by four matches to one.

English sticky wickets were never as terrifying as their Australian counterparts, but in England wet wickets were a way of life, rather than the occasional hazard that they were in the Antipodes. Joe Darling prepared himself for the trials of a tour of England by practising on a net wicket doctored to imitate the conditions he was likely to encounter in England. Contrary to legend, the era was not blessed by perpetual sunshine, and the elements were to add more than a pinch of spice to the season of 1902.

The great bowlers of the golden age were masters of the

wet. Rhodes, Hirst, Haigh, Briggs, Peel, Lockwood, J.T. Hearne, Spofforth and their kind were merciless exponents of the drying wicket. Apprenticed, schooled and brought up in the tradition of cricket played on wickets left open to the elements, they left no escape for any batsman. The great bowlers, then as now, were masters of length and line. On a rain-damaged pitch they went calmly about their business, and only the luckiest, the most gifted, and, perhaps, the most obdurate of batsmen survived for long. The best bad-wicket batsmen of the era, W.G. Grace, Joe Darling, Ranji, Arthur Shrewsbury - and a certain Francis Stanley Jackson - relied not just on technique and courage, but something less quantifiable: genius.

Stanley Jackson was one of the finest bad-wicket batsmen of his day. Technically sound, apparently nerveless - fearless even - at the wicket, his batting on a drying wicket had about it a quality that went beyond the mechanics of batsmanship, or any personal well of courage.

At Headingley in the days after the Test Match, Yorkshire put the Australians on the rack on another rain-ruined wicket. This time it was Jackson, not Rhodes, who was George Hirst's partner in the execution. The start of the game came hard on the heels of the announcement of peace in South Africa, and a huge crowd packed the ground when play started at one o'clock on the first day. The wicket was wet, but the Australians managed to score 131, with Jackson (4 for 30) and Hirst (4 for 35) doing most of the damage.

Jackson had developed the knack of imparting off-spin to what looked like a normal medium-pace delivery; allied to his command of line and length on a helpful pitch, it was a wicked weapon. Yorkshire struggled to 107. Hawke, not wanting to give the Australians a chance to have a slog at Rhodes, handed the new ball to Hirst and Jackson when the tourists batted again.

Hirst made immediate inroads into the Australian batting, and Jackson had Clem Hill stumped, David Hunter whipping off the bails as the left-hander lifted his back foot for a moment as the ball evaded his defensive bat. The Australians reeled to 22 for 6, whereupon Jackson proceeded to wrap up the innings in the space of one famous over. Gregory hit a single off the first ball, A.J. Hopkins was trapped leg before wicket off the second, the third bowled J.J. Kelly, Ernest Jones jammed down at the last moment on the fourth, only to be comprehensively bowled by the fifth, and off the last ball of the over W.P. Howell snicked a catch to Hunter behind the stumps. Australia had been dismissed for 23 runs in 84 deliveries by Hirst (5 for 9) and Jackson (5 for 12). The Tykes needed 48 for a famous victory, a total achieved with five wickets in hand.

Jackson's batting had foundered on that mud-heap of a wicket, with scores of 0 and 6 in the match. The weather, however, amply compensated him for his tribulations with the bat. In his first seven matches of the season he took 25 wickets at a cost of 6.52 apiece.

The rain had a say in Yorkshire's game with Middlesex at Bradford the following week. Jackson took a back seat in the proceedings, out for 1 in the Tykes' only innings, and unlucky not to take more than the one wicket he claimed in the visitors' first knock.

Dismal weather blighted the second Test at Lord's. Rain permitted just one-and-three-quarter hours' play on the first day, and completely washed out the last two days of the match. The Selectors had toyed with the idea of bringing in Yorkshire's Tom Taylor to strengthen the batting, but when the side was finalised on the morning of the match, there was no place for the Cambridge blue, and he never again figured in an England twelve. After a nightmare start in which two wickets had gone down - those of Fry, for his second successive duck, and Ranji - before a run was on the board, England reached 102 for 2, with MacLaren (47) and Jackson (55) at the wicket. Cricket in the golden age was rarely dull; high drama tended to be the rule, not the exception.

The weather gave Somerset the upper hand against Yorkshire the following week. The Tykes laboured to totals of 74 and 84 and lost by 34 runs, in a match in which L.C. Braund took 15 for 71. Jackson could do little with the bat, but he captured 6 for 29 in the Somerset first innings and 8 wickets in the match.

Jackson dropped out of the side for almost two weeks, reappearing in the meeting with Surrey at Headingley in a match that produced the first definite result between the two sides since 1898, a Yorkshire victory by an innings and 102 runs. On a blissfully dry wicket Jackson found some batting form scoring a handsome 54. Later his 4 wickets, captured at a cost of 19 runs, in the Surrey second innings broke the back of the visitors' resistance.

Jackson had been co-opted by the England Selectors before the Second Test. The Selection Committee of Lord Hawke, H.W. Bainbridge and Gregor McGregor, the former Cambridge wicketkeeper, had, by that stage of the season, been swollen by the addition of MacLaren, Fry and A.G. Steel, the President of M.C.C., in a strictly advisory capacity. The seven men were rarely able to convene in the same place at the same time, but, even so, the chopping and changing that afflicted the teams England put into the field in that era rather smacks of too many cooks spoiling the broth. Later that summer the inherent failings of a selection system (which lacked a coherent strategy and so was inevitably prone to the whims of individual members of the Committee) contributed in no small measure to the fall from grace of Archie MacLaren.

Bobby Abel of Surrey and Sidney Barnes of Lancashire were drafted into the side for the third Test at Sheffield at the beginning of July, neither Ranji nor Lockwood being wholly fit. It was the only Test ever played in Sheffield. The Bramall Lane ground was the home of Sheffield United Football Club, although Yorkshire continued to use the ground until 1973, when falling attendances at county games and Sheffield United's expansion plans eventually brought to an end their long association.

As a Test Match venue Bramall Lane was less than ideal. The main problem was the light, which, due to the persistent industrial haze shrouding the city, was adequate on a good day, but not on any other.

The match was attended by controversy. Joe Darling claimed the wicket had been tampered with, illegally rolled on the second and third mornings before the players arrived at the ground. He was at pains to absolve MacLaren from any responsibility for the deed, but it left a cloud over the proceedings. Australia batted first and scored 194, England, having reached 106 for 5 in funereal light on the first evening, struggled to 145 on the second morning. Jackson (3) and Fry (1) were notable failures, but the rest of the England batting lacked inspiration.

Australia, on the other hand, batted like men inspired. They made 289 (Trumper 62 in 50 minutes, and Clem Hill 119) and so set England 339 to win in just under seven hours. MacLaren (63) and Jessop (55) apart, the batting never came to terms with a fiery wicket, and the Australians won by 143 runs. Fry scored 4, and did not play again for England that year. Jackson who had taken 4 for 71 in the match, could manage only 14 in the last innings. England had been outplayed and, some said, outfought by Darling's Australians.

For Jackson the matches in between the third and fourth Tests were odd affairs: he scored 33 and 6, and took 2 for 106 as the Gentlemen were routed by the Players at Lord's; he was out for 11 as Yorkshire ran up a total of 504 against Essex at Bradford and won by an innings; and again he went cheaply, hitting only 8 of the Tykes' 497 runs, against Nottinghamshire in a drawn match at Trent Bridge. In the three matches his bowling claimed 3 victims at a cost of 90.33 apiece.

Before the Fourth Test William Lawies Jackson was created 1st Baron Allerton of Chapel Allerton in the Coronation Honours List, and Jackson, as the younger son of a peer, became The Honourable F.S. Jackson.

England made several changes for the fourth Test. Fry, Hirst, Barnes, and Jessop, whose batting had shamed most of his fellows at Sheffield , were left out, and in came Somerset's L.C.H. Palairet whose inclusion in an England side was long overdue, Ranji, Lockwood, and controversially, F.W. Tate of Sussex. Fred Tate's right-arm medium-pace had taken a hatful of wickets that year; he was a rotund, sound county cricketer to whom the call to represent his country at Manchester came like a bolt from the blue. He was MacLaren's man, called up at the express insistence of the England captain (it was rumoured) in a fit of pique when the other selectors denied him his first preference. The selectors had offered him George Hirst, MacLaren had wanted Barnes.

In many ways the Manchester Test of 1902 was a personal triumph for Stanley Jackson, and an unmitigated disaster for Archie MacLaren. It had rained heavily the day before the match, and the wicket was soft when the captains tossed. Joe Darling won and elected to bat in the sure knowledge that the unsettled weather and underprepared pitch would probably make batting a lottery later in the match.

At luncheon on the first day Australia were 173 for 1, Victor Trumper (103 not out), R. A. Duff (54) and Clem Hill (14 not out). Trumper and Duff had hit up an opening stand of 135 in 75 minutes. Trumper's own century had arrived after just 108 minutes at the crease. Only Lockwood had slowed the run glut; Rhodes, Tate, Jackson and Braund had been powerless to halt Trumper's progress. The pitch was drying slowly, and when play began after the interval, wickets began to tumble. Trumper was the first to go, caught behind off Rhodes for 104. Hill (65) and Joe Darling (51) battled throughout the afternoon, taking the score to 256 for 4 before Lockwood was brought back into the attack, and the Australians collapsed to 299 all out, the Surrey bowler finishing with 6 for 48.

On a lively wicket England lurched to 70 for 5 at the close. Palairet (6), Abel (6), Tyldesley (22), MacLaren (1) and Ranji (2) were out, Jackson (16) and Braund (15) still at the wicket. Hugh Trumble and J.V. Saunders, orthodox right and left-hand spinners respectively, had woven their spell and mesmerised the early batsmen. England's cause was desperate. Yet when Jackson and Braund came to the wicket on Friday, the second day of the match, it soon became apparent that all was not lost. Mixing dogged defence with calculated stroke play, they kept the spinners out, and Darling was forced to resort to Noble and Armstrong as he searched for a breakthrough. As the stand progressed even Trumper's military medium-bowling was drafted into the attack, without effect. The stand lasted two-and-three-quarter hours and took the England score from 44 for 5 to 185 for 6. Braund was the first to go, bowled by Noble for 65 just before lunch. Jackson, however, was immovable, undefeated at the interval with 78 against his name. Noble and Trumble wore away at the England tail in the afternoon but Jackson batted calmly and carefully until, with nine wickets down and 235 on the board, he was joined by Fred Tate. Tate was not a batsman to be depended upon, a stout yeoman to the core, but hardly a batsman. Jackson went for his shots. When he was last man out England had scored 262, his own share being 128 runs compiled in 255 minutes.

Almost single-handed Jackson had wrenched back the initiative from Darling's rampant Australians. Yet cricket was cricket, a game and no more, and as if to put matters in their proper perspective he was fond of recounting a conversation he had at dinner that evening. Jackson found himself sitting next to a lady who remarked, 'I was so disappointed that Ranjitsinhji failed.'

It was a comment on a par with that of another young lady to Archie MacLaren whilst they were dining with a

Harrow master some years before. 'Do you play cricket?' she had asked, innocently, to which MacLaren had replied, 'A little.'

Jackson and MacLaren shared a dry sense of humour that could sometimes seem a trifle arid. It was as much a legacy of Harrow as the fearlessness of their batting.

When Australia commenced their second innings that Friday afternoon Trumper, Duff and Hill fell to Lockwood in 25 minutes for 10 runs. Shortly afterwards Joe Darling put up a steepling catch to Fred Tate. Tate had conceded 44 runs without threatening to take a wicket in the first innings and now, when Darling had made just 6, he spilled the catch that might have won the match. As it was, Darling went on to score 37 and the tourists struggled to 86 all out on the last morning, setting England 124 to win.

Even though the rain had come again in the night, 124 seemed a target within the grasp of what was, after all, a very strong England batting Side. At 72 for 2 England were well on the way, but then MacLaren fell to Trumble for 35. MacLaren stormed back to the dressing room, threw down his bat and, declaring that all was lost, went into his shell and brooded as the wickets fell. At 109 for six Jackson was still there, 7 to his name. The longer they played the worse the wicket became, and when Saunders bowled Jackson a full toss, he crashed the ball away. Unfortunately, he hit the ball straight at Noble, who gleefully clung hold of it. The ninth wicket fell at 116, and with 8 needed Fred Tate rolled out to the middle. Wilfred Rhodes, whose batting was already showing unmistakable signs of what was to come, was Tate's partner in that fateful last wicket stand. The last man, Lilley, had been out to the final ball of the previous over bowled by Trumble, and as the batsmen had crossed while the ball was in the air, Tate had to face the first ball of the new over from Saunders.

Tate threw the bat at the first ball, somehow deflecting it to the fine- leg boundary for 4. He jammed down on his second ball, and allowed the third to go past the outside edge of his bat. The final ball of the match, probably Saunders' top-spinner, kept low and bowled poor Fred Tate.

It was his only Test Match, and Archie MacLaren never really lived it down. England lost by 3 runs and the Ashes were retained by Joe Darling's men. England had now been defeated in four successive Ashes series, and MacLaren's days as captain of England were numbered.

Jackson joined Yorkshire at the Oval at the end of the month, taking an unhurried 77, and 81 not out - during a stand of 155 in 75 minutes with Tom Taylor - off the Surrey attack in Tom Hayward s high-scoring drawn benefit match. In the Roses Match at Old Trafford in the following week, Yorkshire in the absence of an injured Lord Hawke, bowled out Lancashire for 243, and had accumulated 499 for 5 before rain washed out the last day's play. Jackson had hit up 82 in good time, batting at five in the list. After his departure at 321 for 5, David Denton (108 not out) and George Hirst (112 not out) had added 178 in 90 minutes, and broken many a Lancastrian heart.

Jackson dropped out of the Yorkshire side that was scheduled to meet Leicestershire at Leicester - a match that was abandoned without a ball being bowled because of rain - and travelled to London, where the Fifth Test was due to begin on Monday 11th August. Inevitably, there were changes in the England side for the last Test. Tom Hayward came in for Bobby Abel, his Surrey team-mate, Ranji was indisposed and Fred Tate was dropped, so back came Hirst and Jessop. Indeed, the Oval Test was to be Jessop's match.

Australia batted first and at one point were struggling at 82 for 4, but resolute batting from the middle and lower order batsmen eventually put up a total of 324, Jackson taking the wickets of Noble and Armstrong in a spell of 22 overs that cost 66 runs. Heavy overnight rain saw England bowled out for 183 on the second day, with Jackson contributing 2, and when the Australians batted again they were reduced to 114 for 8 by stumps. That evening the England players turned their eyes skyward as a storm broke over their hotel - and their hearts sank.

The last two Australian wickets added 7 runs, and England were left 263 for victory. On a rain-damaged pitch 263 runs was a huge total. MacLaren (2), Palairet (6), Tyldesley (0), Hayward (7), and Braund (2) all fell to the spinners before lunch, England slumping to 48 for 5. It was then that Gilbert Jessop joined Stanley Jackson in the middle. At the luncheon interval the pair had carried the score to 87 for 5, Jessop scoring 29 of the 39 added in the 20 minutes he had been in. When play resumed Jackson batted soundly and solidly while Jessop launched himself at the bowling. Together they put on 109 in 65 minutes before Jackson was deceived in the flight by Hugh Trumble and induced to offer a sharp caught-and-bowled chance that was eagerly accepted by the tall Victorian. Jessop had gone to his 50 in 43 minutes, and had made 75 when Jackson was out for 49. He responded to the dismissal by clouting Trumble into the pavilion twice in an over and raised his century in 85 minutes. His was the seventh wicket to fall with the score at 187, his 104 including a five and 17 fours. George Hirst (58 not out), Lockwood (2), Lilley (16), and Wilfred Rhodes (6 not out) brought England home to victory by the margin of one wicket.

When the two men from Kirkheaton came together in the middle with 9 wickets down and 15 runs still needed, George Hirst and Wilfred Rhodes, phlegmatic characters both, allegedly agreed: 'Weil get 'em in singles.' The runs were duly got, although not exclusively in singles.

The glory belonged to Jessop, it was his finest hour, an hour beyond compare. An immense crowd gathered in front of the pavilion to pay court to England's new hero. The scenes that day were not to be seen again at the Oval until Percy Chapman's triumph in 1924. Jessop took his bow. Later he paid Jackson a fulsome tribute in *A Cricketer's Log* (1922):

> The wicket prior to the interval was in its worst stage, the ball not only turning quickly but getting up abruptly at an awkward height. The batting of 'Jacker' was masterly, and it was his determined defence during this most awkward and trying period which made possible the ultimate astonishing result. One had to be in with 'Jacker' to realise what a great batsman he was in a crisis. He seemed to have an uncanny prescience as to which ball to play at and which to leave alone, and the ball at which he did play even on that tricky wicket seldom collided with any part of the bat except the middle.

The Championship was safely in Yorkshire hands as August drew to a close. Jackson scored 41 in the resounding defeat of Gloucestershire at Cheltenham, 1 in the drawn match at Taunton with Somerset, 0 and 8 against Middlesex at Lord's - a low-scoring encounter won by the Tykes in two days. At Scarborough he hit 23 and 26 for the Gentlemen against the Players, and took 2 for 127 in an exciting draw. For C.I. Thornton's XI against the Australians he hit 72 out of a first innings total of 198, and 11, raising his game to the challenge of the tourists. His season ended with Yorkshire's match against a 'Rest of England' team at Lord's in September in aid of the Cricketers' Fund Friendly Society, of which Lord Hawke was a Trustee. He scored a good-looking 57, and took 2 for 40, but the weather prevented a definite conclusion to a closely fought match.

Jackson's forthcoming marriage promised to be the East Riding social event of the year. Shortly before the happy day the Yorkshire team attended Wighill Park, Lord Hawke's country seat. It was an annual gathering, a celebration of the cricketing year, a Yorkshire tradition. Foremost among the presentations was that of a silver salver to the nervous bridegroom, inscribed 'Presented to The Honourable F.S. Jackson by the Members of the Yorkshire County Cricket Team on his marriage, November 5th, 1902'.

It had been a memorable year: George Hirst and Wilfred Rhodes were presented with silver teapots bearing 'England v. Australia at the Oval, August, 1902. Presented by a few friends of the London Stock Exchange. England won by one wicket.'

Jackson and Hirst were both given half the ball with

which they had bowled out Australia for 23 at Headingley, inscribed: 'Yorkshire v. Australians. Leeds, June 2nd and 3rd, 1902. Hirst five for nine, Jackson five for twelve. Yorkshire won by five wickets.'

The marriage of Francis Stanley Jackson and Julia Henrietta Harrison-Broadley took place at the Church of St Helen's at Welton, near Brough in the East Riding. The ceremony began at a quarter to two, the weather was dull, wintery, and the mood of the occasion was somewhat overshadowed by the recent death of the bride's uncle. The church and the churchyard were crowded. A special train had been laid on for the contingent from Leeds, (the bridegroom's father was a director of the Great Northern Railway!). Lord Hawke officiated as best man, having delayed his departure for New Zealand where he was leading a touring party that winter.

The honeymoon was in southern England, far from the cares of the East and West Ridings, and afterwards the couple returned home to Heworth Hall, near York. With matrimony, the direction of Jackson's life shifted towards a career in politics. His marriage united two of the most influential Unionist families of Yorkshire, and wedded him heart and soul to the Tory establishment. It was his natural home, he was a deeply conservative man whose egalitarian instincts were regulated by his profound respect for the status quo. He was an Establishment man, a man who believed in working for change by consensus from within the system, who viewed politics as a duty that men of his station in society were honour bound to discharge.

For many years he continued to support W.L. Jackson and Co., but few doubted that one day he would follow in his father's footsteps to Westminster, and perhaps, build an equally brilliant Parliamentary career.

13 | The Gentleman Cricketer (1903-1904)

Stanley Jackson played in just nine first-class matches in 1903. His careers in business and soldiery called him, and he responded unstintingly. Since 1899 he had neglected his responsibilities to W.L. Jackson and Co., but now he set about repaying his father's indulgence. Only when he was selected for training with the 3rd Royal Lancasters on Salisbury Plain that summer, did he seek leave of absence from the Buslingthorpe works. In his few spare moments he threw himself into the service of Yorkshire cricket, the most energetic of Vice-Presidents even if the game saw little of him.

That spring there was a movement afoot to widen the wickets from eight-and-a-half inches to nine inches in order to 'afford some relief to the bowlers'. It was Ranji who led the opposition to the change, with Jackson and Archie MacLaren swiftly declaring their support. At the annual dinner of the Scarborough Cricket Club in March, Jackson entertained his hosts with his thoughts on the subject: 'I don't expect it will effect the big players, but it will effect the "rabbits", the eighth, ninth, tenth, and eleventh men. It was ignorance, no doubt, but the average spectator would rather see a man get a hundred runs than see Rhodes do a magnificent performance and get five wickets for thirty runs.'

He contended that what was really needed was not a wider wicket but a quicker game; that the problem of the bat dominating the ball was simply a question of deficient fielding standards; raise the standard of the fielding and the balance between bat and ball would inevitably tilt towards equality. It is pertinent to note that, many years later, when wickets were widened, it made little or no impact on the game.

Jackson made his first appearance of the season at the end of the third week of May in the 6 wicket defeat at the hands of Somerset at Taunton. He scored 16 and 12, and took 4 for 64 in the match. Making himself available for Yorkshire's first three fixtures in June, he struck a vein of his richest bowling form against Lancashire in the Roses Match at Old Trafford. The contest was drawn in the home side's favour, but not before Jackson had taken 6 for 20 on the second afternoon to dismiss the Red Rose county for a score 130 in arrears of the Tykes' first innings total. Later he shared in a stand of 92 with David Denton (84) in 70 minutes, during which both batsmen rode their luck. His own good fortune evaporated when he snicked a catch to the wicket-keeper two runs short of his fifty.

After Yorkshire crashed to defeat in the matches with Middlesex at Lord's and Sussex at Bradford, Jackson retreated to the West Down Camp where he reported to 15th Militia Brigade for training, not to reappear on a cricket field until the end of July, when his bowling was instrumental in brushing aside Warwickshire by 69 runs at Hull.

His return to the Yorkshire colours was timely: apart from the inimitable J.T. Brown with 92, only Jackson had looked at home batting on an awkward pitch in compiling 30 in the Tykes' first innings total of 217. In the visitors' reply he took two cheap wickets as George Hirst (6 for 61) ran through the Warwickshire list and then, when

Yorkshire had contrived to set a stiff target of 211, it was Jackson's mean line and nagging length that claimed 5 for 53, thwarting Warwickshire's hopes.

His occasional Championship outings were hardly conducive to consistency. In the Roses match at Headingley he scored 29 and 12, falling in both innings to Sidney Barnes. A week later at the same ground he hit 4 and 82 not out against Middlesex, and took 4 for 39 as Yorkshire overwhelmed the southern county.

A fortnight later Jackson emerged at Scarborough for a brief, end of season flourish, enriching the festivities with a forthright 54 in a hard-hitting partnership of 102 with Hirst in 50 minutes against M.C.C., as Yorkshire swept to an innings win. His season concluded with the Gentlemen - Players match, in which his two scores of 27 and return of 1 for 83 with the ball against a strong professional side were in a lost cause.

It was the first season since 1892 - excepting 1901 when he had been in South Africa - in which Jackson had failed to register a first-class century. It had been a disappointing year for Yorkshire, a year when the Tyke machine had faltered, and surrendered the Championship to Middlesex.

That winter the M.C.C. sponsored its first official England tour of Australia: Stanley Jackson was asked to captain the side, but he declined the invitation. Business, military and domestic commitments meant he had no option but to decline. It was simply not practical for him to drop everything and embark on a six or seven month tour of Australia.

The M.C.C. offered the captaincy to Plum Warner, who accepted. MacLaren did not feel himself able to tour under the captaincy of a man who was his junior, and in any event could not afford to join the party. Jessop, Ranji, and other leading amateurs Lionel Palairet, E.M. Dowson and H. Martyn were unable, for a variety of reasons, to join the England side. Nevertheless, Warner won back the Ashes, defeating the Australians, under the captaincy of M. A. Noble, by three matches to two.

In the first Test at Sydney, R.E. Foster scored 287 on his debut for England, and not even a virtuoso unbeaten 185 from Victor Trumper could save the Australian cause. In the second Test at Melbourne Wilfred Rhodes took 15 wickets - despite having eight catches put down - and again the home side crumbled to defeat. The Australians had rallied at Adelaide, but a fine all-round performance by England at Sydney had clinched the Ashes. In that fourth Test Noble's Australians had been bowled out in the last innings by J.T. Bosanquet, whose looping leg-spinners and googlies were to introduce a completely new element to the game in the years to come. The fifth Test at Melbourne was turned into a lottery by rain, and England lost by 218 runs, but Australia's hold on the Ashes had been broken.

Jackson followed the fortunes of Warner's side in the papers, too busy to brood on what might have been, although often he must have yearned to be in Australia. Perhaps it was England's unexpected success that spurred him to play more cricket in the new season, reminded him that he was getting older, and that there were young lions aplenty snapping at his heels. He need not have worried, for his stature in the game was undiminished by Warner's achievements in the Antipodes.

C.B. Fry in an article titled 'May Models in Cricket Bags', reproduced in *Cricket*, paid this, somewhat whimsical, tribute to his contemporary:

> A great, big, aristocratic-looking bag is one you may come across on any of the big Yorkshire railway stations; it has three letters on it, 'F.S.J.'. Better runs than come out of that bag so consistently it would be very difficult to find; with the ball, too, who can do better on his day? What a model to take as your own; spotless flannels, blue-white cricket pads and boots, a cool, firm head, with a pair of most resourceful eyes, ready to bat or bowl on any wicket. Watch F.S. Jackson, and learn how to play all-round cricket as it should be played.

In Yorkshire he had thrown his weight behind the idea of a permanent county ground where young players could be coached and their game developed, rather than thrusting them into the fray to sink or swim in a trial match. His sentiments were echoed throughout the county.

However, Jackson's views on the game were not always accepted without demur. His remarks to the effect that current players should not write about their fellows in the Press, rang a rather hollow note since he was a director of the *Yorkshire Post*. Gilbert Jessop penned an open letter pointing out - with the utmost civility - one or two home truths:

> As a director of an influential newspaper you have some connection with journalism, which makes me wonder why you are unsympathetic with him who wields the willow while wielding the pen. The

limited-income amateur, my dear Jacker, is just as enthusiastic on the game as he who is more fortunately placed. In order to still continue his favourite pastime, he has three courses open to him. Firstly, if he is good enough, he may induce the authorities to appoint him to an assistant secretaryship; secondly, if he has any ability whatever in the direction of putting his thoughts on paper he can accept the opportunity of doing so; and lastly, he may become a professional... The public having viewed you through the spectacles of the sporting journalist for many years, like to read what one fellow-cricketer thinks of another. Some fellow-cricketers may not like it, but only they who are possessed of an oversensitive cuticle...

Jackson's comments were rarely ill-judged, in this matter his concern was for the reputation of cricket. If his own financial circumstances were happier than the majority of his fellow 'gentlemen', then he was scarcely going to apologise for the fact.

He turned out for a Yorkshire XI against an XVIII of Northallerton and District at Northallerton in the first week of May. Yorkshire compiled totals of 184 and 111 for 7, Jackson's share being 25 and 14, while the home side struggled to 126, with Rhodes snapping up a dozen wickets before the rain came and put an end to the trial.

A week later he was playing for the Rest of England against M.C.C.'s Australian team at Lord's. The weather was damp and grey, cheerless like only England in May can be. Jackson batted well for his 41 as the Rest replied to M.C.C.'s first innings total of 300. Shortly after the commencement of M.C.C.'s second innings, the game was finally called off, after Jackson had bowled R.E. Foster, spearing his notorious arm ball through Foster's flowing defence in dismal light.

Some two weeks elapsed before Jackson's next appearance, in the Roses Match at Old Trafford. Walter Brearley, Lancashire's fiery amateur fast bowler tore into the early Yorkshire batting, and it took a brave innings of 49 from Jackson to steady the boat as the wickets crashed all around him before lunch on that first day. Later, Rhodes with an unbeaten 94 and Schofield Haigh with 84 carried the Tyke total to the unlikely heights of 293. Thereafter, with Jackson taking 6 for 91, it demanded a majestic century from R.H. Spooner, and rain, to deny Yorkshire victory.

Jackson had quieter matches against Derbyshire at Derby, and Middlesex at Lord's. The elements prevented a conclusion to the Derbyshire match, but at Lord's, Middlesex got the better of their visitors in a low-scoring encounter. At Bradford in the first week of June he registered a duck (caught behind by Herbert Strudwick off the bowling of Walter Lees off the last ball of the first over) against Surrey, but had his revenge in the second knock, scoring 158, including 18 fours, in a 4-hour innings, during which he gave just one sharp chance. In the same innings Wilfred Rhodes hit 107, his first Championship century. The Surrey attack was despatched to all parts as Yorkshire made 398 for 7 before the declaration, with the great Lockwood returning the chastening figures of 0 for 124.

Jackson shared in three punishing stands, hitting 85 with David Denton for the second wicket, then 80 with

Hirst in an hour, and 87 with Rhodes in 50 minutes. Surrey collapsed in the last innings of the match, Jackson (3 for 21), Hirst (3 for 41), and William Ringrose, the right-arm medium-pace bowler (3 for 25), seeing the visitors beaten by 297 runs.

At Sheffield a week later Yorkshire struggled against Sussex, bowled out for 220 in a little less than 4 hours. Jackson alone played with confidence for his 40. Sussex ran up 440 for 9, and the Tykes were left with the task of playing out time. When Tunnicliffe was out early on, and Denton joined Jackson at the wicket, Yorkshire briefly looked defeat in the face. The momentary anxiety passed and the domination of the bat over the ball was quickly, ruthlessly asserted as 171 runs were added for the second wicket. Denton went as stumps approached, but Jackson remained to the end, unbeaten on 110, the Yorkshire tally 218 for 2. Jackson appeared at Hull, eight days after the Sussex match and scored a brisk 84, batting at the top of the order against Somerset. Yorkshire won by 7 wickets, Jackson scoring 20 of the 151 needed on the last day as the runs were made with ease.

Since the match with Middlesex at Lord's at the beginning of June Jackson had resumed his former role as opener in the continuing absence of J.T. Brown. Jack Brown had been dogged by ill-health for many years, suffering from chronic asthma and a heart condition (almost certainly aggravated by his heavy smoking). He was a popular man in Yorkshire, a gifted batsman whose explosive cutting and hooking had once outshone even Archie MacLaren in Australia. Over 40,000 people saw his benefit match at Headingley in 1901, from which he received the then record amount of £2,282. In league with the taciturn Tunnicliffe he had formed the finest opening partnership in the land. He died in November, 1904 at the age of thirty-five.

At the end of June, Hampshire came up to Headingley and were beaten by 370 runs in two days. Yorkshire, batting first on a soft wicket made 194 with Jackson hitting 73 out of the first 97 runs scored in 75 minutes before the lower order collapsed. In the Yorkshire second innings Jackson went for 6, but Tunnicliffe's 94 was the foundation of the side's total of 274. Bowling unchanged in both Hampshire innings Rhodes (10 for 39) and Haigh (10 for 33) dismissed the visitors for 62 and 36.

Jackson then dropped out of the Yorkshire side and went down to Lord's to watch the Eton - Harrow and Oxford - Cambridge matches, to meet old friends, and to prepare for the Gentlemen v. Players match, in which M.C.C. had invited him to captain the amateurs. *Cricket* described the meeting as 'the match of the season.

The Players had first use of what turned out to be a fiery wicket, and did well to score 327. J.H. King, the Leicestershire left-hander, had been drafted into the ranks of the professionals on the morning of the match when injury had forced Tyldesley to stand down. He scored 104 in the Players' first innings, and an undefeated 109 in the second, rivalling the feat of R.E. Foster in the Lord's match of 1900. When the Gentlemen batted it was Jackson's 58 which held the innings together. At one stage the Gentlemen had been reduced to 60 for 5, but Jackson, who batted for nearly 2 hours defended until the ninth wicket fell at 112, whereupon he hit out freely, adding the lion's share of the 59 runs added in a 40-minute stand with H. Hesketh-Pritchard. The innings closed at 171 all out.

Lilley, the captain of the Players, opted to bat again rather than have to bat last on what seemed to be a rapidly deteriorating pitch. He was to rue the decision, although it seemed to have paid off when the professionals managed to set the Gentlemen a target of 412 with a full day left to play.

The Gentlemen picked up the gauntlet and went after the runs, but towards the end of the third morning, the first three batsmen had fallen for 108 and it seemed as if the challenge was beyond them. Then the tall, trim figure of the captain of the Gentlemen walked out to join Ranji.

'To put it mildly, my batting was very streaky,' Jackson said of his work that day. He was missed in the slips when on 33, and again at 53, before Lilley pouched a snick behind when he had made 80. On a lively pitch, on which the ball was coming through at varying heights and speeds, Jackson and Ranji had battled away for two-and-a-half hours to add 194 runs before they were parted at 302 for 4. Although Ranji departed soon afterwards, for 121, the amateurs scraped home by two wickets with the last two fit batsmen at the wicket.

It was the highlight of Jackson's season.

The six remaining Championship matches in which he played were drawn as Yorkshire's year turned sour and Lancashire strode to the title. Jackson's scores of 24 and 0 not out, 33, 8, 13, 7 and 62, and 21 reflected the way both his and his county's season had gone flat. His solitary half-century was against Middlesex at Sheffield, and his bowling seemed bereft of penetration as the season fizzled out. After the Middlesex game he took time off to play for Ranji's XI against XXII of Gilling and District at Gilling. He scored 44 as he relaxed in the less fraught atmosphere of club cricket.

At the end of the season he discovered some form during Scarborough Week, cracking 71 off the M.C.C. and 38 off Frank Mitchell's South Africans. He then left cricket behind to pick up the threads of his other careers. He might have given up the first-class game then, but he hesitated, mulled over his future.

In 1904 he had scored 1,037 runs at an average of 45.08, putting him in twelfth place in the national lists. His bowling had been less successful, although he had captured 33 wickets at the respectable rate of 27.54 apiece. In the field he was fit, trim, very nearly as nimble as ever he had been. However, but for the return of the Australians to English shores in 1905 he might have been tempted to forsake the first-class game, preferring to leave the big stage of English cricket whilst at the height of his powers.

Yet it was not in Stanley Jackson's nature to side-step a challenge. Among Englishmen who had played in more than a handful of Test Matches, only Ranji had achieved a higher batting average than Jackson; 44.95 over fifteen matches against Jackson's 41.95 in the same number of matches (15). Circumstance had denied him the Yorkshire captaincy and he had come to terms with that, but another dream still beckoned, of becoming captain of England.

His future outside the game was mapped out: his career in commerce would be the foundation for a life in politics and public service. Other amateurs agonised over whether or not their financial straits permitted time for cricket - Archie MacLaren had virtually bankrupted himself to tour Australia - but for Jackson the question of when to hang up his cricket boots was not affected by such considerations. He could afford to pick and choose the matches in which he played, invariably filling his diary with a preponderance of fixtures against the stronger county elevens. In many respects he was a typical amateur; he clung to his amateur status as a mark of honour rather than as a badge of rank or wealth. There were many wealthy amateurs, some lived off private incomes like Charles Kortright, the Essex fast bowler, but most worked for a living. It was not uncommon for a humble bank clerk to captain his county side; Jessop and Warner looked to journalism for a living, MacLaren was not above asking the Old Trafford grounds man for a loan, Sammy Woods held the secretaryship of the Somerset Club from 1893 onwards. There was a host of professionals who were at least as comfortably placed, if not more so, than their amateur teammates.

The financial imperative played little or no part in the decisions Stanley Jackson made about his cricket. He had sacrificed four opportunities to tour Australia to his loyalty to his father's business, his political constituents in Leeds, and the call to arms in the Transvaal. Now, as he looked towards the season of 1905, he could be forgiven for thinking, with no little justification, that he owed himself at least one further tilt at the Australian foe on English soil before he turned to other things.

One last campaign.

Then he would bid farewell to the first-class game without regret.

14 | An Appointment with Destiny (1905)

There were rumours abroad in the spring that Stanley Jackson would play little or no cricket in 1905. In the event, however, he was in charge of the Yorkshire side that took on South Wales at Cardiff in a trial match at the beginning of May. Yorkshire won easily enough, the margin of victory being 7 wickets. On a wet pitch batting was never straightforward, and the gallant Welshmen had no answer to Rhodes, Hirst or Haigh. In retrospect it was an unlikely opening to what was a momentous season for Stanley Jackson.

He turned out in the next fixture against Somerset at Taunton, scoring 12 in a total of 549 for 9 declared. Wilfred Rhodes hit 201 not out and the West Country side crumbled away to an inevitable defeat. Jackson's turn to hold centre stage came at Bradford in the middle of the month against Derbyshire, when his 3-hour innings of 111 set up another innings win for the Tykes. On a slow outfield he hit 11 fours, exercising his driving to good effect.

The innings confirmed his form and a few days later Lord Hawke turned to his lieutenant and informed him that he was to captain England in the coming series against the Australians. Warner had covered himself with glory in Australia, but his batting could not justify his inclusion in an England side in England, and he was, in any case, both Jackson's and MacLaren's junior. MacLaren in turn, was passed over in Jackson's favour.

In Jackson the selectors had opted for the one man in England under whom MacLaren could play without having to swallow too much of his pride. The wheel had come full circle. The man whom many had felt ought to have succeeded W.G. Grace as England captain in 1899 had at last received the call to arms.

As fate would have it Yorkshire were due to play the tourists at Sheffield just before the first Test at Trent Bridge. The Australians, with Joe Darling restored to the captaincy, were every bit as formidable a batting side as they had been in 1902, although there were question marks about the penetration of their bowling, which seemed to rely heavily on the fast bowler, Albert 'Tibby' Cotter. The tourists shrugged aside Yorkshire, taking the match by a margin of 174 runs. Jackson, the England captain designate, opened the batting in a Tyke team led by Lord Hawke. He scored 42 in the first innings, a breezy knock which included 7 fours, and 3 in the last innings of the match. His bowling was unusually expensive, his seventeen overs in the tourists'

first innings costing 74 runs, although he had the consolation of having Trumper caught by Tunnicliffe at slip when it seemed nothing could stop the Australian reaching his century.

The England selectors named Jackson, MacLaren, C.B. Fry and A.F.A. Lilley to play in all five Tests that summer, but almost immediately Fry was forced to stand down for the Nottingham match. The XI that eventually emerged was, in batting order:

T.W. Hayward (Surrey), A.O. Jones (Nottinghamshire), J.T. Tyldesley (Lancashire), A.C. MacLaren (Lancashire), F.S. Jackson (Yorkshire), B.J.T. Bosanquet (Middlesex), J. Gunn (Nottinghamshire), G.L. Jessop (Gloucestershire), A.F.A. Lilley (Warwickshire), W. Rhodes (Yorkshire), E.G. Arnold (Worcestershire).

Given that Ranji was in India, and that both Fry and George Hirst were injured, it was a representative side, although critics were swift to point out that it lacked an out-and-out fast bowler.

Joe Darling had withdrawn from the recent Ashes campaign in Australia out of consideration for his family. Warner's defeat of Noble's team had persuaded him to return to the fold. It was his fourth tour of England, his third as captain. He had captained his country in four Test series, three against England, one against South Africa, and won them all. In 1905 Joe Darling was - by any yardstick - the most successful captain in the relatively short history of Test Match cricket. He had led his country in sixteen Tests, won seven, lost just two, and bested Archie MacLaren time and again. There was no more worthy opponent in Christendom than Joe Darling and, as if to rub home the point from the outset, he set about seizing the initiative over the new England captain even as the two men walked out to toss on the first morning of the Nottingham Test.

It was the custom - as it still is - for the home captain to toss the coin and for his opponent to call. Joe Darling, out to test the mettle of the new captain, suddenly produced his own coin, flicked it skyward and invited an astonished Stanley Jackson to call.

'Heads!'

Heads it was and Jackson duly elected to bat. A captain of England - an Old Harrovian captain of England - could do no less.

Back in the pavilion he turned to MacLaren: 'Archie, Darling ought not to have tossed.'

'No,' agreed the other.

'It would be an extraordinary thing if Darling never won the toss in any of the Test Matches,' he mused, out loud. It was a remark that MacLaren was to remind him of at the end of the season.

There is a theory that a captain can do no wrong if he wins the toss. It was a theory tested to destruction that morning as England lurched to 49 for 4 and the new England captain put his bat under his arm and trudged forlornly back to the dressing room.

The wicket had seemed flat and benign to the eye, yet Cotter had roared in to bowl and given the early batsmen a fearful shaking up. Hayward (5) had been bowled by Cotter, Jones (4) and MacLaren (2) had both fallen to Frank Laver's medium pace. Now Jackson was gone without scoring, bowled off the handle of his bat by a rising ball from Cotter. Disaster beckoned. A fighting 56 from Tyldesley, and some solid batting from Lilley and Rhodes carried the England total to a semblance of respectability, but England's 196 looked rather sad when the Australians finished the day on 158 for 4. Things might have been even blacker, for at one point the tourists had stood at 129 for 1 - albeit with Victor Trumper in the pavilion having retired with a back strain at 23 for 1 - at which point Jackson had decided, somewhat belatedly, that it was about time he gave himself a bowl. The match turned upon a single over.

Jackson had Noble (50) caught at the wicket off his first ball, the fourth ball bowled Clem Hill (54), and the last ball of the over caught the edge of Joe Darling's bat and flew into Bosanquet's waiting hands at slip. Neither captain had troubled the scorers.

On the second morning of the game Armstrong and Cotter took their stand for the sixth wicket to 70, but the Australians collapsed and were all out for 221, Jackson's final analysis being 5 for 52. England were back in the match and daring to think of achieving something more than just a draw. As if to press home the initiative, Jackson promoted MacLaren to open with Hayward in the second innings. On the first morning Cotter had unsettled - and very nearly unnerved - the England batsmen. Now as he waited to go out to bat, Archie MacLaren paced the England dressing room muttering defiance: 'I'll Cotter him...'

Hayward and MacLaren saw off the initial attack: Hayward watchful, clinical, content to wait for the bad ball; MacLaren upright, majestic, merciless when the bowler erred in length. They put up 145 for the first wicket before Hayward was out for 47.

Tyldesley arrived on the scene to be greeted by Cotter's return to the attack. A couple of overs were bowled, and MacLaren came down to meet his partner in mid-wicket. 'Johnny,' he declared, 'I've made up my mind about this feller. I'm going to drive him.'

'You do as you please, Mr MacLaren,' said the professional, 'but I'm going to cut him.'

Cotter soon retired from the attack as the runs flowed.

Laver, Armstrong, and McLeod, the hard-pressed Australian medium-pacers, resorted to bowling to heavily guarded leg-side fields to stem the runs, the crowd barracked, the batsmen stepped away to leg and carved the ball through the wide-open spaces on the off-side. MacLaren departed at 222, his 140 his fifth hundred against Australia. Jones came and went for 30, Tyldesley rattled up 61 and was gone. At stumps England were 318 for 5, Jackson on 19, and Rhodes, promoted above Jessop, Gunn and Lilley, on 2. The next morning the two Yorkshiremen batted until the declaration at 426 for 5, when their stand was worth 113. Jackson had redeemed his first innings failure with a robust 82, and Rhodes had been an ideal foil, finishing with 39.

The Australians, set 402 to win in 5 hours might have batted out time but for two particular misfortunes that befell them that day. Firstly, Victor Trumper was unable to bat, and secondly, Bosanquet's googly.

Joe Darling and R.A. Duff put up 60 in good time for the first wicket and it looked as if a draw was inevitable. Then, after the luncheon interval, MacLaren prompted Jackson to put on Bosanquet.

Bosanquet was a tall man who was liable to make the ball bounce awkwardly, but his main weapon - and his claim to cricketing immortality - was his googly. A googly is simply a delivery bowled with a leg-spinner's action that, contrary to a batsman's expectation, spins to the off. Bosanquet had introduced the googly into first-class cricket and its very newness made it a dangerous variation in any bowler's armoury. Unfortunately, Bosanquet's googly was an erratic missile that often cost him dear, and for this reason he tended to use it sparingly. Jackson watched him bowl a couple of overs, and, realising that Bosanquet was bowling within himself to avoid punishment, strode over to him and indicated that he meant to keep him on for most of the afternoon, regardless of the number of runs he conceded. Fortified by the news, Bosanquet set about his task with a will. Darling made 40, Sid Gregory 51, but nobody else came to terms with Bosanquet that afternoon. As the day lengthened so the storm clouds gathered over the ground, threatening to burst as the drama reached its last act. Then, with Australia at 188 for 9, and Bosanquet's tally standing at 8 for 107 with only minutes left, the arrival of the injured Trumper was breathlessly awaited. Trumper limped down the steps, but at the gate he faltered. In agony he could go no further, and had to be assisted back to the dressing room. England had won by 213 runs.

Fresh from his triumph Jackson opened the Yorkshire batting at Lord's against Middlesex the next day, playing under the captaincy of Lord Hawke. He scored 37 and 52 not out as the Tykes won by 7 wickets.

Jackson remained in London to captain M.C.C. against the Australians. Upon winning the toss he elected to bat, and on a damp wicket he hit up 85 in 165 minutes out of the premier club's total of 183 for 8 declared. The rains came and put an end to the match after just one ball of the tourists' first innings, off which J.T. Hearne had bowled R.A. Duff. From Lord's he travelled north to Manchester for the Roses Match, an affair lost by the Tykes by an innings after R.H. Spooner (109) and J.T. Tyldesley (134) had mastered the Yorkshire attack on the first day. Jackson's bat contributed scores of 34 and 2, Rhodes and Denton resisted stoutly, but the Tykes were well beaten. The Lancashire victory was no less galling to the Yorkshiremen for the fact that a ball from Jackson had actually struck Spooner's off stump without removing the bails, when the batsman had made only 37.

The second Test was at Lord's in the middle of June. England made two changes; C.B. Fry came in for Gunn, and Schofield Haigh replaced Jessop. Jessop had made a duck at Nottingham, throwing away his wicket with a wild shot as soon as he got to the middle. Jackson was looking for application, not heroics. A half-fit Victor Trumper returned for the Australians, who went into the match without the injured Cotter.

Rain before the match left the pitch slow, the outfield soft and treacherous, and rain during the match condemned it to a draw. England had much the better of what play was possible, and, it must be said, the conditions. Jackson won the toss, tossing *his* coin, and batted. His personal contribution to his side's 282 all out was a hard- fought 29 in 85 minutes. England reached 258 for 8 at the close of the first day, and were barracked by sections of the crowd. Fry (73), MacLaren (56) and Tyldesley (43) ground out their runs, hamstrung by the dismal light and soggy ground. A thunderstorm broke over Lord's that evening, leaving the ground waterlogged. Australia made 181 when they batted, unable to make much headway against England's Tyke attack of Jackson (4 for 50), Rhodes (3 for 70) and Haigh (2 for 46).

Jackson came and went for another duck in England's second innings, bowled by Armstrong, By then, however, Archie MacLaren's brilliant 79 had carried the total to 151 for 5 at the close of the second day, 252 ahead on a rain-damaged pitch with Rhodes and Haigh warming up their spinning fingers in anticipation of the morrow. As it was, the rain came to Australia's rescue on the last morning, causing the match to be abandoned at lunch time.

In the two weeks before the third Test at Headingley Jackson played in three Championship matches, against Warwickshire at Dewsbury, Sussex at Headingley, and Kent at Hull. His batting was below par, his thoughts perhaps straying towards captaining England on Yorkshire soil. His scores of 7 and 25, 19 and 15, 19 and 0 completed a sequence of ten innings in which his highest score had been 34.

England made four changes for the Headingley Test Match. Archie MacLaren was unable to play, an injured knee ruled out Arnold, a damaged thumb side-lined Rhodes, and A.O. Jones was dropped. In came Yorkshire's David Denton, and the Derbyshire fast bowler A.R. Warren for their Test debuts; George Hirst was recalled, so too was the Kent left-arm spinner Colin Blythe.

Jackson again won the toss. England slumped to 64 for 4 on the first morning. Fry (32) and Hayward (26) had put on 51 for the first wicket, but Tyldesley and Denton had both been dismissed without scoring. The stage was set for a captain's innings and Stanley Jackson rose to the occasion. He batted for 280 minutes, and remained undefeated on 144 (including 18 fours) when the last England wicket fell at 301 just before stumps. It was the first century hit in a Test Match at Headingley.

Jackson always judged his hundred at Manchester in 1902 as his best in Test cricket, hut no innings gave him quite the same measure of satisfaction as this, hit, as it was, in the citadel of Yorkshire cricket. Yorkshire was at his feet.

Australia was bowled out for 195 on the second day and England went in search of quick runs. Tyldesley led the way with a sparkling innings of exactly a hundred, Hayward and Hirst gave him fine support, and although Jackson fell for 17, he was able to declare on the third morning at 295 for 5, setting Darling's men 402 to win in a little less than 5 hours. At Lord's the tourists had been thoroughly bamboozled by Bosanquet; but Bosanquet held few terrors for the Australian batsmen that afternoon, instead it was Colin Blythe who briefly threatened to run through the order. At 224 for 7 off 91 overs at stumps Darling's men had fought a gritty rearguard action, and, by the skin of their teeth, survived.

While Yorkshire took on Somerset at Harrogate Jackson travelled south to London, where, on the Saturday before the Gentlemen v. Players match at Lord's, he made an appearance for the Old Harrovians against Harrow School. The School had slightly the better of the meeting, putting up 290 for 8, against the seniors' 217 for 8. It seems that Stanley Jackson enjoyed less success against his old school than he had recently become accustomed to against the Australians!

He captained the Gentlemen against the Players the following week. It mattered not one jot that the amateurs were roundly beaten, for he was the man of the moment. He scored 6 and 22, had no luck at all with the ball other than to trap Hayward leg before wicket in the Players' first innings, and still found himself cheered whichever way he turned.

In the days before the fourth Test at Manchester, Jackson - captaining Yorkshire in Lord Hawke's absence - shared in a fifth wicket stand of 177 in 165 minutes with George Hirst against Surrey at the Oval. Jackson batted for 3 hours for 87, hitting 1 five and 10 fours before departing to a running catch by Jack Hobbs at third man, off the fast bowling of N.A. Knox. Hirst went on to score an unbeaten 232 as Yorkshire won by an innings.

Jackson always considered the England side that took the field for the fourth Test at Old Trafford to be at least the equal of the 'golden eleven' of three years earlier. In batting order the side was:

A.C. MacLaren (Lancashire), T.W. Hayward (Surrey), J.T. Tyldesley (Lancashire), C.B. Fry (Sussex), F.S. Jackson(Yorkshire), R.H. Spooner (Lancashire), G.H. Hirst (Yorkshire), E.G. Arnold (Worcestershire), W. Rhodes (Yorkshire), A.F.A. Lilley (Warwickshire), W. Brearley (Lancashire).

MacLaren, Arnold and Rhodes were now restored to fitness and their rightful places in the side; Spooner came in to strengthen the middle order, and Walter Brearley, MacLaren's partner in the slips at Old Trafford, was the fastest bowler in the land. The batting seemed endless and the variety of the bowling, irresistible.

Jackson won the toss for the fifth successive call and England at stumps on the first day had reached 352 for 6, with the captain unbeaten on 103. The Australians had brought back Cotter to try and knock the England batting out of its stride, but to no avail. Cotter went wicketless that day and England prospered. When Jackson was finally out for 113 on the second morning he had hit 12 fours in an innings lasting 225 minutes, scoring his runs out of 226 added whilst he was at the wicket.

Rain had fallen early on the second day and when the Australians came to reply to England's formidable total of 446, they struggled. Joe Darling held things together with his 73, hitting out defiantly in his 85-minute stay at the crease, as Australia were dismissed for 197. The wicket had eased by then, but Jackson asked Darling to bat again. Although the Australians reached 118 for 1 at the close, heavy rain on the third morning left them at the mercy of Brearley, Rhodes and Haigh on the last day. England won by an innings and 80 runs and the rubber was won; the Ashes had been retained.

Jackson played a captain's hand in the Roses match at Sheffield. Walter Brearley, who had taken 8 Australian wickets for 126 runs in the Manchester Test, ripped through the Yorkshire batting on the first day at Bramall Lane. Jackson's 30, scored in 50 minutes out of the Tykes' total of 76, was all that stood between the home side and complete humiliation. Jackson snapped up 4 for 15 when the visitors batted, but the old enemy still ran up a total of 177. Yorkshire were soon in trouble on the second day, reduced to 21 for 2 when Jackson joined Denton at the wicket. They added 122 in under two hours, Jackson playing steadily for 45, while Denton chanced his arm and hit up 96. Yorkshire eventually set Lancashire 185 for victory, 135 of which were still required at stumps on the second evening with 8 wickets to fall, both MacLaren and Spooner out, the former bowled by Jackson. It rained overnight and in the morning Jackson set Rhodes and Haigh upon the remaining batsmen. Yorkshire's victory was all the sweeter for having been snatched from the jaws of defeat.

Jackson was again in charge when Yorkshire entertained Surrey at Headingley in the second week of August, and although he had a quiet match, the Tykes won with relative ease, Wilfred Rhodes hitting fifty at a vital time, and taking 10 wickets in the match.

England fielded an unchanged side for the fifth and final Test Match at the Oval. Needless to say, Jackson won the toss and England batted on a wicket that looked full of runs.

It seemed Jackson could do nothing wrong. England stood at 381 for 7 at stumps. It was the long-awaited day when C.B. Fry scored his first century for England, sharing in a partnership of 151 in 125 minutes with his captain for the fourth wicket. For a while it looked as if Jackson, who had ridden his luck that afternoon, might score his third hundred in successive Tests, but it was not to be. Fry was the first to go when he had scored 144 and Jackson soon followed for 76.

The Australian reply to England's 430 all out got off to a bad start when Brearley bowled Trumper for 4. A few overs later Brearley removed Clem Hill for 18, and Australia were 44 for 2. The moment passed, and Duff

(146), assisted by Darling (57), Noble (25) and Armstrong (18), managed to save the follow on, Australia amassing a total of 363.

Drama ensued when England commenced their second innings a few minutes before the close on the second day. Arnold, the night-watchman, was bowled by Cotter, and on the next day MacLaren, Hayward and Fry were quickly sent back to the pavilion. England at 48 for 4 effectively 48 for 5 as Lilley was injured - were just 115 ahead.

Enter Stanley Jackson to turn the tide. He and Tyldesley hit up 55 in quick time and extinguished what little hope remained in the Australian camp. Jackson departed for 31, not a big score, but a score made like so many before it, when his side needed it. Going after the bowling he clouted a ball from Noble into Warwick Armstrong's large, and very safe, hands. As the cheers subsided Spooner (79) came to the wicket and in league with his Lancashire team mate, Tyldesley (112 not out), collared the bowling for 158 in 80 minutes, Jackson's declaration coming hard on the heels of Spooner's dismissal when the score was 261 for 6. Left 329 to win in less than three hours the Australians batted out time, finishing at 124 for 4.

Jackson was the first England captain to win a series against the Australians in England since 1896, and in so doing he had contrived to top both the English batting and bowling averages in the Tests. English cricket had been yearning for success against the colonial foe in England for many years, and now the plaudits deluged upon Jackson's head.

Stanley Jackson took it in his stride. He thanked Archie MacLaren for his help and support during the series, remarked upon how he had turned over the captaincy to his old school fellow whenever he put himself on to bowl.

Jackson captained Yorkshire against Middlesex at Bradford, his last Championship appearance of the season, in a match abandoned after lunch on the third day when Yorkshire, with all their wickets in hand required only 33 to clinch victory. It must have seemed rather tame in the wake of the Test Matches. He scored 17 and bowled himself lightly as Rhodes, Haigh and Hirst made merry in the wet at the expense of the Middlesex batsmen. Yorkshire marched to the Championship that year, although not without moments of discomfort. Against Essex at Leyton in August - in Jackson's absence - the Tykes were obliged to fight a long and desperate rearguard action to stave off an innings defeat. The normally effervescent Ernest Smith batted for an hour without scoring a run on the third evening to deny the home side victory.

At Scarborough at the beginning of September he played under Hawke's captaincy as the Tykes struggled home against the M.C.C. in a close match on a difficult pitch. The grand finale of the Scarborough Week was a match between C.I. Thornton's England XI under Jackson's captaincy against the Australians.

Jackson and Darling had now tossed seven times and the Yorkshireman had won every time. That summer the Australians had grown so used to hearing 'England bats' that they no longer waited to hear the result of the toss, they simply went out to field.

Darling's ill-luck had moved him to exasperation during the Tests, but now, in the midst of the seaside festivities his mood was lighter. So when Jackson strolled over to the Australian tent - in those days at Scarborough cricketers prepared for battle under canvas - on the morning of the match to toss up he was in for a surprise.

'Is Darling about?' He enquired.

'He'd like to see you inside,' the England captain was told.

Jackson marched in and found himself surrounded by Australians. Before him stood Joe Darling, decked out in wrestling attire. No doubt writing it off as some obscure Antipodean eccentricity, Jackson tried not to stare.

'Well, what about tossing?' he asked.

Darling grinned.

'Yes, but this is going to be quite a different toss from our previous efforts. You're too good for me at spinning a coin. We'll wrestle for it this time!'

Jackson contemplated the challenge for a moment. Darling's deep chest and powerful shoulders were better suited for grappling than his own, more linear build.

'Go on, Jacker. Have ago!' Said one and all of Darling's men.

Jackson was not to be swayed.

'In that case I think I'll nominate Georgie to toss for me,' he suggested, not wanting to seem unreasonable. George Hirst was a man constructed rather on the same lines as Darling, if anything, perhaps on a slightly taller, broader scale.

Jackson laughed and shook his head: 'No go? I think we'll toss outside.'

With which he left Joe Darling to don garments more appropriate to the occasion. As the Australian captain emerged in his whites the tourists prepared to take the field. Jackson tossed the coin. Darling called. And Stanley Jackson informed him that England would bat.

There had been heavy rain before the match, and water had seeped under the covers. The wicket was somewhat lively when play began. Throughout the day batting was never straightforward, Cotter in particular extracting unpredictable, and sometimes excessive bounce. He quickly sent back MacLaren and Spooner. The wickets of Tyldesley and Denton fell later that morning, and then Hirst's. It was 88 for 5; the situation demanded a captain's innings and Jackson responded to the challenge. He put down anchor in the middle order, batted slowly, cautiously to raise his fifty in about two hours. Thereafter he took on the bowlers. He was the last man out when the score had advanced to 282, his personal contribution being 123, including 13 fours. The next highest score in the innings was 24.

The Australians batted with great courage and skill in compiling a total of 393, Clem Hill scoring a peerless 181 at the heart of the innings. Jackson's team were left with four hours to bat on the last day to save the match.

Jackson was at the wicket with 31 to his credit when a storm broke over the ground in the late afternoon and caused the abandonment of the match.

It had been Stanley Jackson's season. He had scored 776 runs against the tourists at an average of 70.54, and many had been the times when he alone had carried the fight to the Australians. His Yorkshire grit and Harrow bravado had led England to a famous triumph. He had been a lucky captain, sometimes a very lucky captain, but England demands no more of its captains than that they be lucky.

Joe Darling set his sights on a farm in Tasmania. Stanley Jackson looked towards the twin heights of business and Unionist politics. For both 'cricketing twins' the last match of the Scarborough Festival of 1905 signalled the virtual end of their playing days.

For many the match was the end of the golden age, the end of the 'diamond decade' of English cricket. But it was not, the Great War was its true death knell and that was still far away in some unthinkable, unknowable future.

Not for another twenty years would English cricket experience the same uplifting joy as it had known under Jackson against Darling's Australians: not until the advent of Percy Chapman.

15 | Life after Cricket (1906-1926)

Stanley Jackson played his last first-class match in 1907, but to all intents and purposes his career in the game ended with his triumphs of 1905. He was at the height of his powers, and might yet have succeeded Lord Hawke in the Yorkshire captaincy had it not been for his other commitments. He made no pronouncement; he simply put his bat under his arm and walked off the big stage of English cricket.

However, in 1906 and 1907 he was prevailed upon to turn out in four matches. His first appearance in 1906 was as captain of the Gentlemen against the Players at Lord's in July in a contest celebrating the centenary of the first match played on Thomas Lord's original ground, at Dorset Square. The Kent fast bowler, Arthur Fielder, had the temerity to take all ten wickets in the amateurs' first innings: Jackson countered by batting in his most dogged fashion, scoring 40 in two-and-a-half hours. Lord Harris, watching from the Long Room, rubbed his hands in delight as Fielder's pace and swerve baffled Jackson's fellows and even kept the great man tied down. Two weeks later Jackson joined the Yorkshire XI that met Surrey at the Oval in Walter Lees' benefit match. He was undone by the pace of N.A. Knox in both innings, and his 3 wickets cost him 119 runs. In August he played in J.T. Tyldesley's benefit match against the old enemy at Old Trafford, scoring 31 and 6 as the Tykes ran out the victors by 107 runs.

Stanley Jackson's last first-class match was at

Headingley, fittingly against Lancashire. It was David Denton's benefit match and Jackson opened the batting with John Tunnicliffe. There were 22,810 people in the ground on that first day, and 20,358 on the second as the match unravelled and the Yorkshire openers went out to bat with 133 runs needed for victory. Jackson scored 35, hit up in his best style. By the time he departed to a running catch by R.H. Spooner off the fast left-arm bowling of Harry Dean, the first wicket was worth 58. The match went into a third day, Yorkshire winning by 9 wickets.

In June of that year Jackson had announced that he was unable, 'owing to pressure of business', either to captain England in the forthcoming Test Matches against the South Africans or to lead the England team in Australia that winter. Two years later, in 1909, the M.C.C. turned once more to him to lead England against the touring Australians, and once again he was moved to decline the invitation.

Jackson's absence from the England party sent to Australia in 1907 was one of many sparks that eventually kindled the fires of what has become known as cricket's 'first crisis'. This had been brewing for a long time, and in part at least, was the inevitable consequence of the world-wide spread and startling success of the game in the previous thirty years. Cricket had become an international sport, but its organisation remained if not parochial, then essentially national. M.C.C. had always acted as if it were judge and jury in its own court, and failed to recognise that the times were changing. The flashpoint of the crisis was an English proposal that England, Australia and South Africa should compete in a triangular competition in England in 1909, and that if the

Australian Board of Control felt themselves unable to support the proposal, then the Australian team should stay at home in 1909. The Australians not unreasonably took umbrage since such a tournament would inevitably effect both the economic and cricketing viability of the tour already planned for that season. South Africa was, after all, the junior Test country, and any accommodation which facilitated their touring England in 1909 ought to have been a matter for negotiation between all three countries, rather than the subject of a decree issued by the M.C.C., which the Australians felt was merely the mouthpiece of the sectarian interests of the English first-class counties.

The affair was the more vexed because the twin citadels of the Australian cricketing world, Melbourne and Sydney, were divided, and because M.C.C. took an interminable time to appreciate the fact. The problem was essentially one of communication, with neither M.C.C. nor the warring factions in Australia really understanding the problems of the other, while the South Africans looked on with incredulity and horror at the crisis, powerless to act for fear of being trapped between the two protagonists.

As the crisis fulminated in the summer of 1908 the situation cried out for an injection of common sense, tactfully administered. The circumstances called for a figure respected and trusted by all parties if the matter was to be amicably resolved. There were few suitable candidates. Lords Harris and Hawke ruled English cricket, but both were men too close to the heart of the M.C.C., W.G. Grace was a colossus, a legend in his own lifetime, but almost an outsider. Among the players, MacLaren in Australian eyes remained a heroic figure, but, like Fry, his continued involvement on the playing side undermined his impartiality.

It fell to Stanley Jackson to step into the breach and in July he wrote a famous letter to *The Times:*

> The resolution, as I read it, seems needlessly curt, not to say ungenerous, though I cannot believe it is intended to offend… The Australians have been coming over here regularly for thirty years, and have, I think, always played the game as it should be played to the advantage of cricket and cricketers here. They would in the ordinary course have received an invitation to send a team here next year… The triangular tournament…while received in a kindly spirit…aroused no great amount of enthusiasm…it was, indeed, quietly hinted that its adoption depended entirely on whether or not the Australians would be prepared to take part in the tournament.
>
> We now have Australia's reply. We know that the Australians do not see their way to taking part in such a contest this year… They may think the time inopportune. If they do there are many people in this country who will agree…
>
> But whatever the reasons which may have prompted the action of the Australians, the fact that they have found it necessary to declare themselves unable to take part in the proposed triangular contest is surely no sufficient cause for their being peremptorily told that they must either join in the tournament or stay at home.
>
> Though I hold no brief for the Australians, I do most earnestly plead for the harmony and good

feeling which should and must exist between us and them if international cricket is to flourish… There can be little doubt that a mistake has been made. Why should it not be acknowledged and the resolution withdrawn with no loss of dignity to anyone concerned?

    I sincerely hope that the counties will see their way to extend to the Australian team on the old lines and with no new conditions a cordial invitation to visit this country next year, and, if this is done, I feel certain that the welcome accorded them will be as hearty and generous as it has always been from all lovers of the game.

J.H. Carruthers, President of the New South Wales Cricket Association, warmly welcomed Jackson's remarks in a letter in the next day's *Times*. L.O.S. Poidevin, the Australian Board of Control's representative in London, indicated in another letter that Jackson's thoughts, if translated into practice by the M.C.C., would resolve the affair, and satisfy the honour of all concerned.

    Lord's moved swiftly, too swiftly in the circumstances, in a manner that implies that Jackson's letter and its consequences had been anticipated in high places before it was penned. M.C.C. asserted its voice above that of the counties and it was made known to the Australians that they would be welcomed with open arms in 1909, and the matter of the triangular tournament was deferred. The crisis was defused almost overnight. Stanley Jackson might have retired from playing cricket at the highest level, but he never retired from cricket itself. The game was never far from his heart.

In March 1909, speaking at a dinner in honour of J.J. Oddy, the Bradford MP, he spoke of the Tories' misfortunes in the recent General Election thus:

> At the last 'Test Match' the Conservatives struck a very bad wicket. Our opponents had most of the luck, but I believe we missed a good many chances. Perhaps, the people wanted to see the other side bat. The bowling of the other side was very good, but many are now more than ever convinced that some of the deliveries of our opponents were very unfair...

When the laughter had subsided somewhat he continued:

> The Conservatives are longing for a return match, and providing we have a fairly good wicket...we will win with a good deal to spare.

He spoke with assurance, and a particular natural credibility. Part of the magic was that he was always what he seemed to be. He was a man with little or no side to him, hardly an archetypal politician. He was his own man, too decent and too moral to engage in the brutal intrigues of party politics. In later life these were weaknesses that deprived him of the high office his father had held, but on a public stage his integrity and dignity were priceless assets.

In everything he did he enjoyed the tireless support of his wife. Their only child, christened Henry Stanley Lawies, was born on 15 November 1903. He too followed in his father's footsteps, to Harrow and Trinity College, but there his life and career took a different turning. Henry Jackson became a member of the Mineralogical Society, and rose to Major in the Grenadier Guards during the 1939-45 War.

Stanley Jackson continued to play cricket, albeit at a humbler level than in former years. He religiously turned out for the Old Harrovians against Harrow School. As time went by the runs ceased to flow from his bat, but now and then the blade would flash through the line of delivery and the ball would race away to the boundary to rekindle memories of 1905. In June 1914 he captained the Old Harrovians against the Old Etonians at Lord's, scoring a well-made 55.

Golf became his passion in those years after he retired from first-class cricket. Legend has it that he practised his swing in front of a mirror for a winter and more before he began to compete seriously. In no time at all he was whittling down his handicap, threatening the best golfers of his day. Golf then was not the high-profile international jamboree it is now; it was a private sort of sport, and Jackson's progress went largely unremarked. Contemporaries say he might have been Amateur Champion had he devoted more of his energies to his game. His athleticism and his tenacity on the golf course made him a formidable opponent. But for Jackson golf was never quite the same as cricket; it was more a form of relaxation, more an outlet from the pressures of business and politics that increasingly weighed him down as the years went by.

A perennial partner was Lord Hawke. Together they planned, plotted and charted the affairs of Yorkshire cricket over more than three decades. Often they were partners, although, as with cricket, Jackson's play tended to put his friend's in the shade. Hawke, in his *Recollections and Reminiscences* (1924), recalls a telling incident during a foursome at North Berwick whilst partnering Jackson:

> At the sixteenth hole I had put down a three-yard putt to make us dormy. I have no doubt I was deliberate in my aim, but I duly shoved the ball in the hole.
> Sidney Lane, one of our opponents, said:
> 'How the devil can we play golf when you take so long as that over a putt?'
> Jacker retorted:
> 'Martin, take ten minutes next time.'

Although Jackson only took up golf in earnest after 1905, his handicap was down to four in January 1906. He competed that winter for Yorkshire in the Cricketers' Golfing Society Tournament. In his first match against the Lancastrian E. Rowley at Ganton, he was beaten. The Yorkshire team of three, Ernest Smith and Tom Taylor completing the threesome, won through to the next round, to meet Northumberland. Jackson made up for his debut 'duck,' overcoming another 'four-handicapper, 'John Hansell as the Tykes proceeded on their way to the third round.

Jackson found golf every bit as challenging as cricket. In cricket the glittering prizes had come to him as if by fate. He had captained Harrow, Cambridge and England as if by right. But golf was different, golf was intensely personal;

man against the course and the elements - a man won or lost by dint of his own endeavour. There was always the luck of the bounce, nobody could legislate for that, but otherwise the thing that mattered was the quality of one's game. He could lose himself in golf, shut out everything else in a way that was quite out of the question in cricket.

Yet it was to cricket that he returned whenever the call came. Like Hawke he was a man who passionately believed that the counties should find and develop their own young players and that county cricket should be played by natives of the particular counties. Every year Jackson would be found at the pre-season Headingley nets coaching youngsters, conferring with the county coach (who in later years was the inimitable George Hirst). Successive generations of young Tykes testify to the influence of Jacker. In old age Jackson would demonstrate to youngsters with a furled umbrella the forward defensive stroke, the cut, glance, on and off-drives.

The family business, W.L. Jackson and Co., was sold in 1913 to two brothers called Laycock: William Lawies Jackson had realised that neither of his sons wished to take on the whole burden of the firm. Stanley Jackson held numerous directorships, and his future lay in Unionist politics. His father hardly disapproved of his choice of career and the family business slipped from his hands.

The Great War came soon afterwards. Stanley Jackson returned to the colours. He joined the Territorial Association of the West Riding of Yorkshire on 8 September 1914, reinstated in his previous rank of Captain. He was responsible for raising and commanding the 2/7th (Leeds Rifles) Battalion of the West Yorkshire Regiment.

Promoted to Lieutenant-Colonel he embarked the battalion for France on 8 January 1917. His command in the field was short-lived, sickness forcing him to retire from the front on 2 March 1917. To his chagrin he was never considered fit enough to return to the duties of commanding a front-line battalion.

In 1915 Jackson had been elected Member of Parliament for the Howdenshire Division of Yorkshire, a seat previously held by his father-in-law. Denied the opportunity to play his part in France, he soon earned a reputation for being a hard-working and loyal backbencher in the House of Commons.

In April 1917, William Lawies Jackson died. The baronetcy passed to his elder brother, but the mantle of

politics rested squarely on Stanley Jackson's shoulders. He buried himself in work, combining military with parliamentary responsibilities. He was hampered during this period by lingering ill-health and as late as August 1918, he was obliged to stand down at the last moment from leading his scratch side against Captain P.F. Warner's

XI at Lord's in aid of the Chevrons Club. Some 8,000 people turned up to watch the match, mostly to see the reappearance of the great Jacker. J.W.H.T. Douglas took his place, a man not perhaps blessed with Jackson's gifts, but every inch as much a fighter.

In Parliament he spoke often and on many subjects. His father had enjoyed the patronage of Lord Randolph Churchill, but Jackson was less fortunate. Nevertheless, he rose steadily in the Tory hierarchy, without ever threatening to reach the highest offices. After the war he was briefly Financial Secretary to the War Office, but that was the high point of his parliamentary career. He was a political journeyman, never a rising star in the Tory firmament, never really a threat to the mighty men at the heart of the party.

In 1923 he became Chairman of the party, an onerous post that a more acquisitive, less principled man might have used as a stepping-stone to greater things.

Jackson inherited the chairmanship in the wake of the Tories' disastrous showing in the General Election. He was popular within the party and well-suited to the diplomatic niceties of the job although some were more than a little surprised when he accepted the post, for it was generally understood (even if rarely discussed) that the chairman's role was often rather a nebulous one, requiring a certain sleight of hand. And besides, the affairs of Central Office were in a parlous state at the time and in need of drastic reform. Many wondered if Jackson had the stomach for cutting out the dead wood. He was Bonar Law's man, and Baldwin - an Old Harrovian contemporary - never forgave him for it.

If Jackson's integrity was his strength, it was also his Achilles' heel. His time as chairman, a period of nearly four years, was a time of fluctuating Tory fortunes, a time when it was feared that poverty and injustice might easily breed a British revolution along the lines of the Russian cataclysm. The horrors of the War had very nearly unhinged the nation and the spectre of Bolshevism seemed to lurk in every shadow. Stanley Jackson was not one of nature's born politicians, and he suffered for his naivety. He had triumphs, he had debacles. In cricket, his errors never seemed to rebound on him: in politics, his errors haunted him.

He was a leading member of the lobby that advised Baldwin to go to the country in 1923 on the issue of tariffs, advice that left lasting, damaging scars on the Party. Yet in 1923 a fall from grace must have seemed unlikely. For a long time he had been discussing with Winston Churchill the possibility of his former fag's return to the Tory fold. The two men had always been 'amicable foes' and friends of a kind, a fact that had amused many distinguished Parliamentarians and exasperated a minority of lesser mortals. Lloyd George took immense pleasure in chiding

Churchill about how he had always wanted to meet the man who had given him a sound beating at Harrow. Later Baldwin had given Jackson licence to persuade Churchill to cross to the Tory benches.

It was Jackson who asked Churchill what post he would accept in a Tory Government if he crossed the House. 'Ah, Jacker,' Churchill sighed, 'I'm afraid that the only job that I would want would be the one I shall never get.' Destiny had other plans, however, and Baldwin eventually asked him to be Chancellor of the Exchequer.

When Jackson heard the news that 'Winston has been offered the post of Chancellor, he thought, in his innocence, that Baldwin meant Chancellor of the Duchy of Lancaster: Jackson was never on the same wavelength as Baldwin, a potentially disastrous state of affairs. In the end it finished Jackson's political career. He probably never really understood how Baldwin manoeuvred him onto the boat to Bengal in 1927.

The affair of the 'Zinoviev Letter' brought home to Jackson the harsh realities of his position. His part in the sorry business was hardly honourable. Grigori Zinoviev was head of the Third International, the part of the Soviet Government dedicated to the exportation of the Bolshevik Revolution. In 1924 the British Secret Service got hold of a letter purporting to be written by Zinoviev inciting the British people to rise in rebellion. The Zinoviev Letter implicated the Labour Party and the Trades Union movement in a conspiracy to overthrow parliamentary democracy. The letter was made available to the Press in the throes of the General Election campaign of 1924, and, in the climate of anti-Soviet paranoia, assured the downfall of Ramsay Macdonald's Labour Government.

Even now the facts surrounding the affair are less than clear. However, what is known is that the Secret Service passed a copy of the Zinoviev Letter to Conservative Central Office, which then proceeded to place the document in the hands of selected Fleet Street editors, who then published the letter. Neither the Secret Service nor Conservative Central Office nor the editors who published it made any but the most cursory of enquiries as to the authenticity of the Zinoviev Letter. In the midst of the General Election the behaviour of those concerned in the affair amounts to nothing less than a conspiracy to pervert the electoral process; a direct assault on democracy.

Jackson's role in the affair was as a broker between the Secret Service and Fleet Street. It is unlikely he actually handled the letter, but he knew what it contained, and he actively assisted in passing it on. One suspects that he had his doubts about what was going on, and later, pangs of conscience, but the damage was done by then, Ramsay Macdonald's Government had been swept away and the Tories had inherited the kingdom: Baldwin became Prime Minister.

Jackson had been President of M.C.C. in 1921, following in the footsteps of Lord Hawke, who had held the post through the long years of the War. Afterwards, in the years of Tory upheaval in the mid-1920s he must have longed for the simplicity of those days when the only cloud on the horizon was the dominance of Warwick Armstrong's invincible Australians.

Jackson struggled long and hard to streamline the Conservative Party's organisation. He called in Sir Herbert Blain, an expert in business efficiency, who quickly became unpopular with sections of the party.

During Jackson's time as chairman, the party was forced to expend capital to meet day-to-day costs. The problem was that the party needed root and branch reform, and Jackson was not the man to do it. He held on until the end of 1926, but then, with Baldwin pressing for changes, he stood down.

It was the end of his career in politics.

16 | Life after Cricket (1927-1946)

Knighted for his services to King and Country, Jackson accepted the Governorship of Bengal. He left England in the spring of 1927, wearied by his travails at Central Office, but eager to return to the subcontinent he had last seen thirty years before. It had been in India that he had found himself, come of age as a man and as a cricketer and now he was going back.

The problems he faced in Government House in Calcutta were no less intractable that those which had beset him in Central Office: his journey no more than a voyage from the lions' den to the tigers' enclosure. Bengal was a hotbed of unrest, and Jackson's predecessor, Lytton, had introduced an ill-advised measure known as the 'Bengal Ordinance' in an attempt to forcibly pacify the region. Jackson found himself torn between his desire to implement the liberalising Montagu-Chelmsford reforms and the need to maintain the peace in Bengal.

Eventually, he despaired of the provincial legislature and dissolved it in April 1929, replacing it with a ministry more in tune with the financial and political realities of the administration of the Raj.

Jackson once said of his years in India: 'I have tried my best to keep the scales even.' Given the religious and social enmity of the warring factions in Bengal, it had always been a losing battle.

Indeed, just before his departure from Calcutta in 1932, a girl graduate attempted to assassinate him in the Senate hall of the university of which he was Chancellor.

Some sources suggest that Jackson arrived in India with little awareness of the problems he was going to face in Bengal. This is probably unfair to him; at the time he was installed in Government House in Calcutta the Indian Statutory Commission, a group of seven Members of Parliament under the chairmanship of Sir John Allsebrook Simon – later to be more generally known as the 'Simon Commission' – was due in India to report on the options for the constitutional reform of the Raj. For Indian nationalists and radicals this was like a red rag to a bull, particularly in Bengal which had seethed with unrest in the 1920s.

The arrival of the Simon Commission in India resulted in protests and riots, at one peaceful demonstration the prominent Punjabi author and nationalist politician, Lala Lajpat Rai was injured, and three weeks later died. It mattered not one jot that Jackson was considered, even by Indian opponents in Bengal as an honest broker doing his best to fairly keep the peace.

During his time in India it often seemed that every incarnation of nationalism was stirring, taking to the streets and becoming ever more embedded in the Raj. Like it or not Jackson was as embroiled as any man in what was an entrenched struggle with the Indian freedom movement. In 1930 Gandhi had initiated the Civil Disobedience Movement, the Indian National Congress had declared 'Purna Swaraj' – complete independence – and a young woman called Bina Das was becoming ever more radicalised.

Bina had been born in Krishnanagar four years after Jackson retired from first-class cricket on 24th August 1911. Her father, Beni Madhab Das, was a peripatetic headmaster of several schools (most likely based in Cuttack at that time of her birth), and her mother, Sarala Devi, was a social worker. As girl she had attended St John's Diocesan Girls' Higher Secondary School, and later, Bethune Collegiate School. It was while she was at this latter institution that she joined the *Chhatri Sangha* (Female Students' Association). Initially, influenced by the ideology of Mahatma Gandhi, she took to using the charkha (spinning wheel) and the path of non-violence. It was only after her older sister, Kalyani, had been arrested and imprisoned for distributing 'seditious' – that is, anti-British – pamphlets, that she eschewed non-violence. Still in her teens she was a volunteer at the Calcutta sessions of Indian National Congress, presided over by Motilal Nehru, and it is not beyond the bounds of possibility that her conversion to 'direct action' began after a meeting with Subhash Chandra Bose.

In any event in the years between 1928 and a fateful day in early February 1932, which was to propel her to national notoriety – fame came later – she changed from a non-violent headmaster's daughter into the nationalist revolutionary 'Agnikanya' – *woman of fire.*

During those years Stanley Jackson had been making the best of a bad job and he was probably looking forward to laying down his burden and going home by New Year 1932.

However, life in India was not all strife and woe. He was visited in Calcutta by Lord Hawke and would often seek the advice of his old friend 'Ranji', now the Jam Sahib of Nawanagar. At a dinner of the Calcutta Cricket Club (held at the Bengal Club in 1930) in honour of Hawke and his Yorkshire lieutenant, Jackson rose to speak, prefacing his speech with a few tongue-in-cheek words for his former skipper:

> I've got the first innings today, old man. You bossed me often enough in the past, but I'm boss here!

Jackson and Ranji invariably talked as much cricket as politics in those years. To Ranji, the Governor of Bengal was 'my first captain'. They reminisced about the old days, the way the game used to be played, and the way some men chose to play it in the modern era. During their playing days Jackson's bowling had claimed Ranji's wicket on just three occasions in first-class matches. Near the end of his tenure in India, Jackson put it to Ranji that he thought he had finally worked out a way of getting him out: 'I should bowl at your left elbow and place as many men as possible to leg,' he declared.

'Yes,' Ranji agreed, 'you would get me out. But it would not be cricket.'

Both men detested 'leg-theory'; neither had ever bowled it, nor sanctioned it in any side they had led. 'Bodyline', the most virulent form of leg-theory was anathema to the two old warriors.

While Bina Das had been studying for her English Degree – which on 6th February 1932 she had been due to receive at the very convocation that the Governor of Bengal was due to speak – she and a friend of her sister's, Kamala Dasgupta, had joined an organisation called *Yugantar*, acquired a revolver for the sum of 280 rupees, and received rudimentary training in the use of the weapon.

Thus, on that day she sat with her fellow students,

gowned and awaiting for the moment that Sir Stanley Jackson stepped up to the lectern.

Barely had the Governor of Bengal started to speak when Bina Das rose to her feet and opened fire from only yards away.

The Glasgow herald reported:

'The Governor, who was not injured, owed his escape to his own marvellous coolness and to the fact that the Vice-Chancellor of the University physically grappled with the assailant.'

In fact Jackson had ducked and his assailant's ineptitude – lack of practice with – or abysmal marksmanship, and the courage of the University Vice-Chancellor, Hasan Suhrawardy saved him.

However, before the gun was wrestled from Bina's grasp she had fired five shots.

Jackson was later to quip that it was 'the fastest duck' he had ever made; for him the ordeal was over but no so for his attacker.

Handled roughly by her interrogators Bina [pictured *right*] refused to co-operate with the police or to implicate any of her comrades in the plot.

Given the febrile background of a Raj under threat, and the supposed heavy-handedness of Imperial law and order in the sub-continent, one might have expected, and likely, so did she, to either die in prison, or sooner, at the end of a hangman's rope.

In the event she was tried at the Calcutta High Court and – surprisingly - no real effort was made to prevent her using the dock as a platform for her cause

> 'I can assure all that I could never have any personal grudge against any person or anything on earth; I have no sort of personal feelings against Sir Stanley Jackson, the man and Lady Jackson, the woman. But the Governor of Bengal represents the system of repression which has kept enslaved 300 millions of my countrymen and countrywomen...'

Stanley Jackson served out the rest of his time in Bengal; attempting to be fair, reasonable and to keep his sense of humour; Bina Das was sentenced to nine years of hard labour imprisonment (although she was released in 1939.

The former Governor went back to England, business, M.C.C. and Yorkshire, and during the Second World War occupied himself keeping the skeleton of the national game intact and acting as an emissary to Britain's friends and allies in the sub-continent, shuttling backwards and forwards several times on Sunderland and other flying boats on the long, wearying journeys from war-torn Europe to the heat and noise of India at the behest of his former fag at Harrow, Britain's great wartime leader, Winston Churchill.

Jackson was awarded the Order of Saint John and the order of the Star of India later in 1932; and Hasan

Suhrawardy, his saviour on the day in February was knighted for heroism.

Released from prison, by 1942 Bina Das campaigned for Gandhi's 'Quit India Movement', and imprisoned a further three years for her trouble; one of the heroines of Indian independence. Between 1946 and 1947 she was a member of the Bengal Provincial Legislative Assembly and, from 1947 to 1951, of the West Bengal Legislative Assembly, marrying Jatish Chandra Bhaumik, another activist from the *Jugantar* group in 1947. Pre-deceased by her husband she lived alone in Rishikesh, dying in relative anonymity at the age of seventy-five on 26th October, 1986.

In 1934, now back in England, Jackson was co-opted to the post of Chairman of the England Selection Committee for that year's Tests against the Australians. England were now without Jardine and Larwood. Jardine had brought an implacable purpose to the England side, and Larwood's devastating pace had struck terror into the stoutest of Australian hearts. Without them England were no longer the formidable side that had brought the Ashes back from the Antipodes, and there was very little Jackson and his hard-pressed fellow Selectors could do about it. The days when everything Stanley Jackson touched turned to gold, were long gone.

He took on the Yorkshire Presidency on Hawke's death in 1938, holding the club together through the long years of war - this despite several visits to India.

His final years were quiet, spent largely out of the public eye. The affairs of the Yorkshire club were never far from his thoughts, nor those of his old school and in 1942 he became Chairman of the Governors of Harrow.

He had always thought himself a lucky man, both in his life and in his cricket. Indeed he was away from home the night when the *Luftwaffe* demolished his London house during the Blitz, but not even Stanley Jackson's luck could last forever.

In 1946 he was knocked down by a taxi near Hyde Park, and although he strove manfully to regain his health, he never really recovered. His heart was failing and that winter he fell ill.

He died on 9th March 1947.

Epilogue

At the time of his death Stanley Jackson was the last surviving member of the England team that had contested the Lord's Test in 1896. Cricket had lost one of its great men. The tributes, both during and after his life, were plentiful.

Many years earlier, A.W. Pullin had said of Jackson, in his *History of Yorkshire County Cricket, 1903-1923* (1924):

> In the annals of cricket (he) will always appear on the front page. Next to the late Dr. W.G. Grace, Colonel Jackson represents the ideal of the national cricketer... He played the game as it came; any thought of building up a big score for his personal gratification was absolutely foreign to his idea of cricket and his conception of its ethics.

C.B. Fry once observed that the Jackson household seemed in awe of its master, commenting that if Jackson was the Almighty, then one was bound to say that he was infinitely 'stronger on the leg- side'.

A.A. Thomson in his *Cricket: The Great Captains* (1965) concluded, regretfully:

> Jackson, in personal character and in cricketing genius, was unique. There has been nobody like him since Lionel Palairet, Fry, Gilbert Jessop, Gregor McGregor, Plum Warner, R.E. Foster, Ranji, Frank Mitchell and A.O. Jones were among

Jackson's friends, foes and peers, but he alone had been picked for England while still up at university.

Any separate analysis of Jackson the man apart from Jackson the cricketer is worthless. The man and the cricketer were one, indivisible. Jackson's cricket was played in the same spirit in which he lived his life.

If, in the corridors of power, his morals went into the same mixing pot as his political allies, then it was hardly done in cold blood. No one is perfect, and the roads of commerce and politics are rarely as straight and narrow as those of sport. Sport is, after all, every man and woman's opportunity to compete on equal terms with whomsoever they please. One makes an essential choice in sport which is not always available in the outside world: whether or not to participate. Sport is to do with life, but it is not life and death, it is not everything, it is just a game. Natural gifts can, in sport, transcend barriers of class, colour and creed which in life are often impenetrable.

Stanley Jackson was in many ways the most remarkable of all the gentlemen cricketers of his age; and the mores of post-Great War politics should never be allowed to cloud our picture of Stanley Jackson the cricketer.

Sir Home Gordon attempted to pin down the secret of Jackson's success in *Background of Cricket* (1939):

> I saw him play his first match against Eton - as a fully-fledged cricketer; splendid bat, perfect field, excellent fastish bowler. All others I have heard or seen as cricketers developed, but 'Jacker' never could - there was no scope. He passed from

Harrow to Cambridge, thence to Yorkshire and so to England, merely adapting his own methods to the prevalent conditions but being distinctively the same player all through.

But perhaps no man was better positioned than Lord Hawke, to identify the strengths of his lieutenant's armour. In *Recollections and Reminiscences* (1924), he wrote of Jackson:

> What always impressed me was his tenacity of purpose. He never let a game go, and always had a grip of it even when at a disadvantage. It has often been said that England and not Yorkshire had the very best of his cricket, but at no time was his individuality anything but dominant, and any other cricketer would be proud indeed of his achievement for the shire of broad acres. Many cricketers display delightful skill, but personalities in the game are few and far between. 'Jacker' enters into the most select group.

C.W. Wright, who had toured India with Jackson in 1892, turned one day to Hawke and remarked, ruefully:

> 'Take Jacker; when he gets to the wicket he is already in up to the knees and the bowlers have to dig him out.'

Jackson was a batsman renowned for the ferocity of his hitting, yet he employed a lighter bat than most. By reputation his defence was sound, and given a crisis, his doggedness was legend. But he always strove to keep the scoreboard ticking over; he never let the ball rule his bat. That was the way cricket was supposed to be played and that was the way he played it.

If he lacked the imperious style of MacLaren, the grace of Spooner, the lithe genius of Ranji, the power of W.G. and the savagery of Jessop, then Jackson was the epitome of orthodoxy. His gift was that he was capable of playing all the orthodox strokes with much more power than his fellows. Whether batting, bowling or fielding, he did the simple things superbly.

There is a lesson in Jackson's game for any cricketer. He was an all-round cricketer. But more than this, he was an all-round batsman. He had all the strokes, could play aggressively or defensively going backwards or forwards, could score his runs all around the wicket and play whatever innings the situation demanded. It was the secret of his consistency in Test Matches, the bane of his foes.

He played his cricket as it came and was good enough to get away with it. W.G. Grace is alleged to have said; 'There is no such thing as a crisis in cricket, only the next ball.'

It might have been Stanley Jackson's motto.

Statistical Section

This is an updated, more complete statistical analysis of the great man's first-class career than that which appeared in the first edition of 'F.S. Jackson'; the product of work I carried out to produce the statistical monograph: 'F.S. JACKSON – His Record Innings-by-Innings' (Famous Cricketers Series: No. 89) for the Association of Cricket Statisticians which was published in 2005.

The following 'stats' pages are photocopied from my 'work sheets' for the same and correct a handful of incidental typos which – maddeningly – crept into the original.

BATTING AND FIELDING SEASON BY SEASON

	M	I	No	Runs	HS	Average	100	50	ct.
1890	14	26	2	385	68	16.04	-	2	6
1891	16	29	0	462	62	15.93	-	1	8
1892	19	31	0	751	84	24.22	-	6	15
1892/93	3	5	0	77	39	15.40	-	-	4
1893	21	36	4	1328	123	41.50	4	6	13
1894	24	39	3	1028	145	28.55	2	3	17
1895	22	40	3	1158	122	31.29	1	6	14
1896	27	42	3	1648	117	42.25	3	10	19
1897	29	46	3	1421	124	33.04	2	11	20
1898	29	43	5	1566	160	41.21	5	2	25
1899	28	44	3	1847	155	45.04	5	8	13
1900	1	2	0	176	134	88.00	1	-	1
1902	25	36	3	1089	128	33.00	2	8	17
1903	9	17	1	419	82*	26.18	-	2	3
1904	17	25	2	1037	158	45.08	2	6	8
1905	21	36	3	1359	144*	41.18	4	5	10
1906	3	6	0	109	40	18.16	-	-	2
1907	1	2	0	41	35	20.50	-	-	-
Total	309	505	35	15901	160	33.83	31	76	195

BATTING AND FIELDING SEASON BY SEASON FOR YORKSHIRE IN ALL MATCHES

	M	I	No	Runs	HS	Average	100	50	ct.
1890	3	4	-	78	68	19.50	-	1	2
1891	6	11	-	187	40	17.00	-	-	1
1892	8	12	-	270	76	22.50	-	2	2
1893	8	13	2	321	111*	29.18	1	1	7
1894	16	26	2	686	145	28.58	2	1	12
1895	18	33	3	870	81	29.00	-	5	11
1896	20	31	1	1211	117	40.36	3	6	14
1897	25	40	3	1300	124	35.13	2	10	16
1898	26	38	4	1442	160	42.41	5	2	23
1899	21	33	2	1468	155	47.35	4	7	11
1902	17	22	2	607	101*	30.35	1	5	10
1903	8	15	1	365	82*	26.07	-	2	3
1904	15	22	2	858	158	42.90	2	4	7
1905	13	22	-	600	111	27.27	1	2	9
1906	2	4	-	67	31	16.75	-	-	1
1907	1	2	-	41	35	20.50	-	-	-
Total	207	328	22	10371	160	33.89	21	48	129

BATTING AND FIELDING FOR EACH TEAM

	M	I	No	Runs	HS	Average	100	50	ct.
A.J. Webbe's Team	2	3	0	109	72	36.33	-	1	3
C.I. Thornton's England XI	1	1	0	3	3	3.00	-	-	1
C.I. Thornton's XI	8	14	1	693	123	53.30	2	4	6
Cambridge University	35	65	3	1649	123	26.60	2	8	22
England XI	1	1	0	57	57	57.00	-	1	1
ENGLAND	20	33	4	1415	144*	48.79	5	6	10
Gentlemen	20	36	3	1052	134	31.87	1	5	15
Gentlemen of England	1	2	0	18	10	9.00	-	-	-
I Zingari	2	4	0	60	34	15.00	-	-	3
Lord Hawke's Team	3	5	0	77	39	15.40	-	-	4
Lord Sheffield's XI	1	2	1	112	95*	112.00	-	1	-
M.C.C.	3	4	1	143	85	47.67	-	2	-
North	3	4	0	88	36	22.00	-	-	1
North of England XI	1	2	0	13	13	6.50	-	-	-
Rest of England	1	1	0	41	41	41.00	-	-	-
Yorkshire (Championship)	178	283	17	8956	160	33.66	18	40	110
Yorkshire (Other matches)	29	45	5	1415	133	35.37	3	8	19
	309	505	35	15901	160	33.83	31	76	195

BATTING AND FIELDING ON EACH GROUND

	M	I	No	Runs	HS	Average	100	50	ct.
Allahabad	1	1	0	34	34	34.00	-	-	-
Bath	2	3	0	146	91	48.67	-	1	3
Blackheath	1	1	0	2	2	2.00	-	-	-
Bombay	2	4	0	43	39	10.75	-	-	4
Bradford	25	38	3	1370	158	39.14	5	3	15
Bramall Lane	24	43	4	1568	160	40.21	4	5	14
Bristol	6	8	1	276	76	39.43	-	3	4
Canterbury	3	5	1	81	35	20.25	-	-	3
Cheltenham	1	1	0	41	41	41.00	-	-	-
Chesterfield	1	1	0	14	14	14.00	-	-	-
Derby	3	4	0	74	51	18.50	-	1	5
Dewsbury	7	12	2	366	82	36.60	-	3	7
Edgbaston	4	5	0	225	117	45.00	1	1	3
Fenner's	28	50	4	1599	133	34.76	4	7	20
Halifax	1	1	0	24	24	24.00	-	-	-
Harrogate	2	4	0	73	39	18.25	-	-	4
Hastings	1	2	1	83	45*	83.00	-	-	-
Headingley	29	49	2	1310	145	27.87	2	6	14
Hove	11	18	1	695	131	40.88	2	3	7
Huddersfield	9	13	0	222	68	17.08	-	2	5
Hull	4	7	0	161	84	23.00	-	1	2
Kennington Oval	23	37	1	1177	118	32.69	2	7	11
Leicester	2	2	0	224	147	112.00	1	1	3

	M	I	No	Runs	HS	Average	100	50	ct.
Leyton	4	7	2	268	101*	53.60	1	1	2
Lord's	42	72	5	2090	133	31.19	1	13	16
Maidstone	2	4	0	62	38	15.50	-	-	1
Old Trafford	16	26	1	925	128	37.00	2	4	5
Scarborough	31	51	4	1898	139	40.38	5	9	28
Sheffield Park	1	2	1	112	95*	112.00	-	1	-
Southampton	3	4	0	106	55	26.50	-	1	6
Taunton	7	9	1	274	124	34.25	1	1	5
The Parks	1	1	0	0	0	-	-	-	2
Tonbridge	2	4	0	46	33	11.50	-	-	-
Trent Bridge	10	16	1	312	82*	20.80	-	2	6
	309	505	35	15901	160	33.83	31	76	195

BATTING AND FIELDING AGAINST EACH OPPONENT

	M	I	No	Runs	HS	Average	100	50	ct.
A.J. Webbe's Team	2	4	1	44	21	14.67			-
All India	1	1	0	34	34	34.00	-	-	-
An England XI	1	2	0	17	9	8.50	-	-	1
AUSTRALIA	20	33	4	1415	144*	48.79	5	6	10
Australians	16	27	3	981	123	40.88	1	7	6
C.I. Thornton's England XI	1	2	0	67	36	33.50	-	-	2
C.I. Thornton's XI	5	10	0	388	101	38.80	1	3	4
Cambridge University	8	13	1	616	133	51.33	2	3	6
Derbyshire	7	9	0	343	111	38.11	1	2	9
Essex	9	14	2	458	101*	38.17	1	2	7
Gentlemen of England	4	8	1	138	43	19.71	-	-	5
Gloucestershire	16	23	3	797	160	39.85	1	5	11
H.T. Hewitt's Team	1	2	0	13	10	6.50	-	-	2
Hampshire	6	9	1	253	73	31.63	-	3	6
Kent	16	27	1	510	81	19.62	-	2	9
Lancashire	23	39	1	1122	134*	29.53	1	4	4
Leicestershire	4	4	0	274	147	68.50	1	1	3
M.C.C.	22	34	3	1074	111*	34.65	2	6	15
Middlesex	22	38	1	1346	155	36.38	4	6	12
Nottinghamshire	16	27	2	793	145	31.72	2	3	10
Oxford University	6	11	1	207	57	20.70	-	1	4
Parsis	2	4	0	43	39	10.75	-	-	4
Philadelphians	1	1	0	4	4	4.00	-	-	0

	M	I	No	Runs	HS	Average	100	50	ct.
Players	20	36	3	1052	134	31.87	1	5	15
Rest of England	1	1	0	57	57	57.00	-	1	0
Somerset	17	24	1	833	139	36.22	2	3	16
South Africans	2	2	0	46	38	23.00	-	-	-
South of England	4	6	0	146	38	24.33	-	-	3
Surrey	25	42	1	1358	158	33.12	2	9	10
Sussex	19	33	4	1095	131	37.76	3	3	11
Warwickshire	8	12	0	332	117	27.67	1	1	6
Yorkshire	4	7	1	45	23	7.50	-	-	4
	309	505	35	15901	160	33.83	31	76	195

BATTING AND IELDING SEASON BY SEASON IN THE COUNTY CHAMPIONSHIP FOR YORKSHIRE

	M	I	No	Runs	HS	Average	100	50	ct.
1890	2	3	0	10	8	3.33	-	-	2
1891	6	11	0	187	40	17.00	-	-	1
1892	7	10	0	264	76	26.40	-	2	1
1893	6	9	1	152	59	19.00	-	1	4
1894	15	25	2	659	145	28.65	2	1	9
1895	17	31	3	853	81	30.46	-	5	10
1896	16	25	1	1030	117	42.91	3	5	13
1897	22	35	2	1089	124	33.00	2	7	14
1898	23	32	3	1326	160	45.72	5	2	21
1899	16	25	0	1149	155	45.96	2	7	10
1902	15	19	2	544	101*	32.00	1	4	8
1903	7	14	1	311	82*	23.92	-	1	3
1904	12	19	2	741	158	43.58	2	3	6
1905	11	18	0	530	111	29.44	1	2	7
1906	2	4	0	67	31	16.75	-	-	1
1907	1	2	0	41	35	20.50	-	-	-
Total	178	282	17	8953	160		18	40	110

BATTING AND FIELDING ON EACH GROUND IN THE COUNTY CHAMPIONSHIP FOR YORKSHIRE

	M	I	No	Runs	HS	Average	100	50	ct.
Bath	2	3	-	146	91	48.66	-	1	3
Blackheath	1	1	-	2	2	2.00	-	-	-
Bradford	24	36	3	1303	158	39.48	5	3	15
Bramall Lane	20	37	3	1464	160	43.05	4	5	12
Bristol	6	8	1	276	76	39.42	-	3	4
Canterbury	3	5	1	81	35	20.25	-	-	3
Cheltenham	1	1	-	41	41	41.00	-	-	-
Chesterfield	1	1	-	14	14	14.00	-	-	-
Derby	3	4	-	74	51	18.50	-	1	5
Dewsbury	7	12	2	366	82	36.60	-	3	7
Edgbaston	3	4	-	172	117	43.00	1	-	2
Halifax	1	1	-	24	24	24.00	-	-	-
Harrogate	2	4	-	73	39	18.25	-	-	4
Hastings	1	2	1	83	45*	83.00	-	-	-
Headingley	24	41	1	1101	145	27.52	1	6	12
Hove	7	11	1	498	131	49.80	2	2	5
Huddersfield	9	13	-	222	68	17.07	-	2	5
Hull	3	6	-	153	84	25.50	-	1	2
Kennington Oval	11	17	1	489	87	30.56	-	3	4
Leicester	2	2	-	224	147	112.00	1	1	3
Leyton	4	7	2	268	101*	53.60	1	1	2
Lord's	9	16	-	451	133	28.18	1	1	2

	M	I	No	Runs	HS	Average	100	50	ct.
Maidstone	2	4	-	62	38	15.50	-	-	1
Old Trafford	12	19	-	600	82	31.57	-	4	3
Scarborough	1	1	-	139	139	139.00	1	-	-
Southampton	3	4	-	106	55	26.50	-	1	6
Taunton	7	9	1	274	124	34.25	1	1	5
Tonbridge	2	4	-	46	33	11.50	-	-	-
Trent Bridge	7	10	-	204	59	20.40	-	1	5
	178	283	17	8956	160	33.66	18	40	110

BATTING AND FIELDING AGAINST EACH OPPONENT IN THE COUNTY CHAMPIONSHIP FOR YORKSHIRE

	M	I	No	Runs	HS	Average	100	50	ct.
Derbyshire	7	9	-	343	111	38.11	1	2	9
Essex	9	14	2	458	101*	38.16	1	2	7
Gloucestershire	16	23	3	797	160	39.85	1	5	11
Hampshire	6	9	1	253	73	31.62	-	3	6
Kent	16	27	1	510	81	19.61	-	2	9
Lancashire	23	39	1	1122	134*	29.52	1	4	4
Leicestershire	4	4	-	274	147	68.50	1	1	3
Middlesex	22	38	1	1346	155	36.37	4	6	12
Nottinghamshire	15	25	2	775	145	33.69	2	3	10
Somerset	17	24	1	833	139	36.21	2	3	16
Surrey	20	33	1	1015	158	31.71	1	6	8
Sussex	15	26	4	898	131	40.81	3	2	9
Warwickshire	8	12	-	332	117	27.66	1	1	6
Total	178	283	17	8956	160	33.66	18	40	110

BATTING AND FIELDING
IN TEST MATCHES AGAINST AUSTRALIA
SEASON BY SEASON

	M	I	No	Runs	HS	Average	100	50	ct.
1893	2	3	0	199	103	66.33	1	1	2
1896	3	5	0	110	45	22.00	0	0	4
1899	5	8	1	303	118	43.38	1	1	0
1902	5	8	1	311	128	44.42	1	2	3
1905	5	9	2	492	144*	70.28	2	2	1
	20	33	4	1415	144*	48.79	5	6	10

BATTING AND FIELDING
IN TEST MATCHES AGAINST AUSTRALIA
ON EACH GROUND

	M	I	No	Runs	HS	Average	100	50	ct.
Bramall Lane	1	2	-	17	14	8.50	-	-	
Edgbaston	1	1	-	53	53	53.00	-	1	
Headingley	2	3	1	170	144*	85.00	1	-	
Kennington Oval	5	8	-	426	118	53.25	2	1	
Lord's	5	8	1	334	91	47.71	-	3	
Old Trafford	4	7	1	325	128	54.16	2	-	
Trent Bridge	2	4	1	90	82*	30.00	-	1	
	20	33	4	1415	144*	48.79	5	6	

SUCCESSFUL BOWLERS

The following bowlers dismissed Jackson on 5 or more occasions:

26	J.T. Hearne
11	W. Attewell
10	H. Trumble
10	J.T. Rawlin
10	T. Richardson
10	W.H. Lockwood
9	G.L. Jessop
9	J. Briggs
9	W.R. Cuttell
8	F. Martin
7	A. Hearne
7	A.W. Mold
7	E. Jones
7	L.C. Braund
7	W. Mead
6	A.E. Trott
6	E.J. Tyler
6	R. Peel
5	A.E. Relf
5	F.W. Tate
5	H.I. Young
5	J.J. Ferris
5	W. Brockwell
5	W.A. Humphreys
5	W.P. Howell

SUCCESSFUL FIELDERS

The following fielders caught or stumped Jackson on four or more occasions:

F.H. Huish 5
H. Trumble 5
H. Wood 5
W.R. Cuttell 5
A.F.A. Lilley 4
G. MacGregor 4
H.R. Butt 4
J.H. Board 4

MODES OF DISMISSAL AS A BATSMAN

Jackson was dismissed 470 times in the following fashion:

Bowled	175 (37.23%)
Caught In the outfield: 179 (38.08%) C&B: 26 (5.53%) Caught behind: 47 (10%)	252 (53.61%)
Stumped	9 (1.91%)
LBW	11 (2.34%)
Run Out	23 (4.89%)

BOWLING SEASON BY SEASON

	5-ball overs	6-ball overs	Mdns	Runs	W.	Average	Best bowling	5WI	10 WM
1890	295.3	-	110	643	37	17.37	7-53	2	1
1891	427.3	-	128	914	45	20.31	6-53	4	1
1892	625.2	-	197	1495	80	18.68	6-37	4	-
1892/93	87	-	41	133	4	33.25	1-15	-	-
1893	538.4	-	186	1172	57	20.56	8-54	4	-
1894	417	-	138	814	55	14.80	7-41	3	1
1895	600.1	-	204	1204	67	17.97	7-63	4	1
1896	560	-	195	1129	48	23.52	4-30	-	-
1897	698.4	-	209	1628	75	21.70	7-78	4	2
1898	904	-	362	1630	104	15.67	7-42	7	-
1899	630.4	-	217	1372	45	30.48	6-51	2	-
1900	-	4	1	18	-	-	-	-	-
1902	-	426.3	109	1067	58	18.39	6-29	4	-
1903	-	295.1	74	698	32	21.81	7-61	2	-
1904	-	359.5	93	909	33	27.54	6-91	2	-
1905	-	291.1	71	756	31	24.38	5-52	1	-
1906	-	48	6	161	3	53.66	3-98	-	-
1907	-	7	2	24	-	-	-	-	-
Total	5785.1	1431.4	2343	15767	774	20.37	8-54	42	6

BOWLING SEASON BY SEASON FOR YORKSHIRE IN ALL MATCHES

	5-ball overs	6-ball overs	Mdns	Runs	W.	Average	Best bowling	5WI	10 WM
1890	33	-	13	78	7	11.14	3-21	-	-
1891	108	-	28	245	12	20.41	3-33	-	-
1892	245	-	88	548	19	28.84	5-20	1	-
1893	124.1	-	37	296	18	16.44	5-42	1	-
1894	198.4	-	68	371	27	13.74	5-37	1	-
1895	451.1	-	159	821	58	14.15	7-63	4	1
1896	466.4	-	163	929	44	21.11	4-30	-	-
1897	600	-	184	1384	66	20.97	7-78	4	1
1898	783.1	-	314	1407	91	15.46	7-42	5	1
1899	476.1	-	161	1018	39	26.10	6-51	2	-
1902	-	279.2	78	607	47	12.91	6-29	4	-
1903	-	262.1	66	615	31	19.83	7-61	2	-
1904	-	299	77	764	28	27.28	6-91	1	-
1905	-	180.2	50	437	16	27.31	4-15	-	-
1906	-	44	6	146	3	48.66	3-98	-	-
1907	-	7	2	24	-	-	-	-	-
Total	3486.2	1071.5	1494	9690	506	19.15	7-61	25	3

BOWLING FOR EACH TEAM

	5-ball overs	6-ball overs	Mdns	Runs	W.	Average	Best bowling	5WI	10 WM
A.J. Webbe's Team	60.2	-	19	138	8	17.25	3-33	-	-
C.I. Thornton's England XI	31	-	19	40	6	6.66	5-27	1	-
C.I. Thornton's XI	90	20	29	275	9	30.55	3-52	-	-
Cambridge University	1241.1	-	421	2713	153	17.73	8-54	12	2
England XI	5	-	1	15	-	-	-	-	-
ENGLAND	162.3	129	77	799	24	33.29	5-52	1	-
Gentlemen	434	189.5	175	1483	50	29.66	7-41	3	1
Gentlemen of England	34	-	14	57	-	-	-	-	-
I Zingari	60	-	22	174	2	87.00	2-96	-	-
Lord Hawke's Team	87	-	41	133	4	33.25	1-15	-	-
Lord Sheffield's XI	22	-	6	49	1	49.00	1-40	-	-
M.C.C.	25.3	-	6	45	3	15.00	3-29	-	-
North	46	-	12	109	6	18.17	3-52	-	-
North of England XI	-	-	-	-	-	-	-	-	-
Rest of England	-	21	7	47	2	19.15	1-6	-	-
Yorkshire (Championship)	3094	890.5	1329	8311	431	19.28	7-42	20	3
Yorkshire (Other matches)	392.2	181	165	1379	75	18.39	6-24	5	-
	5785.1	1431.4	2343	15767	774	20.37	8-54	42	6

BOWLING ON EACH GROUND

	5-ball overs	6-ball overs	Mdns	Runs	W.	Average	Best bowling	SWI	10 WM
Allahabad	51	-	27	61	2	30.50	1-25	-	-
Bath	52.3	-	18	102	9	11.33	4-24	-	-
Blackheath	4	-	2	2	-	-	-	-	-
Bombay	36	-	14	72	2	36.00	1-15	-	-
Bradford	385.2	175.3	204	1046	47	22.26	6-30	1	-
Bramall Lane	323.1	160.2	143	1084	58	18.69	6-29	3	-
Bristol	94.2	-	33	179	9	19.89	4-23	-	-
Canterbury	118	-	40	246	24	10.25	7-63	3	2
Cheltenham	-	2	-	14	-	-	-	-	-
Chesterfield	65	-	34	78	7	11.14	4-52	-	-
Derby	70	11	25	167	1	167.00	1-23	-	-
Dewsbury	140.1	37	65	301	19	15.84	5-32	1	-
Edgbaston	111.3	4	44	220	6	36.67	2-34	-	-
Fenner's	868	-	299	1922	122	15.75	8-54	11	2
Halifax	-	-	-	-	-	-	-	-	-
Harrogate	82	-	35	167	8	20.88	5-73	1	-
Hastings	32	-	8	67	4	16.75	3-44	-	-
Headingley	349.3	178	188	1035	72	14.38	7-42	5	-
Hove	344	-	101	881	29	30.38	5-25	2	-
Huddersfield	88.1	2	22	270	16	16.88	4-38	-	-
Hull	-	100.1	32	230	12	19.17	5-53	1	-
Kennington Oval	365.1	90.2	105	1205	38	31.71	5-39	1	-
Leicester	65.3	-	17	130	14	9.29	5-20	1	-

	5-ball overs	6-ball overs	Mdns	Runs	W.	Average	Best bowling	5WI	10 WM
Leyton	61.3	1	23	107	7	15.29	5-46	1	-
Lord's	866.2	236.1	367	2399	102	23.52	7-41	3	1
Maidstone	45.4	-	14	101	5	20.20	3-49	-	-
Old Trafford	240.1	145	125	874	39	22.41	7-61	2	-
Scarborough	432	195	174	1506	66	22.82	6-24	2	-
Sheffield Park	22	-	6	49	1	49.00	1-40	--	-
Southampton	77.4	-	29	130	18	7.22	6-19	2	1
Taunton	73	40.2	32	307	8	38.38	3-44	-	-
The Parks	26	-	8	64	4	16.00	3-33	-	-
Tonbridge	23	-	7	52	-	-	-	-	-
Trent Bridge	271.2	53.5	102	699	25	27.96	5-42	2	-
	5785.1	1431.4	2343	15767	774	1431.4	343103	42	6

BOWLING AGAINST EACH OPPONENT

	5-ball overs	6-ball overs	Mdns	Runs	W.	Average	Best bowling	5WI	10 WM
A.J. Webbe's Team	51	-	11	124	6	20.67	4-75	-	-
All India	51	-	27	61	2	30.50	1-25	-	-
And England XI	24.3	-	11	44	6	7.33	6-24	1	-
AUSTRALIA	162.3	129	77	799	24	33.29	5-52	1	-
Australians	187	57	72	531	25	21.24	5-12	1	-
C.I. Thornton's XI	142.2	-	48	308	15	20.53	6-53	1	-
Cambridge University	168.3	-	55	425	22	19.32	6-51	2	-
Derbyshire	191.3	11	85	350	12	29.17	4-52	-	-
Essex	163.3	41	71	431	18	23.94	5-46	1	-
Gentlemen of England	133	-	48	359	14	25.64	8-54	1	-
Gloucestershire	260.1	20	105	531	33	16.09	5-73	1	-
H.T. Hewitt's Team	33.4	-	8	106	7	15.14	4-87	-	-
Hampshire	81.4	-	29	148	18	8.22	6-19	2	1
Kent	344.4	35.1	132	737	55	13.40	7-63	5	2
Lancashire	341.3	210.3	184	1206	69	17.48	7-61	3	-
Leicestershire	88.3	2	32	171	16	10.69	5-20	1	-
M.C.C.	424.2	89	159	1185	64	18.52	6-37	2	-
Middlesex	243.3	156.2	121	879	44	19.98	7-42	1	-
Nottinghamshire	455	44	169	976	40	24.40	5-37	3	-
Oxford University	206.3	-	75	384	21	18.29	4-71	-	-
Parsis	36	-	14	72	2	36.00	1-15	-	-
Philadelphians	19	-	8	35	-	-	-	-	-

	5-ball overs	6-ball overs	Mdns	Runs	W.	Average	Best bowling	5WI	10 WM
Players	434	189.5	175	1483	50	29.66	7-41	3	1
Rest of England	-	15	3	40	2	20.00	2-40	-	-
Somerset	257.3	102.5	113	824	50	16.48	6-29	2	-
South	46	-	12	109	6	18.17	3-52	-	-
South Africans	-	61	19	117	4	29.25	1-8	-	-
South of England	44	-	9	129	5	25.80	3-88	-	-
Surrey	452.3	109.5	165	1237	56	22.09	5-39	3	-
Sussex	401	107	142	1282	38	33.74	5-25	2	-
Warwickshire	156.3	51.1	83	366	17	21.53	5-53	1	-
Yorkshire	182.3	-	81	318	33	9.64	7-53	5	2
	5785.1	1431.4	2343	15767	774	20.37	8-54	42	6

BOWLING SEASON BY SEASON IN THE COUNTY CHAMPIONSHIP FOR YORKSHIRE

	5-ball overs	6-ball overs	Mdns	Runs	W.	Average	Best bowling	5WI	10 WM
1890	12	-	1	50	2	25.00	2-50	-	-
1891	108	-	28	245	12	20.41	3-33	-	-
1892	234	-	86	511	18	28.38	5-20	1	-
1893	77.1	-	28	160	13	12.30	5-42	1	-
1894	180.2	-	64	336	25	13.44	5-37	1	-
1895	426.3	-	148	777	52	14.94	7-63	3	1
1896	392.4	-	140	778	37	21.02	4-30	-	-
1897	550.3	-	170	1270	62	20.48	7-78	4	2
1898	697.3	-	287	1217	80	15.21	7-42	4	-
1899	414.4	-	143	844	30	28.13	5-98	1	-
1902	-	244.2	72	525	36	14.58	6-29	3	-
1903	-	241.1	56	564	28	20.14	7-61	2	-
1904	-	200	51	529	19	27.84	6-91	1	-
1905	-	154.2	47	335	14	23.92	4-15	-	-
1906	-	44	6	146	3	48.66	3-98	-	-
1907	-	7	2	24	-	-	-	-	-
Total	3094	890.5	1329	8311	431	19.27	7-42	21	3

BOWLING ON EACH GROUND IN THE COUNTY CHAMPIONSHIP FOR YORKSHIRE

	5-ball overs	6-ball overs	Mdns	Runs	W.	Average	Best bowling	5WI	10 WM
Bath	52.3	-	18	102	9	11.33	4-24	-	-
Blackheath	4	-	2	2	-	-	-	-	
Bradford	358.2	175.3	195	1000	45	22.22	6-30	1	-
Bramall Lane	304.1	121.1	132	904	53	17.05	6-29	3	-
Bristol	94.2	-	33	179	9	19.88	4-23	-	-
Canterbury	118	-	40	246	24	10.25	7-63	3	2
Cheltenham	-	2	-	14	-	-	-	-	-
Chesterfield	65	-	34	78	7	13.14	4-52	-	-
Derby	70	11	25	167	1	167.00	1-23	-	-
Dewsbury	140.1	37	65	301	19	15.84	5-32	1	-
Edgbaston	111.3	-	42	213	6	35.50	2-34	-	-
Halifax	-	-	-	-	-	-	-	-	-
Harrogate	82	-	35	167	8	20.87	5-73	1	-
Hastings	32	-	8	67	4	16.75	3-44	-	-
Headingley	315.3	146	170	904	59	15.32	7-42	4	-
Hove	160.4	-	51	414	10	41.40	3-28	-	-
Huddersfield	88.1	2	22	270	16	16.87	4-38	-	-
Hull	-	68.1	22	168	10	16.80	5-53	1	-
Kennington Oval	185.2	57.2	58	594	19	31.26	4-101	-	-
Leicester	65.3	-	17	130	14	9.28	5-20	1	-
Leyton	61.3	1	23	107	7	15.28	5-46	1	-
Lord's	124.4	73.2	61	435	23	18.91	4-53	-	-

	5-ball overs	6-ball overs	Mdns	Runs	W.	Average	Best bowling	5WI	10 WM
Maidstone	45.4	-	14	101	5	20.20	3-49	-	-
Old Trafford	202.3	122	110	691	36	19.19	7-61	2	-
Scarborough	37	-	12	68	4	17.00	3-47	-	-
Southampton	77.4	-	29	130	18	7.22	6-19	2	1
Taunton	73	40.2	32	307	8	38.37	3-44	-	-
Tonbridge	23	-	7	52	-	-	-	-	-
Trent Bridge	200.2	34	72	500	17	29.41	5-42	1	-
	3094	890.5	1329	8311	431	19.28	7-42	21	3

BOWLING AGAINST EACH OPPONENT IN THE COUNTY CHAMPIONSHIP FOR YORKSHIRE

	5-ball overs	6-ball overs	Mdns	Runs	W.	Average	Best bowling	5WI	10 WM
Derbyshire	191.3	11	85	350	12	29.16	4-52	-	-
Essex	163.3	41	71	431	18	23.94	5-46	1	-
Gloucestershire	260.1	20	105	531	33	16.09	5-73	1	-
Hampshire	81.4	-	29	148	18	8.22	6-19	2	1
Kent	344.4	35.1	132	737	55	13.40	7-63	5	2
Lancashire	341.3	210.3	184	1206	69	17.47	7-61	3	-
Leicestershire	88.3	2	32	171	16	10.68	5-20	1	-
Middlesex	243.3	156.2	121	879	44	19.97	7-42	1	-
Nottinghamshire	421	44	155	919	40	22.97	5-37	3	-
Somerset	257.3	102.5	113	824	50	16.48	6-29	2	-
Surrey	325.1	109.5	127	934	40	23.35	5-98	1	-
Sussex	217.4	107	92	815	19	42.89	3-28	-	-
Warwickshire	156.3	51.1	83	366	17	21.52	5-53	1	-
	3094	890.5	1246	7945	414	19.27	7-42	21	3

BOWLING IN TEST MATCHES
AGAINST AUSTRALIA ON EACH GROUND

	5-ball overs	6-ball overs	Mdns	Runs	W.	Average	Best bowling	5WI	10 WM
Bramall Lane	-	22.1	3	71	4	17.75	3-60	-	-
Edgbaston	-	4	2	7	-	-	-	-	-
Headingley	16	12	9	51	2	25.50	1-10	-	-
Kennington Oval	38	33	20	226	3	75.33	2-66	-	-
Lord's	34	15	12	119	4	29.75	4-50	-	-
Old Trafford	37.3	23	15	183	3	61.00	2-26	-	-
Trent Bridge	37	19.5	16	142	8	17.75	5-52	1	-
	162.3	120	77	799	24	33.29	5-52	1	-

BOWLING IN TEST MATCHES
AGAINST AUSTRALIA SEASON BY SEASON

	5-ball overs	6-ball overs	Mdns	Runs	W.	Average	Best bowling	5WI	10 WM
1893	16	-	4	43	-	-	-	-	-
1896	27	-	11	62	-	-	-	-	-
1899	119.3	-	42	284	5	56.80	3-57	-	-
1902	-	61.1	12	209	6	34.83	3-60	-	-
1905	-	67.5	8	201	13	15.46	5-52	1	-
	162.3	129	77	799	24	33.29	5-52	1	-

BATSMEN DISMISSED

The following batsmen were dismissed by Jackson on 6 or more occasions:

12 W.H. Lockwood
10 C.W. Wright
10 W. Storer
 9 L.C.H. Palairet
 9 W. Gunn
 8 A. Hearne
 8 A. Ward
 8 W.L. Murdoch
 7 A.C. MacLaren
 7 A.J. Webbe
 7 J.T. Tyldesley
 7 W. Attewell
 7 W. Brockwell
 7 W. Mead
 7 W.G. Grace (sen.)
 6 C. Hill
 6 C.B. Fry
 6 G.R. Baker
 6 J. Briggs
 6 J.A. Dixon
 6 J.R. Mason
 6 J.T. Brown
 6 J.T. Hearne
 6 J.T. Rawlin
 6 M.A. Noble
 6 V.T. Trumper
 6 W. Flowers
 5 F. Marchant

SUCCESSFUL FIELDERS FOR JACKSON

The following fielders caught or stumped batsmen off Jackson's bowling at least 6 times

54	D. Hunter (including 8 st.)
40	J. Tunnicliffe
23	E. Wainwright
19	G.H. Hirst
16	D. Denton
12	G. MacGregor
12	E. Smith
10	J.T. Brown
10	F.W. Milligan
10	C.M. Wells
9	Lord Hawke
9	L.H. Gay
9	E.C. Streatfield
8	R. Peel
7	S. Haigh
8	A.L. Bairstow (including 1 st.)
6	W. Rhodes
6	D.L.A. Jephson

MODES OF DISMISSAL AS A BOWLER

Jackson's 774 wickets were taken in the following fashion:

Bowled	321 (41.47%)

Caught
  In the outfield: 288 (37.20%)
  C&B: 39 (5.03%)
  At the wicket: 86 (11.11%)
	413 (53.35%)

Stumped	10 (1.29%)
LBW	30 (3.87%)

Miscellaneous Statistics

1. Stanley Jackson bowled in 289 of his 309 first-class matches, bowling in 464 innings.
2. Although he normally fielded outside the close catching ring, he held 195 catches. His best catching return in an innings was 3, which he achieved on 9 separate occasions.
3. His best match haul was 4 catches, held for Yorkshire against Derbyshire at Derby in June 1896
4. He made his side's highest score in 101 of the 505 innings in which he batted.
5. In his first-class career his team won 142 and lost 71 of its matches.
6. Two final measures of Jackson's eminence as a Test Match batsmen. At the time of Jackson's retirement from the game in 1905 he was one of only seven men to have scored 500 or more runs in Test Matches, listed in order of average Jackson and his 6 contemporaries were:

BATSMAN	M	I	NO	RUNS	HS	AVERAGE	100
F.S. Jackson	20	33	4	1415	144*	48.79	5
K.S. Ranjitsinhji	15	26	4	989	175	44.95	2
T.W. Hayward	13	22	2	763	137	38.15	2
J.T. Tyldesley	11	20	1	719	138	37.84	3
W.G. Grace	19	31	2	934	170	32.21	2
A.C. MacLaren	15	25	2	706	140	30.70	1
C.B. Fry	12	19	1	540	144	30.00	1

7. Jackson's tally of 5 centuries in Ashes Test Matches in England remained unequalled until Geoffrey Boycott caught up with him at the Oval in 1981.

Bibliography

A Country Vicar, *Cricket Memories* (Methuen, 1933), *The Happy Cricketer* (Frederick Muller, 1946)
Altham, H.S. *A History of Cricket* (Allen and Unwin, 1926)
Ashley-Cooper, F.S. *Curiosities of First-Class Cricket* (Edmund Seale, 1901)
Bailey, P; Thorn P.; Wynne-Thomas, P., *The Who's Who of Cricketers* (Newnes Books in association with the Association of Cricket Statisticians, 1984)
Beldam, G.W.; Fry, C.B., *Great Batsmen: Their Methods at a Glance* (Macmillan, 1905),
Great Bowlers and Fielders: Their Methods at a Glance (Macmillan, 1907)
Betham, J.D. *Oxford and Cambridge Scores and Biographies* (Simpkin, Marshall, 1905)
Bettesworth, WA. *Chats on the Cricket Field* (Merritt and Hatcher, 1910)
Blake, R. The Conservative Party: From Peel to Churchill (Eyre and Spottiswoode, 1970)
Brodribb, G. *The Croucher* (London Magazine Editions, 1974)
Chester, L.; Fry, S.; Young, H., *The Zinoviev Letter* (Heinemann, 1967)
Coldham, J.D. *Lord Harris* (Allen and Unwin, 1983)
Coldham, J.P. *F.S. Jackson* (Crowood Press, 1989), *Lord Hawke* (Crowood Press, 1990)
Cotton-Minchin, J.G. *Old Harrow Days* (Methuen, 1898)
Darwin, B. *W.G. Grace* (Duckworth, 1934)
Darling, D.K. *Test Tussles On and Off the Field* (D.K.

Darling, 1970)

Down, M. *Archie: A Biography of A.C. MacLaren* (Allen and Unwin, 1981)

Fingleton, J.H. *The Immortal Victor Trumper* (Collins, 1978)

Fischer-Williams, J. *Harrow* (George Bell, 1901)

Fletcher, J.S. *The Making of Modern Yorkshire: 1750-1914* (Allen and Unwin, 1918)

Ford, W.J. *A History of the Cambridge University Cricket Club: 1820-1901* (William Blackwood, 1902)

Frindall, W. *The Wisden Book of Test Cricket: 1876-77 to 1977-78* (Macdonald and Janes, 1978)

Fry, C.B., *Life Worth Living* (Eyre and Spottiswoode, 1939)

Gibson, A. *Jackson's Year* (Cassell, 1965)

The Cricket Captains of England (Cassell, 1979)

Gordon, Sir Home (ed.) *Eton v. Harrow at Lord's* (Williams and Norgate, 1926)

Gordon, Sir Home *Background of Cricket* (Arthur Barker, 1939)

Hawke, Lord *Recollections and Reminiscences* (Williams and Norgate, 1924)

Holmes, Revd R.S. *The History of Yorkshire County Cricket: 1833- 1903* (Constable, 1904)

Howson, E.W.; Warner, G.T. (eds) *Harrow School* (Edward Arnold, 1898)

Hutchinson, H.G. (ed.) *Cricket* (Country Life, 1903)

Hutton, Sir Leonard *Fifty Years of Cricket* (Stanley Paul, 1984)

James, R.R. (ed.) *Memoirs of a Conservative: J.C.C. Davidson's Memoirs and Papers, 1910-1937* (Weidenfeld and Nicholson, 1969)

Jessop, G.L. *A Cricketer's Log* (Hodder and Stoughton, 1922)

Kilburn, J.M. *Yorkshire County Cricket* (Convoy Publications, 1950) *A History of Yorkshire Cricket* (Stanley Paul, 1950)

Leveson-Gower, H.D.G. *Cricket Personalities* (Williams and Norgate, 1925)

Lilley, A.A. *Twenty-four Years of Cricket* (Mills and Boon, 1912)

MacLaren, A.C. *Cricket Old and New* (Longmans, Green and Co., 1924)

Mangan, J.A. *Athleticism in the Victorian and Edwardian Public School* (Cambridge University Press, 1981)

Martin-Jenkins, C., The Complete Who's Who of Test Cricketers (Orbis, 1987)

Midwinter, E.C. W.G. Grace: His Life and Times (Allen and Unwin, 1981)

Middlemas, K.; Barnes, J. Baldwin (Weidenfeld and Nicholson, 1969)

Morrah, P. The Golden Age of Cricket (Eyre and Spottiswoode, 1967)

Noble, M.A., *The Game's the Thing* (Cassell, 1926)

Pavri, M.E. *Parsi Cricket* (J.B. Marzban, 1901)

Pentelow, J.N. *England v. Australia: 1877 - 1904* (Arrowsmith, 1904)

Pullin, A.W. *History of Yorkshire County Cricket: 1903-1923* (Chorley and Pickersgill, 1924)

Pollard, J. *Australian Cricket: The Game and its Players* (Hodder and Stoughton, 1982)

Ramsden, J. *The Age of Balfour and Baldwin: 1902-1940* (Longman, 1978)

Ranjitsinhji, K.S. *The Jubilee Book of Cricket* (William Blackwood,1897)

Roberts, E.L. *Yorkshire's 22 Championships: 1893-1946*

(Edward Arnold, 1949)
Rogerson, S. *Wilfred Rhodes* (Hollis and Carter, 1960)
Ross, A. *Ranji: Prince of Cricketers* (Collins, 1983)
Standing, P.C., *The Honourable F.S. Jackson* (Cassell, 1906), *Anglo-Australian Cricket: 1862-1926* (Faber and Gwyer, 1926)
Stevenson, M. *A History of County Cricket: Yorkshire* (Arthur Barker, 1972)
Thomas, P. *Yorkshire Cricketers: 1839-1939* (Derek Hodgson, 1973)
Thomson, A.A. *Cricket: The Golden Ages* (Stanley Paul, 1961), *Cricket: The Great Captains* (Stanley Paul, 1965), *Cricket: The Wars of the Roses* (Pelham Books, 1967)
Trumble, R. *The Golden Age of Cricket* (R. Trumble, 1968)
Warner, Sir Pelham *Cricket Reminiscences* (Grant Richards, 1920), *My Cricketing Life* (Hodder and Stoughton, 1921), *The Book of Cricket* (Dent, 1922), *Cricket Between the Wars* (Chatto and Windus, 1942), *Lord's: 1787-1945* (Harrap, 1946), *Gentlemen v. Players: 1806-1949* (Harrap, 1950), *Long Innings* (Harrap, 1951)
Wild, R., *The Biography of His Highness S.S. Ranjitsinhji* (Rich and Cowan, 1934)
Woods, S.M.J. *My Reminiscences* (Chapman and Hall, 1925)

Newspapers, Periodicals & Annuals

Ayres' Cricket Companion
Cricket: A Weekly Record of the Game
The Cricket Field
The Cricketer

The Harrovian
James Lillywhite's Cricketers' Annual
James Lillywhite's Cricketers' Companion
The Times
Vanity Fair
Wisden's Cricketers' Almanack
The Yorkshire Post

Author's Endnote

My father, James D. Coldham, began work on a biography of Sir Stanley Jackson in the mid-1980s, but for various reasons, the project never advanced beyond the preliminary stages. When my father died his work became the starting point for my own research, resulting in this book, the first edition of which was published by Crowood Press (now defunct) in 1989.

Jackson was a remarkable man: sportsman, businessman, soldier, politician, and imperial pro-consul. This is a book primarily about Jackson the cricketer, and cricket in his age. In this sense it is not perhaps the book my father would have written.

I have written about Jackson and his place in the golden age of English cricket; my father might have chosen a broader perspective. The words are mine; the spirit in which they were written reflects, I hope, our shared love of the great summer game.

Prosaically, one other 'note': I have pursued the convention of spelling place names 'as they were' *at the time*, rather than attempting to track their etymological progression in the years since.

Finally, thank you for reading this book. I hope you enjoyed it; if not, I apologise. In either event, I thank you; a reader does an author and his subject no greater compliment than by reading his, or her work. Civilisation depends on people like *you!*

James Philip
Spring, 2017.

Other Books by James Philip

NON-FICTION CRICKET BOOKS

Lord Hawke

Cricket Books edited by James Philip

The James D. Coldham Series
[Edited by James Philip]

Books
Northamptonshire Cricket: A History [1741-1958]
Lord Harris

Anthologies
Volume 1:   Notes & Articles
Volume 2:   Monographs No. 1 to 8

Monographs
No. 1 - William Brockwell
No. 2 - German Cricket
No. 3 - Devon Cricket
No. 4 - R.S. Holmes
No. 5 - Collectors & Collecting
No. 6 - Early Cricket Reporters
No. 7 – Northamptonshire
No. 8 - Cricket & Authors

WORKS OF FICTION

The Timeline 10/27/62 World

The Timeline 10/27/62 - Main Series
Book 1:   Operation Anadyr
Book 2:   Love is Strange
Book 3:   The Pillars of Hercules
Book 4:   Red Dawn
Book 5:   The Burning Time
Book 6:   Tales of Brave Ulysses
Book 7:   A Line in the Sand
Book 8:   The Mountains of the Moon
Book 9:   All Along the Watchtower
Book 10: Crow on the Cradle
(*Available 27th October 2017*)

Timeline 10/27/62 - USA
Book 1:   Aftermath
Book 2:   California Dreaming
Book 3:   The Great Society
Book 4:   Ask Not of Your Country
Book 5:   The American Dream
(*Available 27th October 2017*)

Timeline 10/27/62 – Australia
Book 1:   Cricket on the Beach
Book 2:   Operation Manna
(<u>Both</u> *Available 2017-18*)

Other Series and Novels

The Guy Winter Mysteries
Prologue: Winter's Pearl
Book 1:   Winter's War
Book 2:   Winter's Revenge
Book 3:   Winter's Exile
Book 4:   Winter's Return
Book 5:   Winter's Spy
Book 6:   Winter's Nemesis
(*Available 2017-18*)

The Bomber War Series
Book 1:   Until the Night
Book 2:   The Painter
Book 3:   The Cloud Walkers

Until the Night Series
Part 1:   Main Force Country – September 1943
Part 2:   The Road to Berlin – October 1943
Part 3:   The Big City – November 1943
Part 4:   When Winter Comes – December 1943
Part 5:   After Midnight – January 1944

The Harry Waters Series
Book 1:   Islands of No Return
Book 2:   Heroes
Book 3:   Brothers in Arms

The Frankie Ransom Series
Book 1:   A Ransom for Two Roses
Book 2:   The Plains of Waterloo
Book 3:   The Nantucket Sleighride

The Strangers Bureau Series
Book 1:   Interlopers
Book 2:   Pictures of Lily

Audio Books of the following Titles are available (or are in production) now

Aftermath
A Ransom for Two Roses
Brothers in Arms
California Dreaming
Heroes
Islands of No Return
Love is Strange
Operation Anadyr
The Nantucket Sleighride
The Plains of Waterloo
Winter's Exile
Winter's Pearl
Winter's Revenge
Winter's War

Details of all James Philip's books and forthcoming publications will be found on his website www.jamesphilip.co.uk

Printed in Great Britain
by Amazon